THE INDUSTRIAL ARCHAEOLOGY
OF GALLOWAY

THE INDUSTRIAL ARCHAEOLOGY
OF THE BRITISH ISLES
Series Editor: E. R. R. GREEN

Derbyshire, by Frank Nixon
The East Midlands, by David M. Smith
Galloway, by Ian Donnachie
Hertfordshire, by W. Branch Johnson
The Lake Counties, by J. D. Marshall and M. Davies-Shiel
Lancashire, by Owen Ashmore
Scotland, by John Butt
Southern England (second edition, revised), by Kenneth Hudson

ASSOCIATED VOLUMES
The Bristol Region, by R. A. Buchanan and Neil Cossons
Dartmoor, by Helen Harris
Gloucestershire Woollen Mills, by Jennifer Tann
Stone Blocks and Iron Rails, by Bertram Baxter
The Tamar Valley (second impression, revised), by Frank Booker
Techniques of Industrial Archaeology, by J. P. M. Pannell

OTHER INDUSTRIAL HISTORY
The British Iron and Steel Industry, by W. K. V. Gale
The Early Factory Masters, by Stanley D. Chapman
The Engineering Industry of the North of Ireland, by W. E. Coe
The History of Water Power in Ulster, by H. D. Gribbon
All these books are in uniform format

The Industrial Archaeology of

GALLOWAY

(South-west Scotland, including
Wigtown, Kirkcudbright and
adjoining parts of Dumfries)

IAN DONNACHIE

DAVID & CHARLES : NEWTON ABBOT

ISBN 0 7153 5126 5

Set in Imprint, 11pt 2pt leaded
and printed in Great Britain by
Latimer Trend & Company Limited Plymouth
for David & Charles (Publishers) Limited
South Devon House   Newton Abbot   Devon

Contents

List of Illustrations

PLATES

Plates not otherwise acknowledged are from the author's own collection

IN TEXT

SECTION ONE

CHAPTER ONE

The Regional Economy of Galloway 1700-1900

GALLOWAY is located in south-west Scotland, bordered by the Solway Firth to the south, the Firth of Clyde to the west, the broad sweep of the Southern Uplands to the north, and the Dumfriesshire dales to the east. By late medieval times Galloway consisted roughly of the modern county of Wigtown, the Stewartry of Kirkcudbright and adjoining parts of Dumfriesshire—a remote, mysterious region, reaching from 'the Brae of Glenapp to the Brig End o' Dumfries'. The eighteenth century saw the ultimate demise of warring clans, gypsies, smugglers and coastal raiders, while a more sedentary population concerned itself with economic development.

Population 1755–1901

Year	Wigtown	Kirkcudbright	Dumfries
1755	16,466	21,205	39,788
1801	22,918	29,211	54,597
1821	33,240	38,903	70,878
1851	43,389	43,121	78,123
1881	36,062	42,127	76,140
1901	32,685	39,383	72,571

Following a marked rise during the era of agrarian improvement and of developing industry and trade, the population of the Galloway counties reached its peak of 164,000 in 1851, having more than doubled since 1755. Rural depopulation, as in most regions of Scotland outside the central belt, has been a notable feature of the south-western counties since the middle of the nineteenth century. In Galloway population decrease has been greatest from the most marginal farming land of the upland interior, while the larger towns, like

Dumfries, Castle Douglas, Newton Stewart and Stranraer, have increased considerably in size and population.

The historical evolution of the regional economy of Galloway over the two centuries which are the concern of this study was primarily a reflection of its location and factor endowments. Isolated from the rest of Scotland by an upland interior, penetrable only by high valley passes, by the Dumfriesshire dales and by the narrow western coastal fringe, the inhabitants of Galloway early looked to the Solway for coastwise communication with neighbouring regions of the British Isles. Regions surrounding the Irish Sea had a profound influence on the regional economy of Galloway, in particular Ulster, Cumberland, Lancashire and the west of Scotland—the latter approached through the Firth of Clyde, rather than by landward communication. Despite the drawbacks presented by upland moors and poor soils over considerable areas, the region is endowed with fertile coastlands and river valleys which provide good farming conditions. Galloway's greatest advantage for farming is its mild climate, particularly in respect of excellent pastureland which is a feature of the south-west. Agriculture dominated the regional economy in the past, as it does at present, because land and climatic advantage are the most lasting resources with which the region is endowed. Other factor endowments were less lasting in effect, but were nevertheless of great significance to the regional economy during the period 1770–1850. The most tangible, water power, was a vital prime mover during the era of the classic industrial revolution. It had the same effect in the generation of industries in Galloway as Mantoux and others since have noted elsewhere.[1] Minerals and building stone were widely dispersed throughout the region, the former of minor importance and the latter of considerable significance in the nineteenth-century economy.

The regional economy of Galloway moved through the stages of growth reflected in the emerging national economy: the development of market-oriented farming; investment in ancillary and processing industries; a build-up in social overhead capital in the form of transport links to markets; and the development of new manufacturing

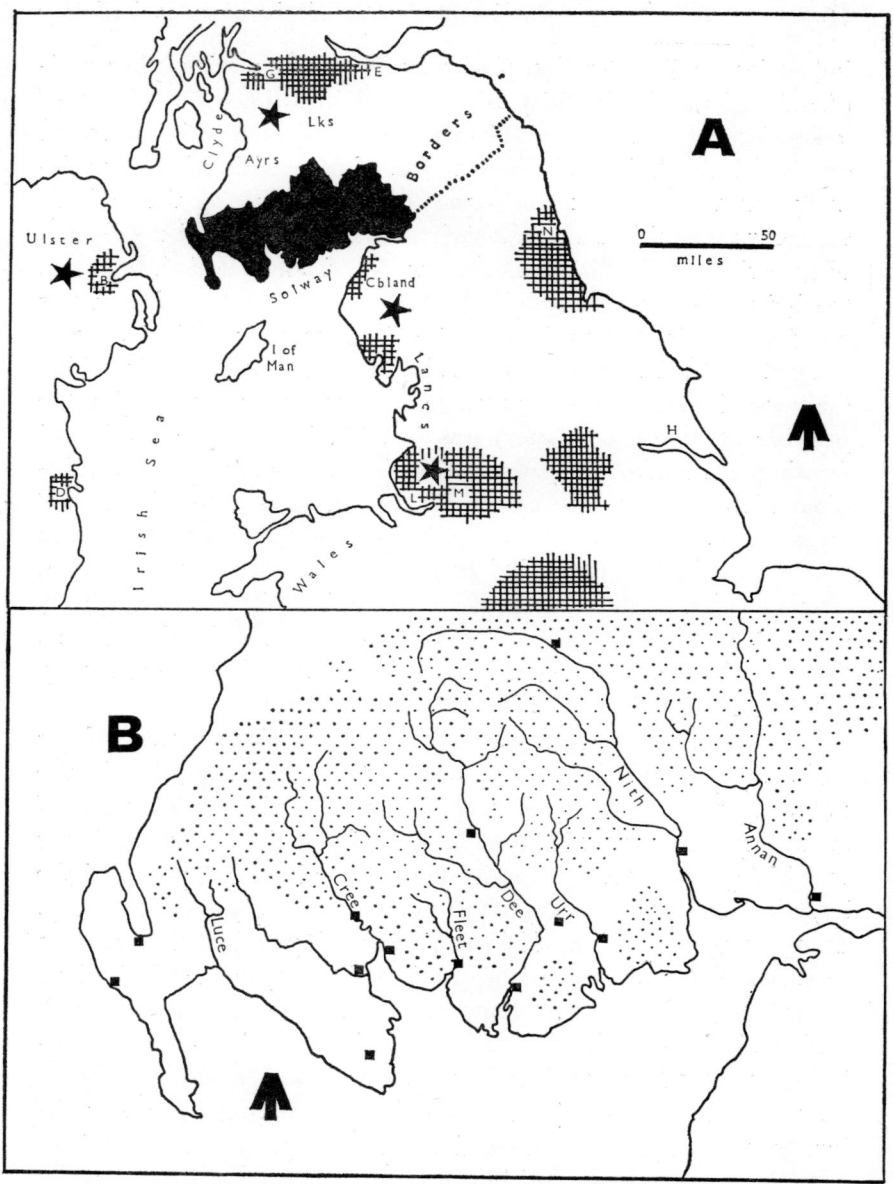

The Setting—A shows the regional setting, with the key industrial areas of greatest influence to the Galloway economy. B indicates the relationship of relief and settlement within the region (dotted area land above 500ft)

industries, such as textiles. Galloway, in common with other peripheral regions of the British Isles, shared for a time the elements of 'take-off' best seen in the industrialisation of Lancashire and west central Scotland. But this early period of industrialisation was relatively short-lived, for technological forces at work on the national economy soon robbed the region of its advantages. With the exception of agriculture, on which the economy was firmly based throughout, the industrial sector was dependent on a narrow range of resources and factor endowments. Participation in inter-regional trade, moreover, demanded increasing specialisation, and the sector in which Galloway had the clear advantage over all other areas (with the possible exception of Ulster) was in agriculture.[2] The specialised farming economy which was beginning to emerge by the mid-nineteenth century was essentially a return to a 'pre-industrial' economy in which capitalistic farming was dominant. This was accelerated in the latter half of the nineteenth century by agricultural reorganisation during and after the 'Depression'. As the Galloway economy became increasingly an appendage of a national economy, the diversified rural-industrial base of the late eighteenth and early nineteenth centuries gradually disintegrated.

In order to trace the main elements in the development of the regional economy of Galloway and its ultimate integration in the national economy, it is necessary to examine the determinants of growth at various periods in the past. Undoubtedly the critical factor in initial growth was the rise of the cattle trade, which provided the key stimulus to agrarian improvement in the early eighteenth century. Increasing external demand from neighbouring regions, like western Scotland and the north of England, had by 1790 transformed an essentially regional, subsistence agriculture to export-orientated, capitalistic farming. During the period of the classic industrial revolution (1780–1820) ancillary industries were developed (mainly by farmers and landowners), such as milling, tanning and leatherworking, brewing and distilling—and the surplus profits accruing from agriculture were channelled into this sector.[3]

Page 17   (above) *Port William Mill—typical of the larger meal mill in Galloway. Note the high kiln ventilator and wheel-house;* (below) *derelict machinery, Mill of Borgue, near Kirkcudbright*

Page 18 (left) *Detail of millstone casing and meal hopper, Monksmill, New Abbey;* (right) *cast-iron waterwheel at Grennan Mill, Dalry—14ft in diameter and installed c 1834*

Galloway had a long tradition of woollen-textile production, and this was probably the first manufacturing industry to be revitalised by capital investment. Several water-powered mills were built after the 1770s, mostly by local entrepreneurs or merchants, a good example being Wauk Mill at Kirkcowan, Wigtownshire, established about this time by the Milroy family. Established textile skills, an expanding local market, good links with other regions and water power also encouraged the development of both linen and cotton-textile production. The latter took root in the 'cotton-spinning mania' of the late 1780s, when three cotton mills were built at Newton Douglas, Gatehouse of Fleet, and Castle Douglas, while numerous other smaller mills were built elsewhere in the region. In the development of cotton spinning and weaving, local initiative and capital played an important role, though the interest of entrepreneurs from outside Galloway, attracted by or already familiar with the region's advantages, was probably paramount. Linen and paper manufacture were never very successful in Galloway.

Galloway's mineral resources did not escape the notice of both local landed gentry and outside speculators, but despite their unyielding efforts, profits were never large in this sector. More remunerative was the building-stone quarrying trade, which developed rapidly after 1820, and following a period of decline, revived during the late-Victorian building boom after 1870. Other extractive industries, such as brick and tile making, were small-scale and little more than an adjunct to the farming economy.

Transport was at all times vital to regional economic growth. Until the 1860s navigation through the Solway ports was the economic lifeline of the region, land communication being limited (at least till the development of turnpike trusts) to local traffic. The railway (contemporaneous with the onset of the 'Depression') brought about a radical reorientation in markets towards urban areas in central Scotland and northern England, and coastwise trade declined rapidly. By the turn of the century its demise was virtually total.

The image of farming in Galloway in the immediate post-medieval

B

period is one of stagnation, backwardness and outright depression common to most of Scotland at the time. Yet land improvements began early in the region and enclosures began to be made as early as the latter half of the seventeenth century. The key activity—apart from subsistence farming on the run-rig system—was cattle breeding and fattening, and it was this which provided the initial impetus to improvement and rationalisation of holdings.[4]

With the active encouragement of local landed gentry (like William Craik of Arbigland, the earls of Selkirk, Galloway and Stair, James and Alexander Murray of Broughton & Cally and Patrick Millar of Dalswinton) and the more active and progressive farmers, agrarian change proceeded apace during the eighteenth century, despite the unrest caused by the Levellers who broke down dykes in the early part of the century.[5] Enclosing, drainage, embanking and general reclamation brought wide areas into productive farming. Systematic rotation and the introduction of green crops resulted in better-quality pasture and increased yields from cultivated land. Improved grasses and new crops, such as turnips and potatoes (the latter very important in Wigtownshire), were introduced and considerable areas given over to the cultivation of oats, barley and wheat. The mixed farming economy came to typify the south-west at this time. During the period 1770–1850 crop surpluses were sent coastwise to north-west England and central Scotland.

The Galloway cattle trade also benefitted from improvements, reaching its peak in the half-century before 1840. Galloway-bred cattle and beasts imported from Ireland were driven south to English markets in vast herds, often as many as 30,000 per annum. The main towns such as Stranraer, New Galloway, Kirkcudbright and Dumfries served as collecting points on the droving routes, which ran the length of Galloway from Portpatrick (the key landing place from Ireland) to Carlisle. The cattle trade has left its own heritage of lonely drove roads across the hills of Galloway.[6] With the development of steam shipping, the droving trade fell away, although meat export continued to be important. By the early nineteenth century beef-cattle, upland sheep and pigs were shipped from the region in considerable numbers to the markets of the north of England.

Stock-rearing declined after the coming of the railway in the 1860s and the production of new breeds elsewhere, like the Aberdeen-Angus and Shorthorn. The development of grain and cattle farming in North America, Australasia and other parts of the world affected farming in Galloway in much the same way as it did other parts of Britain after 1870. A mixed arable-livestock agriculture with specialisation in dairying was gradually created. 'Depression certainly exists,' wrote John Spier in his report to the Royal Commission on Agriculture in Scotland (1895), 'but dairying is spreading rapidly . . . and nothing like total collapse can be pointed to.'[7]

The dairy industry certainly helped to cushion the Galloway farming economy from the worst effects of the 'Depression', but despite improved marketing techniques and the establishment of creameries large and small, the dairy industry remained relatively unstable till the 1930s. Following the establishment of the Scottish Milk Marketing Board in 1933 the situation improved and Galloway remains as important an area of liquid milk and dairy product manufacture as it was in the 1890s.

Agrarian improvement and the consequent extension of arable land in the latter half of the eighteenth century brought new stimulus to a formerly localised rural craft—milling—which was among the first of a wide range of processing industries to benefit from increased investment. The region became a grain exporter and numerous mills were built or reconstructed. Between 1770 and 1850 the milling industry enjoyed a period of great prosperity as farmers pushed crops of oats and barley on to once marginal land. As the nineteenth century progressed, arable production became unprofitable and only the major grain mills survived. By the early decades of the present century the industry was concerned with the production of animal feeding stuffs, fertilisers and some edible grain in large mills centred on Stranraer, Dalbeattie and Kirkcudbright.

An obvious adjunct of the extensive Galloway cattle trade was the development in the late eighteenth century of the skinning, tanning and leather-curing industry. Practically every market town in the region had at least one tannery, hides being obtained locally and also imported from Ireland. The main centres at the beginning of the nineteenth century were Stranraer, Gatehouse, Castle Douglas and Dumfries. Associated industries, such as leather-cutting, leather-working, saddlery, shoe and clog making were widely dispersed throughout the region, fulfilling local demand for leathergoods. Tanning was an important industry in Dumfries, which in the 1860s processed nearly 30,000 hides per annum.[8]

Two other primary processing industries which were of some consequence were brewing and distilling. Brewing was a long-established rural industry and the majority of breweries established in the late eighteenth century appear to have been small production units catering for very local markets. The existence of this industry, like distilling, was a stimulus to barley growing, particularly in the more fertile areas of southern Wigtownshire and Kirkcudbrightshire. The principal centres of brewing in the early nineteenth century were Dumfries, Gatehouse and Stranraer, in addition to smaller, more localised plants at Kirkcudbright, Newton Stewart and Wigtown.[9] The small Galloway industry did not survive the rise of the large city breweries and the extension of markets as a result of improved communications in the mid-nineteenth century. Small distilleries developed in the late eighteenth century and the industry was centred on Stranraer, Wigtown, Kirkcudbright and Dumfries. Malt whisky was produced from local and imported barley and, despite the vagaries to which the industry was inevitably exposed, was certainly highly profitable. Only one distillery, however, survived the imposition of more severe Excise duties and the rise of whisky blending in the late nineteenth century. Bladnoch's annual output in the 1880s was around 51,000gal.[10]

Textiles made an important contribution to the regional economy in the period 1785 to c 1820 and again in the latter half of the nineteenth century, when tweed manufacture was important in several towns. Evidence of the increasing importance of the woollen industry in the eighteenth century are the numerous 'wauk mills' which were established throughout the region to process local wool. At first widely dispersed, the industry later became concentrated in the main centres in considerably enlarged factories, at Dumfries, Sanquhar, Newton Stewart and Kirkcowan. After 1840 the wool industry became a major source of employment in Dumfries and production concentrated on tweed and hosiery. By the end of the century the Dumfries tweed industry rivalled that of the Border.

The linen industry was never of any great importance in Galloway, largely as a result of unsuitable climate and soil for flax production. Only in Annandale and the Rhins district did it achieve more than local significance and in both areas water-powered lint mills and associated bleachfields were established. Even at its peak c 1780, the linen production of the three Galloway counties represented a mere fraction of Scottish output.[11]

Cotton textiles were of more lasting importance than linen and brought to the Galloway countryside the direct effects of the industrial revolution. Local landed interests, attracted by the benefits and profits of rural industry and encouraged by entrepreneurs from Lancashire and the west of Scotland, established cotton-spinning mills at several locations. The most important centre was Gatehouse, where an enlightened landed proprietor, Murray of Cally, and Yorkshire cattle dealers joined forces. Two other mills, Newton Douglas and Castle Douglas, were associated with William Douglas, a former merchant, who went into partnership with David Dale in at least one of his unsuccessful schemes.

The Galloway region has a wide range of mineral ores which have been exploited with varying degrees of economic success during several periods in the past two hundred years. The most significant were lead, iron, copper and barytes, all found in a variety of locations throughout the area. Lead mining in the Wanlockhead district dates back to the sixteenth century, although systematic exploitation only began in the eighteenth century.[12] Lead prices fluctuated considerably throughout the nineteenth century and the activity of the Galloway mines was very much geared to the general climate in the industry, but as late as 1910 lead mining in the south-west employed over 250 workers, producing nearly 3,000 tons of lead and 12,500 oz of silver. Farther west, lead was worked in many places around Gatehouse and Newton Stewart and in the interior at Carsphairn. Lead and zinc were still actively mined in the area around Newton Stewart in 1918, but production ceased shortly after. Copper was worked at several places around Gatehouse, but had ceased to be important by 1860, and attempts to work iron-ore were equally short-lived. The majority of mines have long been abandoned due to uneconomic exploitation, but the existence of mineral mining in Galloway provides an interesting opportunity to study entrepreneurial optimism in the face of considerable economic odds.

From being an industry of little more than local significance in the eighteenth century, building-stone quarrying developed into a major economic activity in the nineteenth century. Granite from the Stewartry and sandstone from Dumfriesshire were exported to many parts of Britain and beyond, to meet the demands of urban building programmes and for major engineering projects such as docks, bridges and lighthouses. The earliest systematic quarrying of granite took place near Dalbeattie and later c 1830 other large quarries were opened in Kirkmabreck parish. For nearly eighty years one of the Creetown quarries employed 180–300 men and had an average output of 10,000 tons per annum, most of which was shipped to the Mersey for harbour works. The industry became very important around Dalbeattie in the late nineteenth century, and the economic prosperity of the town was very dependent on employment in the quarries. As late as 1900 over 60,000 tons of granite were quarried in the Stewartry. Production and employment in the industry declined rapidly after World War I and its main function became the supply of road-metal.[13]

Coal-mining took place in the Sanquhar–Kirkconnel and Canonbie districts of Dumfriesshire, neither strictly within Galloway, but nonetheless of some importance to the whole of the south-west. Systematic exploitation began in the early nineteenth century and large-scale working at Sanquhar was underway by 1848. The opening of the Glasgow & South-Western Railway led to further successful developments. Despite the drawbacks of bad faulting and thin seams the pits in upper Nithsdale continued to be an important source of employment until recently. The important Fauldhead pit closed in 1968.[14]

Limestone quarrying and burning depended heavily on local coal supplies and the Nithsdale industry provided an important 'means of improvement' to eighteenth-century Galloway agriculture. The principal quarries operating at the beginning of the nineteenth century were those at Barjarg, Closeburn and Porterstown. The limestone was mined at Closeburn and burned in nearby kilns. Such was the demand for lime for agrarian improvement at this period that it was transported widely, even to districts in the interior of Galloway. Limestone for agricultural purposes formed an important element of import from north-west England, particularly from Cumberland. Smaller quarries and limeworks operated in the late eighteenth and early nineteenth centuries in the Kirkbean district of southern Kirkcudbrightshire and at various places in the Rhins of Galloway where limestone deposits exist. The majority of the larger Nithsdale quarries were closed by the end of the century and by 1900 the remaining ones were worked only sporadically.[15]

Improvements in agricultural techniques also provided the initial impetus for the development of another small-scale industrial activity —brick and tile making. Numerous small clay-pits were opened and tile works erected to meet this demand. An adjunct to this at several works was brickmaking, again supplying an essentially local market. The largest works were at Stranraer, Dumfries, Sanquhar and Kirkconnel, the remainder in Galloway proper being relatively small units, often with as little as a single kiln. Buccleuch brickworks at Sanquhar, which dates from the 1850s, used local clay and produced a fine-quality terracotta brick. Few of the smaller works (at, for example, Gatehouse and Dalbeattie) survived till the present century.

As late as the eighteenth century, Galloway was a remote area,

isolated from the rest of the country by physical barriers. Its main
links with other regions of the British Isles were by sea through the
Solway ports, and by poor, unreliable pack routes across the upland
interior. General Roy's Military Survey of Scotland c 1750 indicates
that a pattern of roads and routeways existed, linking the main centres
within Galloway and affording communication with other parts of
central and southern Scotland and the north of England. The first
constructed road in the region was the Military Road, built for
essentially strategic purposes and completed c 1765, which linked
Dumfries with Portpatrick, then the principal harbour for Ireland.
The cattle-droving trade engendered the development of other routes,
but it was not until the establishment of Turnpike Trusts after 1780
that Galloway began to acquire a good network of roads. This basic
network remains little altered to the present time, and the majority of
bridges still in use date from the turnpike era. The industrial archaeology of transport in Galloway is thus particularly worthy of study.[16]

Shipping provided vital linkages between the regional economy
and the broader, more rapidly expanding national economy, particularly in the period 1750–1850. The majority of the region's external
trade was seaborne and numerous ports and harbours developed
along the Solway coast. The most important were Dumfries (with its
outports at Kingholm and Glencaple) on the Nith, Kirkcudbright on
the Dee and Stranraer at the head of Loch Ryan. Others of secondary
significance, like Dalbeattie, Gatehouse and Wigtown, were equally
handicapped by the Solway tides, which made navigation precarious
and limited shipping to comparatively small tonnage. In the early
nineteenth century steamship services were introduced between the
Solway ports and Whitehaven, Liverpool and Glasgow. These continued the traditional export of agricultural produce and import of
fertilisers, coal, timber and supplies. The tragic history of Portpatrick
harbour, which from the 1770s served as the main packet station for
Ireland, ended in 1862 when the service was formally transferred to
Stranraer and the great harbour walls were left to the mercy of the
seas. Even after the building of railways after 1850 coastal shipping

on the Solway continued to serve relatively isolated communities until the turn of the present century. Now the majority of the old harbours are deserted, though there has been a revival of activity at several ports, notably Kirkcudbright, Palnackie and Glencaple, while fishing and sailing craft use many others.[17]

The earliest railway development took place on the periphery of the region, when the Glasgow & South-Western Railway opened the Nithsdale route in 1850. The building of the Dumfries & Castle Douglas Railway in 1859, followed by a cross-country link provided by the Portpatrick Railway (opened 1861), tapped not only local Galloway traffic, but also connected with the Irish steam-packet boats. Several important branch lines were built, notably those from Castle Douglas to Kirkcudbright (1864) and from the main line to Stranraer harbour (1863). The Wigtownshire Railway, a largely locally promoted scheme to provide the Machars with better communications, was finally opened to Whithorn in 1877. The final link was established when the Girvan & Portpatrick line was opened to traffic in 1877. Ultimately all lines in the region were worked by and eventually amalgamated with the G & SW railway, which had an important effect in the reorientation of Galloway's economic linkages away from the Solway towards central Scotland.[18]

By 1900 few of the earlier industrial ventures survived. Agriculture had become again the main economic activity of the region, and only in the larger towns, like Dumfries, was manufacturing of any significance. Wool, tweed and hosiery continued to be prosperous until World War I, and there was a brave attempt to establish an off-shoot of the doomed Scottish motor-car industry at Dumfries (Heathhall) and Kirkcudbright (Tongland) after 1905. Further in the future, and of more economic and social value, was the construction of the Galloway Hydro-Electric Scheme (1930–6) at a cost of £13 million providing five power stations supplying electricity to much of the region. After the development of the railway network the area became accessible to growing numbers of Victorian and Edwardian tourists and Galloway established an industry which was to prove of vital importance to its future economic prosperity.[19] Galloway's industrial archaeology was the creation of economic and structural change within the region and beyond. Two centuries of changing economic circumstance have left a physical heritage of outstanding importance to the economic historian. The detailed examination of this industrial heritage makes possible some understanding of the real impact of technical and economic change in Galloway, and is vital to any analysis of the evolution of its regional economy.

(*See pages* 243–4 *for notes*)

CHAPTER TWO

Agricultural Processing and Rural Crafts

AGRICULTURE was and is the dominant feature of the regional economy of south-west Scotland. It is hardly surprising therefore that a large element of its more recent physical heritage reflects the importance of farming. The broad-based farming economy which was characteristic of the region down to 1850 engendered a wide range of processing activities. Today Galloway agriculture is still dominated by an essentially mixed husbandry, but with a distinct emphasis on dairying. It was the rise of the latter specialisation before and during the age of agricultural 'Depression' in the late nineteenth century which has created many of the rural features found in such profusion throughout the region: corn kilns; threshing mills of every kind; meal mills, large and small; windmills; and a wide range of traditional farm architecture. The dairy industry has engendered its own archaeology, for technical developments in milk processing and the growth of large-scale factory creameries in recent years have contributed to the demise of the cheese-maker, the cheese-loft (a feature of many Wigtownshire farms) and the small country creamery.[1]

Other essentially primary processes reflect the balanced nature of the Galloway farming economy in the past. Tanning and leather-working were, as already indicated above, old-established crafts which derived new importance in the latter half of the eighteenth century from the growth of cattle-rearing and the meat export trade. Timber sawing and woodworking, traditional crafts of long standing, were stimulated by the revitalised forest resources of the region, particularly on estates where extensive planting was carried out. Brewing and distilling reflected the local importance of barley growing and although the former succumbed to outside competition the latter was much more in line with national trends in the distilling industry. Finally, the sea-

29

shore crafts of kelp-burning and salt-making illustrate the strong and lasting influence of the Solway in Galloway and emphasise the relative isolation of the region even by the end of the eighteenth century.

In the broadest sense, the total landscape of Galloway reflects the changing nature of its regional farming economy over 250 years. Dry-stane dykes, symmetrical field patterns, drainage ditches, hedges and woodlands, estate roads, farm steadings, country mansions and planned villages are part of a broader pattern of evolution which is beyond the scope of this inquiry, but nevertheless constitute part of a wider and equally rich heritage. The microcosm of changes in transportation over the last two hundred years is reflected in a deserted harbour in some isolated bay on Solway shore and likewise in farming by the broken-down ruin of a meal mill near an abandoned farmstead, surely on the very margin of cultivation even in the age of 'high farming'.

MILLING AND OTHER PROCESSING

Meal or grain milling was probably the earliest processing activity undertaken in the Scottish countryside, and in Galloway, as elsewhere, mills existed in considerable numbers from medieval times. Every sub-stantial ferme-toune had its mill and the town mill was a feature of most burghs, as for example at Dumfries. Water power was the basic prime mover and remained so until the ultimate demise of the smaller country mills in the early part of the present century. Windmills were much less common in the west of Scotland than in the east (especially the Lothians and Fife), but south-west Scotland shared the pattern of development common to the rest of the country, and indeed to Ireland and much of the north of England.[2] Other basic farm processing, like threshing, shared a variety of forms of motive power, the most common being the waterwheel, followed by horse power in the ubiquitous horse-mill or gin. The threshing barn with its round horse-gin house is almost as common in the drier parts of Wigtownshire as the lean-to wheelhouse is in the Stewartry. Only rarely does the steam-engine stack appear on farm outbuildings in Galloway—a reflection of costly coal imports. This latter factor was probably also critical to the survival, until at least the 1850s, of the primitive stone-built corn kiln in the isolated upland districts or on farms remote from a meal mill.

There were three distinct phases in the development of milling in Galloway and at least two in its decline after 1850. In the medieval phase, mills were adjuncts of religious houses, burghs or estates, and their function was fairly strictly limited to the processing of grain from astricted tenants or burgesses. The second era, in the late seventeenth and early eighteenth centuries, was one of expansion in arable production, essentially a response to population growth in and beyond the region and the exploitation of external markets to the south. The third phase, covering roughly the century 1750–1850, was simply an extension of the second phase of growth, although milling developed rapidly as an industry and the number of mills doubled to reach about 140 at the close of the period. Galloway became an important grain-exporting district, with its main markets in Cumberland, Lancashire, Ireland and the west of Scotland, the traditional outlets for the agricultural surpluses of the region. After the 1850s came a phase of slow decline, accompanied by the closure of many small mills, as arable farming was abandoned for less economically hazardous dairying. The rise of pasture farming after the 'Depression' contributed to the decline of milling and to its increasing concentration in larger units at Stranraer, Dalbeattie and Dumfries. Only a handful of country mills are still at work.

There are numerous references to mills in later medieval Galloway, which indicate the importance of milling in the agrarian economy of the time. The mill of Innermessan, for example, was granted under royal charter to Andrew Agnew c 1429, while the mill of Busby in the parish of Whithorn is mentioned in a sasine of 1545. Most of the medieval burghs, like Dumfries and Kirkcudbright, had mills which provided an important part of civic revenue.[3] Surviving estate records show clearly the importance of mills in the lands of Galloway by the seventeenth century.

The Hay of Park papers provide good documentary illustration of the expansion of grain milling within the Hay estates in the parish of Glenluce during the late seventeenth and early eighteenth centuries. The mill of Kirkchrist is first mentioned in a tack of 1636 and the more important Bridgemiln of Glenluce, some years later in 1676.[4] Milnton of Larg appears in 1730, an indication of the expansion of arable farming on to the higher districts of the Luce valley. Tacks and leases of mills become increasingly more frequent after 1700 and multure disputes are also more common. One particularly interesting multure dispute shows that the distant Grennan Mill near Balmacllelan was at that time held by the Hays, for in 1725 Sir Charles Hay sued John Hannay of Grennan for payment of £43 10s (Scots) in multures.[5]

On the Lochnaw lands of the Agnews there was a similar growth in mill tacks, indicative not only of the increasing importance of a money economy where grain formed an important element of rent but also of a growing respect for legal agreements. The earliest mill mentioned is Soleburn (near Leswalt), which was leased in 1673 to Quentin Shenane whose descendants held it till 1729. In 1692, Matthew Torbrane of Lochans Mill in the parish of Inch was granted a tack of the mill of Lochnaw. Much firmer evidence of expansion in the early eighteenth century is provided by a 'Survey of Milns' in Leswalt parish 1718–41, where Galdenoch was described in 1719 as 'a sufficient miln new built in timber and stone'.[6]

The larger and much more widely dispersed Broughton and Cally estates illustrate much the same pattern of development in milling. In 1677, for example, the mill of Plunton was leased to John Hannay and John Douglas, and numerous other mills appear in the records thereafter—such as Broughton, Barley (Gatehouse), Enrick (Girthon) and Kirkandrews. Bonds of thirlage, another indication of the growing significance of mills on Galloway estates, also occur in considerable numbers after the beginning of the eighteenth century. A good illustration is provided by that of Alexander Gordon of Carleton, thirling the lands of Littletoune to the Mill of Enrick in 1729.[7]

The meal mill was probably the most common feature of the eighteenth-century 'improved' landscape in Galloway, indicative of

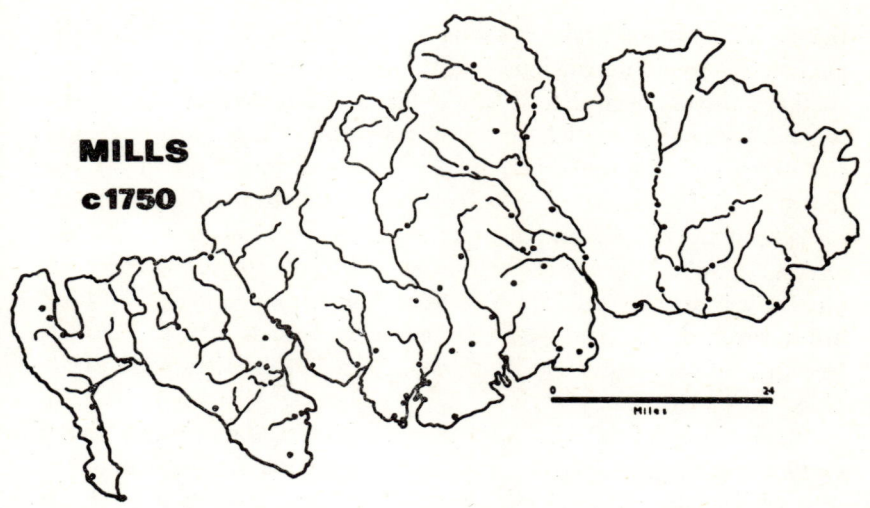

MILLS
c1750

0   24
Miles

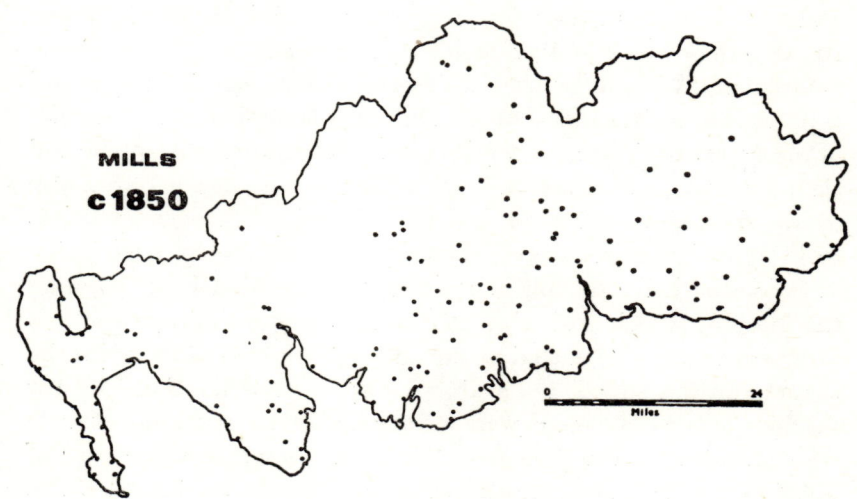

MILLS
c1850

0   24
Miles

the significance of grain growing in the regional economy of the period. The rapid expansion of milling 1750–1850 is some measure of the key position occupied by arable farming during that century—in what is today an essentially pastoral district. Perhaps most striking is the extension of grain growing on to the marginal upland farming districts of, for example, the Glenkens and central Machars. Comparison of the figures on page 33 serves to emphasise the expansion which took place during the traditional era of prosperity to 1850, and particularly in the period 1790–1815. The demands of surrounding areas reached such heights that even the much reduced returns brought by oats and barley cultivation in such districts were profitable.[8]

The majority of mills in Galloway date from the late eighteenth and early nineteenth centuries, although many were reconstructions of much older fabrics. New mills were built in some number and old ones refurbished widely in the latter half of the eighteenth century—a real indication of the growing local and external demand for oats and barley. Typical of the older mills which were reconstructed in the late eighteenth century and the early decades of the nineteenth are Grennan (Balmaclellan), Milldriggan (Kirkinner) and Monksmill (New Abbey), all of which occupy medieval millsteads.

Grennan Mill near St John's Town of Dalry dates from 1506 and is perhaps one of the oldest meal mills in the upland Glenkens district of the Stewartry (plate, page 18). It is a small, two-storey, rubble and slate structure, built into the valley side of the Garple Burn. The overall dimensions are about 30ft by 40ft and the main range seems to be original, though it has clearly undergone extensive reconstruction at various periods. The mill is powered by water from a lade taken off the burn by a weir and originally had a wooden undershot wheel. Grennan was reconstructed in the late eighteenth century when the square kiln was added, and again in 1834 when much of the present machinery and waterwheel were installed. The main entrance at first-floor level leads on to the stones floor, where there are three sets of millstones. The stairway leads to the basement or meal floor, where

Page 35 (above) *Former brewery, Newton Stewart, dating from the early nineteenth century;* (below) *Bladnoch Distillery, on the bank of the River Bladnoch, near Wigtown*

Page 36 (above) *Logan estate sawmill, Kirkmaiden. The rim-drive, overshot wheel is 20ft in diameter;* (left) *Maidenholm Forge, Dalbeattie, dates from the early nineteenth century and formerly manu-factured agricultural implements*

the gear cupboard is situated. Most of the internal gearing is complete and in working order, though the stones would require to be re-set and realigned. The machinery is driven by a high-breast, cast-iron wheel, made in ten sections with cast-iron cross-spars and axle, 14ft in diameter by 3ft 4½in wide. Water falls from a wooden trough 3ft 3½in wide. The zinc buckets of the wheel were badly damaged in a spate in 1964, when the wheel 'ran away' for nearly two days. Grennan last operated as a meal mill about 1950 when it was worked by the McDowall family of Milldriggan, Kirkinner.[9]

Milldriggan, in the central Machars district of Wigtownshire, is marked on Timothy Pont's 'Gallovidia' map of the 1680s, and is thus one of the oldest mill sites still in use in Galloway. Milldriggan was reconstructed in the early nineteenth century by William Routledge, a miller from Cumberland who settled in Galloway. Routledge later acquired the larger Elrig Mills in nearby Mochrum and sold out Milldriggan to the McDowalls, an old established family of Galloway millers who formerly worked the Mill of Garlies in the parish of Minnigaff. Milldriggan has remained with the McDowalls for over 130 years and they still operate it as a family business. The building is a typical three-storey and attic range in whitewashed rubble with a local slate roof. A large kiln (16ft long by 24ft wide) adjoins the main range. The internal wheel was last used in 1965, although an electric motor has been the main source of power since 1940. The cast-iron wheel was produced locally at the Castle Douglas Foundry of J. & R. Wallace (well-known millwrights in Galloway) and is probably about 100 years old. It is high-breastshot and measures 20ft in diameter by 3ft 10in wide.[10]

Monksmill is so named because of its long association with the Abbey of the Sweetheart, established by Lady Devorgilla in the early fourteenth century. There were at least four mills near the Abbey, one being Monksmill, situated in New Abbey village (plate, page 18). The present structure probably dates from about 1700 but was extensively reconstructed in the early part of the nineteenth century. It has a number of interesting features, including stones by famous north-

c

country millwrights, W. J. & T. Child of Leeds and a kiln by a local maker in Dumfries. The interior is in very good order but the wheel and water works have unfortunately been allowed to deteriorate. With its pond, lade, trough and high-breast wheel, Monksmill exhibits the classic features of the Scottish country meal mill.[11]

Although the expansion of milling in Galloway was most marked in the last decades of the eighteenth and the early part of the nineteenth centuries, mill building and reconstruction continued in Galloway until the 1870s. The Stair estates afford two good examples of mill building as late as the 1850s and 1860s in Ravenston meal mill, near Kirkinner, and Sandmill in the Rhins of Galloway. Ravenstone was built in 1850 and had all the features of the mid-nineteenth-century mill, with three floors supported on cast-iron columns and virtually all internal machinery of the same material. On one gable was the overshot waterwheel and on the other a square kiln, fitted with cast-iron plated floor. The figure below shows how functional the building was—the only departure being the ornate kiln ventilator. Sandmill was a larger building, designed and built for the Earl of Stair

RAVENSTON MILL

0   50

by J. & A. Taylor, Ayrshire millwrights and agricultural engineers in 1861. This was also of three storeys, and as the figure below indicates the mill had four sets of stones. Sandmill had a substantial kiln, 20ft square, the fitments being of cast iron.[12]

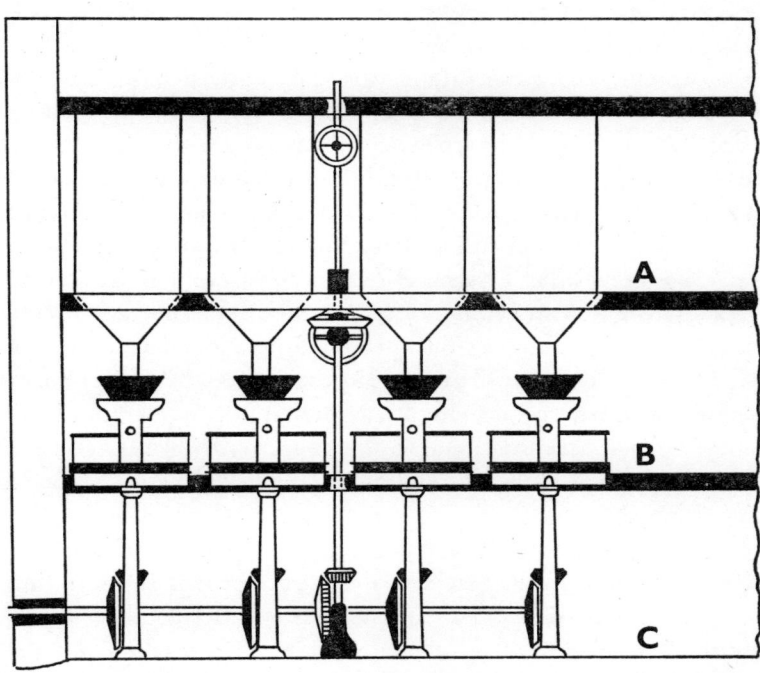

Machinery in Sandmill Grain Mill 1861—Drawn by J. & A. Taylor, Engineers & Millwrights. This plan (which lacks a scale), approximately $\frac{1}{2}$in to 4ft, shows the layout of milling machinery and drive-gearing in a typical mid-nineteenth-century mill. There are three floors (A, hopper; B, stones; C, meal) and cast iron is used in both gearing and supporting columns (from SRO, RHP 4951)

The country meal mill of Galloway did not disappear overnight with the onset of the 'Depression'—for the grain export trade continued as before, though at a much reduced level. The rise of the railway and of pasture farming brought about a decline in arable production, and although mixed farming was still the order of the day, there was a suggestion made by the Royal Commission on Agriculture in Scotland (1895) 'that old buildings in the shape of meal or other mills', preferably near the railway, would be readily converted to 'cooperative cheese and butter factories at a comparatively small outlay'.[13] Nonetheless, changing consumer demand both within Galloway and elsewhere brought about the slow demise of the meal mill. Those that survived after 1914 changed over almost entirely to the production of animal feeding stuffs and were invariably merged with larger concerns. The three largest firms still operating in the area are all long-established. James Carsewell & Sons of Barrbridge, Dalbeattie, date from 1837 and produce meal and flour for human consumption as well as animal feeding stuffs. Thomas Biggar, also of Dalbeattie, started in 1840 as bone and artificial manure manufacturers, but now process a wide variety of grain and other products for animal feeding. James Wyllie & Son of Stranraer have the largest grain and fertiliser business in the south-west, and although production is concentrated in their modern mills at Stranraer, Garlieston and Dumfries, they still maintain several small mills throughout Galloway as local stores and distribution centres.[14]

The omnipresence of water power and the cheapness of horse levers and mills to drive farm machinery did not prevent the building of windmills at several locations in the south-west (see page 41). The pattern of development illustrated by the survivals in Galloway is broadly similar to that of Scotland as a whole.[15] Three main types are represented, all being tower mills: the vaulted tower mill, a type apparently peculiar to Scotland; the tower mill proper (mostly of eighteenth-century date); and the farm windmill, powering threshing and other farm machinery. Andrew Symson explains the reason for the building of Logan windmill in the Rhins of Galloway, almost certainly the first in the district:

The countrey hereabouts especially in the summer time is very defective of mills, by reason that the little bourns are then dried up; to supply which defect the Laird of Logan hath lately built an excellent windmill, which is very useful not only to his own hands but to the whole countrey there-abouts.[16]

Logan windmill is a fine example of the vaulted windmill built in the late seventeenth and eighteenth century throughout Scotland. It consists of a large rubble tower (about 30ft high) on a basement, set into a natural mound overlooking Luce Bay. The figure on page 42 provides a section and reconstruction of Logan windmill with its sails. The Whithorn windmill was probably similar (though much more substantial) and a print in the Priory Museum shows the mill complete with sails c 1825.[17]

Although the threshing machine invented by Andrew Meikle had its precursors, the mill which he perfected by 1786 quickly spread throughout the arable districts of Scotland. Using his earlier experience of millwrighting, he had experimented with various types of

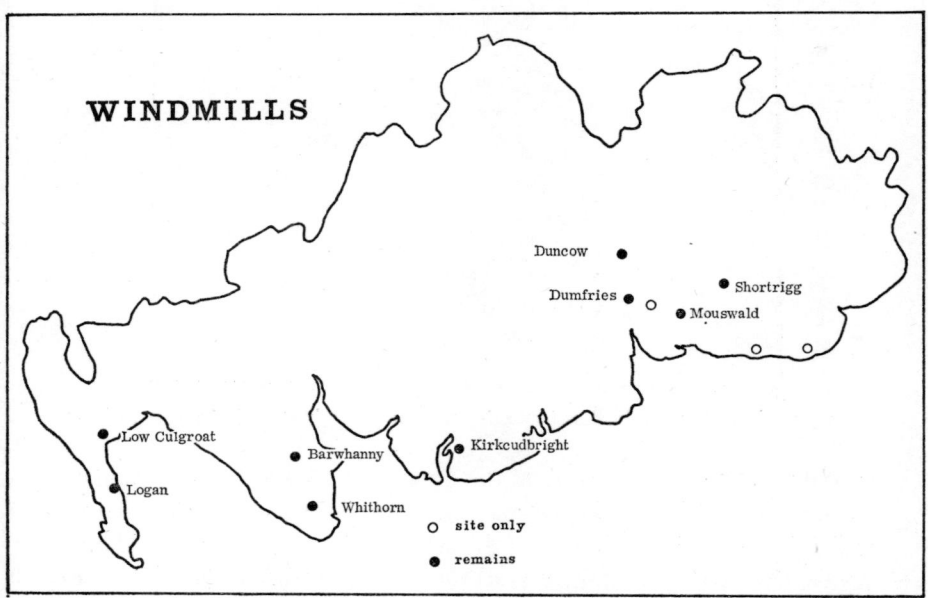

WINDMILLS

Duncow
Dumfries
Shortrigg
Mouswald

Low Culgroat
Barwhanny
Kirkcudbright
Logan
Whithorn

O site only
● remains

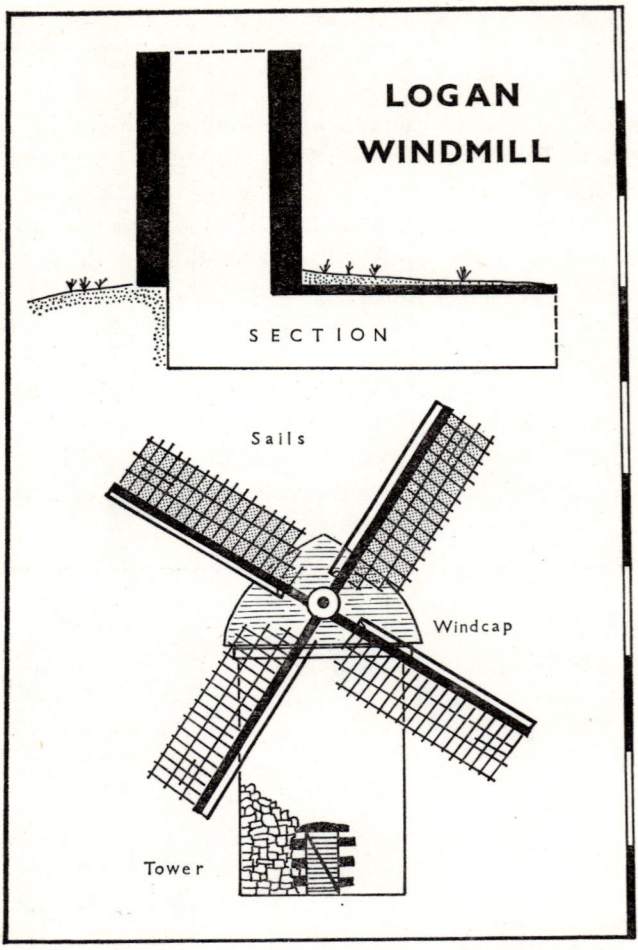

Logan windmill: section and reconstruction (marginal scale in 10ft units)

machine which beat or rubbed the grain. Rotary motion was the key
to success, and his perfected machine incorporated revolving drums
which knocked the grain free of the straw and chaff. The great advantage of the Meikle machine was its relative cheapness and adaptability

to various forms of power. It could be driven by horse-levers, water-wheel, wind power—and later by steam engine.[18] Many machines were driven by horse and water power in the south-west, the windmill being much more exotic. A few machines combined two forms of power, but this was rare in Galloway as elsewhere. Galloway had its own threshing-machine designer (c 1794) in William Gladstone of Castle Douglas, a smith and millwright who built over 200 farm mills in the south-west and elsewhere.[19]

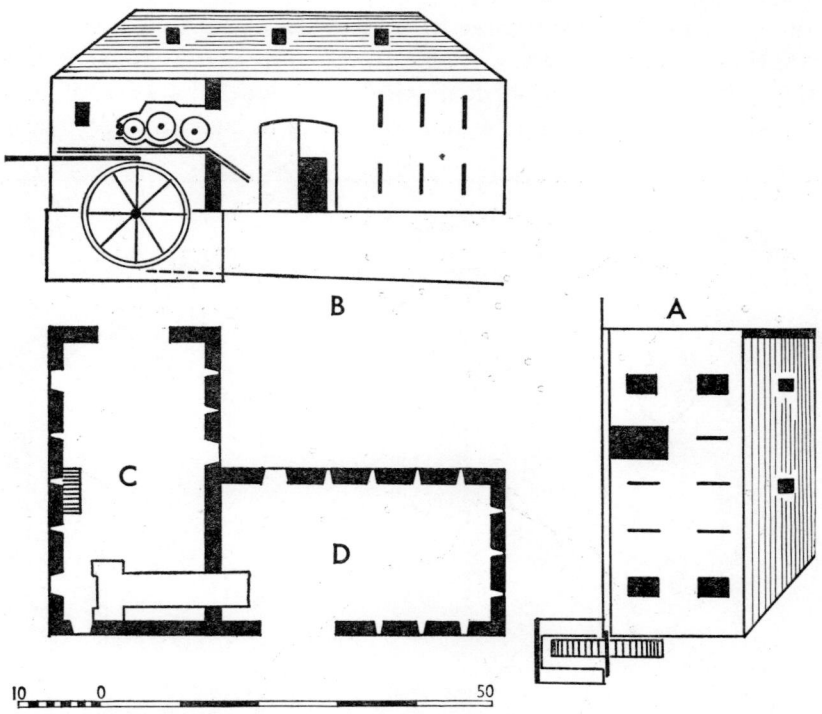

Threshing barn and strawhouse—this undated plan (c 1850) from the Stair Papers, shows the layout of a typical water-powered farm threshing mill. It shows: A, the elevation of the mill, with 14ft waterwheel at side; B, strawhouse with cutaway showing threshing machinery; C, the mill barn, adjoining; D, the strawhouse. The scale is in feet (from SRO, RHP 4915)

Before 1800 threshing machines on the Meikle design were uncommon in Galloway, but even a decade or so later 'even in the higher parts of the country where corn is less plentifully sown, they are very common'.[20] 'When water can be secured as the moving power it is always preferred,' wrote Singer, 'but many of these mills are moved by horses.' A wide variety of horse threshing machines existed in the south-west, including the open type (common in Wigtownshire) and the roofed and enclosed types in a range of shapes and sizes (both round and hexagonal). Most of the enclosed gin houses, built of local rubble and slate, adjoin the threshing barn and strawhouse, to which power was transmitted by gears or levers. In this respect it was exactly like the water-powered version, common throughout the region and illustrated on page 43. A fine example survives at Blairbuie farm near

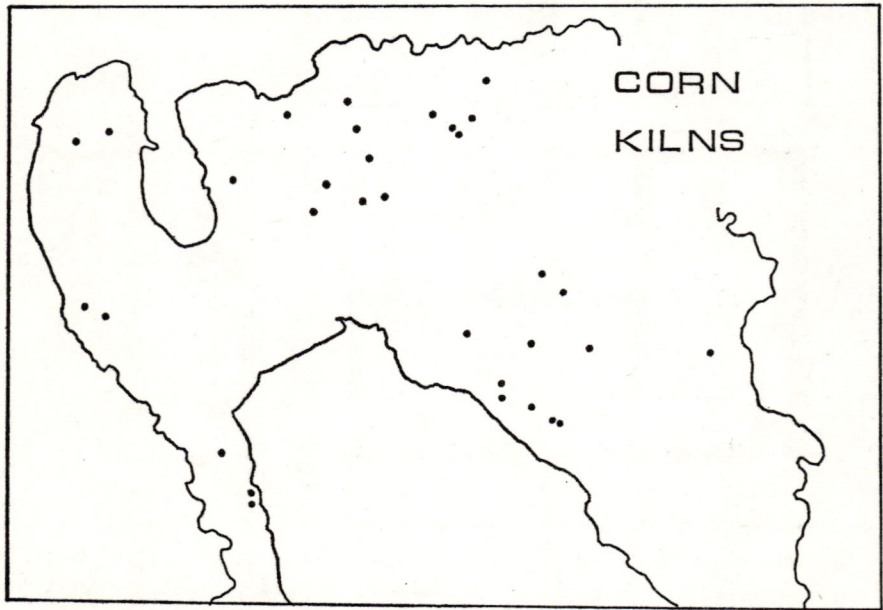

Corn kilns c 1850—These primitive kilns for drying corn were once common in isolated farming districts of Galloway

Monreith, where the threshing machine was only recently removed. Threshing mills, in various states of repair, can be found on most large farms, the majority now used as stores or machine sheds. In Wigtownshire there were nearly 180 threshing mills and at least twice as many in the Stewartry c 1850. The most interesting survivals are described in Section Two.

TANNING AND LEATHERWORKING

Tanning and leatherworking were old-established country crafts in Galloway, where since medieval times beasts occupied a position of importance in the agrarian economy of the region. There are many references to skinners in the various burghs, particularly during the late seventeenth century, when the cattle trade with the South was beginning to assume some significance. Among the most interesting is in the Minute Book of the Stewartry Covenanting War Committee 1640–1, which records the 'Actes anent Hydes, schoes, Bootes and tanning of Leather' issued by the Scottish Parliament. Another entry lays down the price of finished leather, a further indication of Galloway's important role in this industry.[21] Symson outlines the 'peculiar custome' then prevalent of tanning hides with heather instead of oak-bark, probably an indirect consequence of the erosion of woodland in the region. The process much resembles that described in the Whithorn tanners' case mentioned below. Hides were limed to remove hair, thoroughly scoured and cleaned, then tanned in open vats. When processed, hides were ready for use—to be sent to 'countrey shoemakers'.[22]

The existence of long-established techniques provided a vital precondition for the development of tanning and leather-finishing on a larger, more capital-intensive scale during the latter half of the eighteenth century. Another important factor was the growth of the cattle trade, both for breeding in Galloway and for droving to English markets. Small tan works were established in most market towns and by the 1790s the industry had assumed some importance, especially in Dumfries and Stranraer, the former having three tanneries which had 'succeeded pretty well'.[23]

One of the earliest tanneries was that established in the infant industrial village of Gatehouse c 1768, when James Murray granted a lease of land for 15 years to John Borrowdale (a tanner in Wigtown) and his partner George Atkenson (also a tanner from Westmoreland), 'to enable them to sink tanpits and erect buildings'. Murray became a partner and over £400 was invested in building the tannery and laying out tanpits on sloping ground at the foot of Front Street near Fleet Bridge. Later another tanner, James Davitts, joined the firm, and when the lease expired he agreed to manage the business which was bought over by Murray. Davitts prospered and in 1797 he feued the tannery from Murray. He ultimately became its proprietor and realised a substantial fortune. The long, low range of tannery buildings still survive.[24]

There are numerous pointers to the prosperity of the leather business at this period. That astute observer, Robert Heron, described tanning as 'a species of manufacture sufficiently suitable to the circumstances of the country' because 'an abundance of hides are obtained in Galloway' or could easily be imported from Ireland, and bark from oakwood, 'which though greatly weeded away is as plentiful here as in most parts of Scotland'. Other evidence speaks for itself: the long-established Newton Douglas tannery was 'managed with great judgement and sufficient success'; while that in Kirkcudbright had 'enriched its proprietor'. Clearly, however, there were failures in the tanning industry, though far fewer than in the highly volatile cattle trade. In Heron's native town of New Galloway, a tannery failed through lack of capital, for finished leather had found easy sale in the surrounding Glenkens.[25] Likewise, the firm of Hugh Gibson & Co, curriers and leatherworkers in Newton Stewart, were declared bankrupt in 1804.[26] The cattle droving trade had strange consequences, for as the minister of Whithorn pointed out in 1795, the local tanner 'sees our own cattle driven to England and sets off for Ireland to buy hides'.[27]

A remarkable case regarding the possession of a tannery in Whithorn, discloses a wealth of technical information about contemporary tanning processes. It also emphasises that a fairly long-term tie-up of capital was common, which inevitably exposed the leather business to regional and national market fluctuations. John Milroy in 1784 obtained a $17\frac{1}{2}$ year lease of a tanyard in Whithorn, which had previously been let by its owner, Anthony Donnan, to Archibald McNeil & Co, who had been in business as tanners for some time and had built a barn and sunk several tanholes. Milroy (a local merchant involved in wool and cotton spinning) entered into partnership with Anthony Sloan to run the tannery. Later the partnership was dissolved, Milroy purchased the property and rented the tannery to Sloan at a rent of £2 10s per annum. Sloan meantime resolved to go into business on his own and in summer 1799 bought a piece of ground in Whithorn on which to build his tannery. Although his lease had not expired he began to dismantle the original works and remove it for re-erection on his own premises, his argument being that because 'some hides are fully two years in the pits', he would require to start operations at his new plant some considerable time before he vacated Milroy's tannery.[28]

Tanning is a fairly complicated process, as the following description from Anthony Sloan's petition to the Court of Session well illustrates:

> The hides are laid smooth in heaps for one or two days in summer and five or six days in winter. They are then hung on poles in a close room called a smokehouse in which is kept a smouldring fire of wet tan; this occassions a small degree of putrefication, by which means the hair is easily got off by spreading the hide on a sort of wooden horse or beam and scraping it with a crooked knife.

When the hair had been removed the hide was thrown into a water-filled pit to clean out the dirt and it was then scraped on the beam to remove 'grease, loose flesh and extraneous filth'. Thereafter the hides were

> . . . put into a pit of strong liquor called ooze. prepared in pits, called ketches or taps, kept for the purpose, by infusing ground bark in water; this is termed clouring. After which they are removed into another pit, called a scouring, which consists of water strongly impregnated with vitriolic acid or with a vegetable acid prepared from rye or barley. This operation (which is

called raising) by distending the pores of the hides occassions them more
readily to imbibe the ooze, the effect of which is to astringe and condense
the fibres, and gives firmness to the leather.

The hides were then removed from the scouring and spread out flat
in another water-filled pit (called a cinder) with a layer of ground bark
between each hide. After a month or six weeks the hides were lifted
out of the pit, and the whole process repeated. In the following six to
eight months re-tanning might take place at least twice. Hides would
only be 'completely tanned' after a further three months 'unless they
are so stout as to want an additional pit or lair'. Depending on the
weight and texture of the hide, tanning could take from 11 to 18 months
and often up to two years. After removal from the pits, hides were hung
up to dry on poles and 'after being compressed with a steel pin [were]
beat out smooth by wooden hammers called beetles'. Tanning, from
hide to finished leather, might take 18 months, and even more pliable
skins took about six months. Hence Sloan's anxiety to see his new
tannery operating well before his lease on Milroy's expired.[29]

This interesting description not only illustrates the long-term tie-up
of capital and time involved in tanning, but also gives clues to the type
of building in which the process was carried out. The small country
tannery of the type common in Galloway would often be located near
the local slaughter house or cattle market, on the bank of a river, or
near wells for water supply. Most of the nine Dumfries tanneries c 1830
were in the Whitesands district or on the other side of the Nith in
Maxwelltown. The typical tannery was a long, low building of no more
than two storeys, the upper being timber-framed and slatted to allow
free circulation of air. In towns where tanning was important (eg
Dumfries), the skinning process was carried out in a separate plant,
and hides often went direct to the tannery. The tanyard itself was
often in the open, pits being sunk at regular intervals and fitted with
pumps for filling and emptying. On the ground floor was the oak-bark
mill, and above, beating machines, rollers and stocks, probably driven
by water power or steam engine. In nearby currying shops skins were
finished and dressed before sale.[30]

TANNERIES

Tanneries 1825

Tanneries were fairly numerous and well distributed in Galloway, market towns like Stranraer, Whithorn, Newton Stewart, Castle Douglas, Langholm and Sanquhar having at least one and often more (see above). Dumfries undoubtedly dominated the regional industry and according to one contemporary estimate the tan and skin works there represented a capital of £25,000 in 1812. Half the hides were obtained locally and the rest imported from Ireland or farther afield. Apart from sales in neighbouring markets, leather was exported to Edinburgh, Glasgow, Carlisle, Liverpool, Dublin, Newcastle and London. Tanneries in Lockerbie and Annan carried on a trade in leather valued at nearly £3,000 per annum.[31]

The decline of the cattle trade and the rise of competitors in large urban centres (eg Glasgow, Edinburgh and Liverpool) brought in its wake the decline of the small country tanneries of Galloway, particularly after the coming of the railways. Although many of the tanneries mentioned in parish accounts of the 1790s were still operating

in the 1830s (and even survived till mid-century) decline had long set
in. An early casualty was that at Creetown, which had been 'long given
up' by 1845.[32] Concentration of the industry in Dumfries began early
in the nineteenth century and became significant after the 1850s—a
direct consequence of its dominating market function in cattle and
increasingly in sheep. The annual value of leather manufactured in
Dumfries rose from £30,000 in 1832 to £80,000 in 1870.

By the 1870s the Dumfries tanning industry was concentrated in
four firms: T. D. Currie; A. & C. Wallace; H. Murphy; and Fallas
& Co, the latter also operating a large saddlery business. About a
hundred workers were employed and output averaged 30,000 hides
per annum. Most of the raw material was imported, mainly through
Liverpool and Leith. Later, Murphy bought over two tanneries and
in 1895 the Dumfries Tannery Co took over the entire industry and
fitted out large premises 'with the latest machinery'. The company
concentrated exclusively on tanning and flourished for a while, but
like the local tweed industry, was unable to compete with larger units
elsewhere and succumbed to economic depression after 1920.[33]

One old-established skinworks in Langholm is still working but
elsewhere only tannery buildings remain, mostly converted to other
uses. Two in Gatehouse and a smaller one in Whithorn are particularly
interesting. Strangely enough, one associated rural craft which was
very common in Galloway, clog-making, is still carried on in Dumfries
—a reminder of the importance of tanning and leatherworking in the
past agrarian economy of the region.

BREWING AND DISTILLING

'The liquor industries were essentially agrarian in origin', and
Galloway shared in both widely dispersed rural activities. Brewing was
of early origin, whereas distilling was essentially a growth of the latter
half of the eighteenth century.[34] The small town breweries common
in the local market centres of south-west Scotland during the late
eighteenth and early nineteenth centuries quickly succumbed to their

larger city counterparts in central Scotland and northern England and few remained by the turn of the present century. The small regional distilling industry shared the fortunes and misfortunes of distilling in general. Four malt distilleries survived the rise of blending in the late nineteenth century, though only one at Bladnoch near Wigtown is still working (plate, page 35).

Material and documentary evidence on the history of brewing in Scotland outwith the context of the larger town and city breweries of Edinburgh, Alloa and Glasgow is remarkably scant. David Bremner in his classic account of the history of industry in Scotland to 1869 naturally devotes some space to brewing, but his remarks are mostly confined to activities in and around Edinburgh. A more recent analyst of the English brewing industry, Peter Mathias, followed suit, remarking that 'brewing in Scotland was above all an urban industry'.[35] As was the case with distilling, government policy aimed to eliminate the small—and often illicit—country operator, so that brewing, particularly after the rise of malt duty 1760–80, became increasingly formal and concentrated in large production units.[36]

Even after the imposition of higher malt duties, poorer Scottish barley was still allowed half duty and in Galloway (where barley was an important rent crop) domestic brewing remained common. In the 1780s innkeepers in the area still brewed their own beer from locally grown barley and malt, making necessary 'numerous and regular surveys by the Officers of Excise'. Among a variety of other related legislation, the Sale of Beer Act (1795) virtually put an end to private manufacture and irregular sale of ale, by requiring the licensing of premises for such purposes. According to Singer, writing in 1812 of Dumfriesshire, brewing in the district 'fell into a few hands and public breweries increased in number'.

One Dumfries merchant, a former provost, who capitalised on the tightening grasp of the Customs & Excise (Robert Burns included) was Gabriel Richardson, who started porter brewing in 1783 and was very successful. His product was well known and its quality considered 'very superior to what is often made in Scotland under that name'.

Nearby Maxwelltown had two breweries in 1791 and though Gate-house probably had its own too, ales, porter and wines were regularly imported by sea.[37] A more useful guideline to the distribution of the industry is afforded by early nineteenth-century commercial directories. The location of the seventeen small breweries operating in south-west Scotland in 1825–6 is indicated below. The dominance of Dumfries and Maxwelltown is an indication of its growing significance as a market centre for the whole region. At least one Dumfries brewer, Charles Barry, had connections with distilling, a family business carried on in the town by Wm Barry & Sons. Revenue from ale and malt in the Dumfries collection in 1809–10 totalled £7,297.[38]

The regional brewing industry had contracted considerably by the

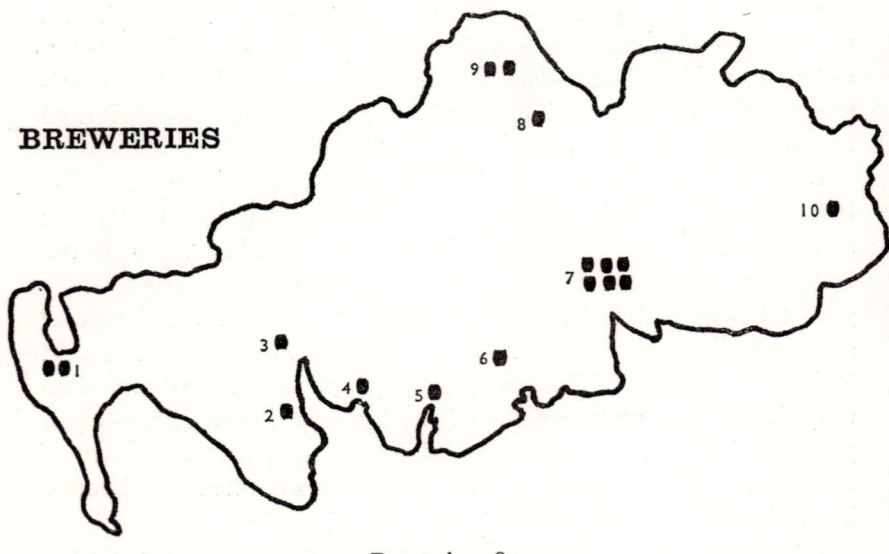

Breweries 1825

Key:
1 Stranraer
2 Wigtown
3 Newton Stewart
4 Gatehouse
5 Kirkcudbright
6 Castle Douglas
7 Dumfries
8 Thornhill
9 Sanquhar
10 Langholm

Page 53 (right)
*Cumloden Waulkmill,
Minnigaff, near New-
ton Stewart. A three-
storey granite mill
range;* (below) *spin-
ning and weaving
machinery for the
manufacture of
blankets was powered
by an internal, over-
shot waterwheel*

Page 54 (above) *Waulk Mill, Kirkcowan, built by the Milroys in 1821 and extended in 1835. Note the large attic and cast-iron window frames, typical of the period;* (below) *part-roofless remains of Mount Pleasant paper mill, Dalbeattie*

mid-1830s. Although several breweries survived in Dumfries, few of the small town ones were operating with the exception of those at Gatehouse and Newton Stewart. The brewery at Gatehouse dates back to 1784 and probably originated as a private enterprise encouraged by James Murray. It was still operating in 1870, when its owner was Thomas McKean. The building survives, a stark, two-storey and attic structure with hipped roof adjoining the lade above the cotton mill complex. The Newton Stewart brewery has long since ceased to produce beer but retains its links with the past, for it is used as a store by Campbell, Hope & King, the Edinburgh brewers (plate, page 35).[39]

In common with much of Scotland during the latter half of the eighteenth century Galloway had numerous country distilleries—licit and illicit—producing for both local and export markets. Barley was often the main rent crop in the better arable districts of Galloway (eg Kirkpatrick-Irongray and Sorbie parishes, to name but two), while in Dumfriesshire it was grown on all but marginal land. Combined with good water supplies and ready access to markets in England and Ireland the availability of local barley supplies provided stimuli for the establishment of distilling in Galloway.[40]

According to Alfred Barnard, author of the best account of the distilling industry, the first distillery was established in the south-west at Langholm in 1765. The *Statistical Account* affords ample evidence of expansion in the period immediately before the imposition of notoriously high duties during the early years of the French Wars.[41] The 'stillatory' of Anthony and Thomas McGuffogg & Co at Small-hill, Whithorn, paid £729 per annum in revenue 'besides malt duty' (1795), while in Kirkgunzeon parish a small distillery at Lochend had just been opened in 1793. Near Kirkcudbright on the River Dee 'a gentleman of remarkable mechanical genius under the patronage of Lord Daer' built a distillery which was short-lived and was soon converted to a cotton mill. Maxwelltown had at least two malt-houses which no doubt supplied both local distilleries and breweries.[42]

Undoubtedly the majority of small country distilleries in Galloway

D

were casualties of the high spirit duty imposed during the period 1799–1822. Among the first was the Smallhill distillery of Anthony and Thomas McGuffogg, who 'carried on a considerable business, it was generally supposed with prosperity and success'. Sequestration in 1801 arose as a result of debts to William Hyslop, a Dumfries corn merchant and distiller, and the McGuffoggs' other creditors included a number of farmers and landowners in the Machars who had been similarly abused. Unfortunately little about business operations at Smallhill is revealed in litigation.[43] No Dumfries Collection distilleries are mentioned as active in the Scottish distilleries report 1798–9, which suggests that those which were not operating illicitly had succumbed to heavier spirit duties imposed at this time.

(a)   *Galloway Distillers and Production 1823–6*

Wm. Barry & Sons	Dumfries	8,886 gal
James R. Marshall	Ecclefechan	11,325
J. & T. McLelland	Bladnoch	28,956
J. McKie Jnr & Co	Stranraer	12,077
John Finlay	Bank	2,250
Finlay & Stein	,,	2,192
Arnott & Co	Langholm	35,255
Wm. Curl	,,	5,426
John McVitie	Ecclefechan	—
		106,367 gal

(b)   *Distillers and Output 1826–7*

Wm. Barry & Sons	436 gal
J. & T. McLelland	9,792
J. McKie	8,956
J. Finlay	1,475
Arnott & Co	2,974
	23,633 gal

Source: PP 1826–7, XVII, *Account Relating to Malt & Spirits*, 405, 498

Galloway shared in the sharp revival of distilling following the

DISTILLERIES

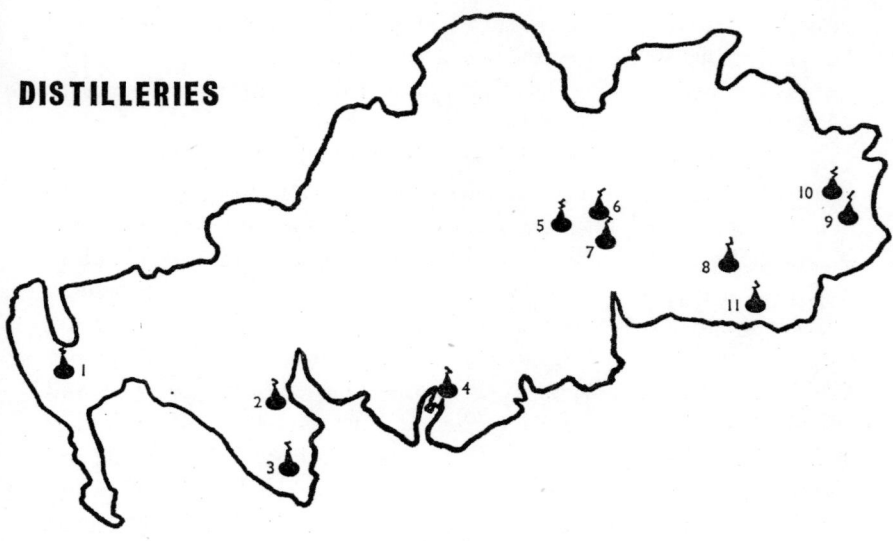

Distilleries

Key:
1 Stranraer
2 Wigtown
3 Whithorn
4 Kirkcudbright

5 Glenessland
6 Glencarrick
7 Dumfries
8 Ecclefechan

9 Glentarras
10 Langholm
11 Annandale

reduction of duty after the Napoleonic Wars, particularly after 1823. By this date there were at least six distilleries in the south-west at Langholm, Ecclefechan, Dumfries, Kirkcudbright, Bladnoch and Stranraer (see table on page 56). Bladnoch, founded in 1817 by the brothers John and Thomas McLelland, was probably the earliest, though the older Langholm distillery of Arnott & Co had the largest output in 1823–6. The latter company was a casualty of this phase of rapid expansion, for the partners John Arnott and James Kennedy went bankrupt in 1826. Their debts totalled £4,850, the main creditors being the Leith Banking Co and Connell & Co, bankers in Carlisle. Other creditors included the local cooperage, a maltster and a nearby colliery, which would probably indicate that too much of the firm's capital was tied up in bonded whisky. Activities soon revived and Langholm distillery operated for a time under the management of James Kennedy & Co, who also founded the nearby Glentarras distillery c 1839.[44]

A number of ventures originated in the early 1830s, the majority short-lived. In the Nithsdale parish of Kirkmahoe, John Miller established Glencarrick distillery 'on the banks of a romantic rivulet'. It was described in 1834 as being 'on a judicious and moderate scale' and in 'full and prosperous operation'. Near the neighbouring village of Dunscore a distillery was erected in 1830 at Glenessland 'on a pretty extensive scale' and prospered for a few years after which its owner died and operations ceased. 'It consumed a large quantity of grain and afforded a ready and convenient market', but it was 'doubtful whether it would have proved a profitable concern'. Both Glencarrick and Glenessland were unsuccessful but another Dumfriesshire distillery established in this era of rapid expansion, Annandale, built by George Donald in 1830, survived for at least a century.[45]

The only distillery to survive in Galloway is one of the oldest, Bladnoch near Wigtown, which survives much as it was when Barnard visited it in the 1880s (plate, page 35). He described it as 'a square pile of buildings round a courtyard' covering about two acres, and even the huge red gates still survive as they were. Bladnoch shared the period of bad fortune from which the other Galloway distilleries failed to recover after the 1890s and following some years of closure, re-opened in 1957. It is again producing the fine Lowland malt for which it was long famed, though all but a few precious bottles are for blending.[46]

TIMBER AND TIMBER CRAFTS

The timber resources of south-west Scotland have long been important, although in the past forestry was probably of much less significance in the regional economy than it has become over the last thirty years. In the eighteenth century landowners throughout Galloway, but particularly in the upland districts of Wigtownshire and Kirkcudbrightshire, began to plant trees to replace the deprivations of the original forest lands which had been going on since medieval times. Most large estates, such as those of the Earl of Stair, the Earl of Galloway, the Murrays of Broughton & Cally and the Duke of Buccleuch, had extensive plantations by the 1790s.

Despite the survival in the late eighteenth century of wide areas of virgin woodland, timber was imported for use in Galloway from both New England and the Baltic. The *Statistical Account* contains several interesting references to timber import at Solway harbours. The largest vessels trading from Stranraer (1792) imported 'deals, planks and large timber' from the Baltic for domestic use and for shipbuilding, while ships from the Baltic loaded with timber for Dumfries were too large to enter the Nith and generally unloaded their cargoes at Carsethorn. At Annan, farther up the Solway, imported 'timber in deals from Gottenburgh' was sold locally, and Sarkfoot, a small creek nearby, annually imported £7,500 worth of timber from 'Riga and Memel'.[47]

Timber exploitation for charcoal led to the depletion of forests throughout much of highland Britain during the eighteenth century and Galloway was for a time an important source of supply of charcoal. Its main markets seem to have been the Cumberland and North Lancashire iron furnaces, which also had important links with two charcoal ironworks farther north in the Scottish Highlands at Bonawe and Craelacken. According to the writer of the *Statistical Account for Carsphairn* (1793) wood formerly abounded and in the same district small-scale iron smelting was carried on until charcoal resources were exhausted. The Earl of Galloway's woods (mostly natural stands of oak and ash) in Minnigaff parish were sold for £6,000 c 1792, mostly to be 'charred' and exported. Small timber from Kirkpatrick-Irongray, worth £1,600 in 1792, was made into charcoal to be sent to the furnaces at Whitehaven. A similar export from the Kells district was transported down Loch Ken by boat to the ports of the Solway on the River Dee.[48]

Another important use of timber resources in Galloway was the exploitation of oak-bark for tanning. Anderson in his classic study of

Scottish forestry mentions that the district was particularly suited to oak growth and notes that there were still extensive stands of native oak woodland in the south-west even in the eighteenth century. Oak for tanbark was a common export at the time of the *Statistical Account*, and Webster says (1794) that 'the sale of wood is pretty considerable in some parts'. Even so late as the 1830s tanbark was exported from Galloway, Minnigaff parish being a good example.[49]

Signs of the re-development of Galloway's woodland and of an expanding home timber trade are seen in the rapid growth of sawmills after 1800. Most of the larger estates had at least one sawmill and even the smaller ones began to be equipped with mills after the 1820s. There are few references in Galloway estate papers to sawmills before 1800 and none in the *Statistical Account* of the 1790s. Where wood was exploited prior to this time, the commonest method of preparing it for use was the large two-man cross-cut saw worked over a saw pit. The most favoured motive power for rotary-saw mills was the waterwheel and many timber mills of this type were built in Galloway during the first half of the nineteenth century.[50]

Of a total of 35 sawmills operating in the two Galloway counties c 1860, 21 were located in the Stewartry. Among the largest was Kingan's Mill at New Abbey (still operated by the same family), where a 17ft diameter waterwheel powered the rotary saws. In the mid-1830s it had an important export trade to Liverpool. Probably more typical was Glen Mill on the Cargen Water near Lochrutton, where a small sawmill was worked from the same wheel as lint-scutching and wool-carding machinery. There are many good surviving examples of estate sawmills, the best being Logan (plate, page 36), Galloway House and Kirkdale. The only working sawmill is at Drumburn, where a water-wheel still drives the rotary saw.[51]

Woodworking crafts have long been important in Galloway, as in most rural districts where timber was plentiful. Probably among the oldest, clog-making was particularly important in Dumfries and Annan, clogs being widely used in country districts instead of boots and shoes. Several clog-makers are still active in Dumfries, though much of the output today is for industrial use in chemical works, tanneries and similar plants.[52] Bobbin and pirn manufacture probably began as a response to demands of the local textile trade in the late eighteenth century, but afterwards expanded into manufacture for export to other textile areas. The founders of the industry and largest firm were Thomas and William Helme of Dalbeattie, natives of Cumberland (another centre of bobbin manufacture), who settled in Galloway about 1840. By 1870, the firm had bobbin mills at Gatehouse and Dalbeattie, a large sawmill and woodyard at Dalbeattie, as well as several smaller sawmills in the neighbourhood.[53] Later the industry expanded considerably in Dalbeattie and until recently there were three firms producing a wide variety of bobbins for the textile trade.

The extension of forestry since the inter-war years has brought about a revival of the timber industry and of sawmilling in south-west Scotland and forestry is now one of the key industries of the region.

SEA-SHORE CRAFTS

Kelpmaking, a rural industry described in the context of the Highland economy by Malcolm Gray as one of 'windfall profits', was carried on in Galloway during the late eighteenth and early nineteenth centuries. Its contribution to the economy of the region was probably relatively insignificant, being little more than a seasonal occupation along the coast. The conditions necessary for kelpmaking in the Highlands were duplicated farther south in Galloway:

> A raw material supply fairly easily reached from existing settlements and replenished by natural growth, a technique of production that was laborious but demanded no elaborate equipment, and a product cheaply transportable in its final concentrated form.[54]

On Solway shore there was an abundant supply of seaweed, and readily available supplies of peat provided the other main raw material of the industry. The main locations of kelp manufacture are shown in the figure on page 62, the most important being Kirkmaiden and Stoneykirk in the Rhins, Luce Bay, Wigtown Bay, Borgue and Kirk-

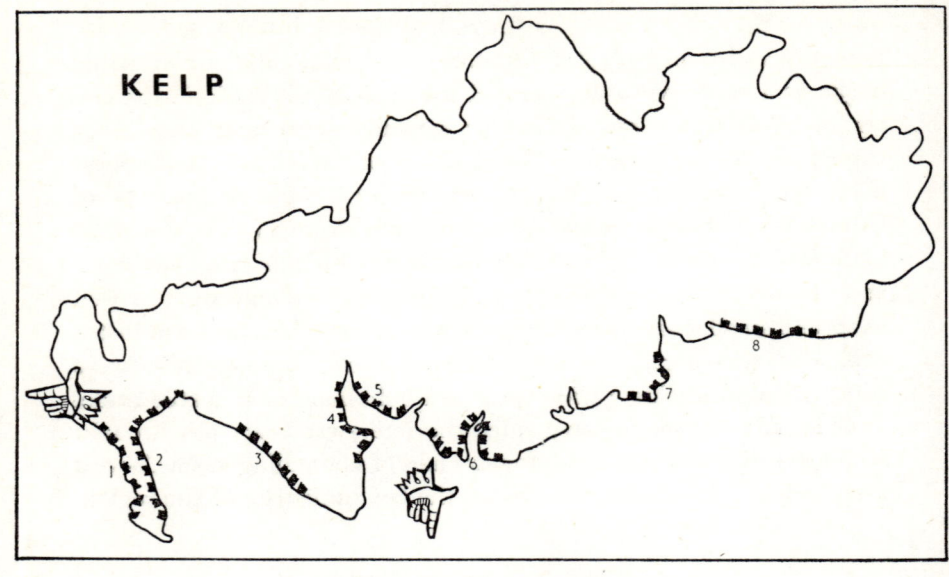

Kelpmaking shores in Galloway

Key:
1 Logan shore   3 Mochrum   5 Kirkmabreck   7 Southerness
2 Luce Bay   4 Wigtown/   6 Borgue   8 Ruthwell
                     Baldoon

cudbright. At Kirkbean kelpmaking was probably combined with lime and shell burning and on Ruthwell shore with salt boiling.[55]

There is little documentary information about kelp manufacture in Galloway and virtually no data on production. In Kirkmaiden, kelp was made 'in considerable quantities', while the kelp shore of Mochrum was rented at £100 per annum in 1796. In the Borgue district production concentrated at Ross, Brighouse, Kirkandrews and Knockbrex bays, and the sands at the head of Luce Bay were a focus of seaweed collection and burning.[56] The main market for Galloway kelp was probably the small native linen industry and it is possibly no accident that the most important kelping areas were in the Rhins, where linen was of some significance. There were four flax mills and a bleachfield in Stoneykirk c 1792, the latter no doubt supplied by local kelpmakers. Another important outlet was Ireland, where the bleachfields of Ulster ensured ready sale. Lastly, there was the omnipresent English market, where Galloway kelp was sold at £5 per ton c 1795.[57]

The primary locational factor in the growth of the Scottish salt and brine industry was the availability of fuel, hence the marked concentration of salt pans in the Forth basin, near readily exploitable coal measures.[58] But salt making was not confined to the coasts of the Forth and Clyde, and in Galloway it survived as a seasonal sea-shore craft till the early nineteenth century.

Several salt works functioned at different times in the Rhins of Galloway from the seventeenth to the nineteenth centuries (see page 64). Uchtred Agnew of Galdenoch made a contract c 1640 with Alexander Osborne to establish a salt pan and works on Galdenoch shore. Osborne was to erect 'a sufficient works', while the laird was to give him an acre of ground and liberty to cut peats for the salt pan. Logan salt pan is mentioned in 1688, when it was 'set' to James Mitchell 'with liberty to cast 3000 loads of peats yearly' in the moss of Logan, 'of qwich moss one horse is able to keep the pann daily going'. Symson says of the same works that 'good salt is made with peits instead of coals'. Galdenoch was still working in 1791 when 'two dwellings houses and the salt pan' were valued at £2 per annum and 'a pann house and large hole digged in the rock' at 10s.[59]

Modern place-names reveal the location of several other salt works which operated during the eighteenth century. At Airies in Kirkcolm is Salt Pan Bay, and near Ardwell is Salt Pans where before 1792 salt had been manufactured in two pans. Even Galdenoch survived till the early nineteenth century, producing 'very excellent salt from seawater'. A salt pan at Port William survived long enough to be marked on the first OS six-inch map and several others around Luce Bay appear on the Ainslie map of the 1780s.[60]

Salt making survived in Galloway primarily because of the complex

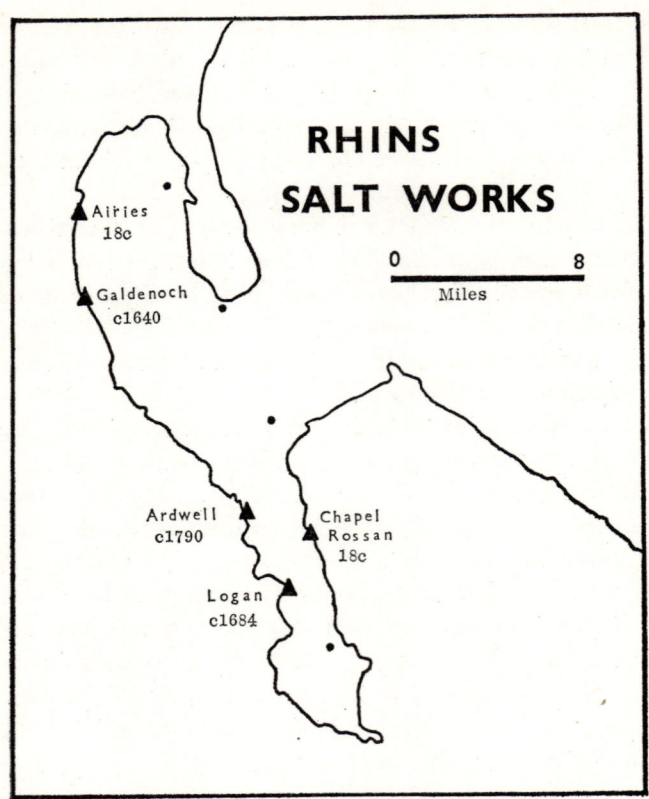

**RHINS
SALT WORKS**

0 _____ 8
Miles

Airies
18c

Galdenoch
c1640

Ardwell
c1790

Chapel
Rossan
18c

Logan
c1684

Salt works in the Rhins of Galloway

'Salt laws', which kept prices high and encouraged illicit manufacture and smuggling—both of which were apparently rife in Galloway. Heron, for example, remarks that salt making 'might be successful were it not for a smuggling importation of Irish salt'. The Annandale salt-manufacturers, farther up the Solway, had exemption from salt duty under an act of the Scottish Parliament in 1671 and this was never contested until final repeal of English laws came in 1825. Local demand for Galloway salt seems to have been maintained by its use for salting meat, bacon and hams—all key exports from the region in the late eighteenth and early nineteenth centuries.[61]

Highly seasonal and intermittent in operation, the Solway and Rhins salt works were probably of little more than local significance. As an industry, and perhaps more as a rural craft, it has left little to interest the industrial archaeologist, with the exception of rock-cut salt pans at the cliff-foot on lonely Galdenoch shore.

Economic change and technological farming methods have together endowed Galloway with a valuable heritage of rural 'archaeology', which despite the apparent tranquillity of the landscape, is rapidly disappearing from the scene. Yet sufficient has survived and been recorded to emphasise the important role of farmers, millers, mill-wrights and other craftsmen in the evolution of the regional economy over the past two hundred years.

(See pages 244–6 for notes)

CHAPTER THREE

Textiles

GALLOWAY had clear advantages for the development of a local woollen industry: fine local wool from moorland sheep; soft water for the various finishing processes; and power to drive machinery from the same rivers and burns. The development of linen production was much less obvious in this wet south-western corner of Scotland. Only small areas were suited to flax growth, especially the Rhins district of Wigtownshire and lower Annandale in Dumfriesshire. Unlike most other parts of western Scotland the relatively small linen industry of the region had a separate identity from the early eighteenth century. Cotton textiles were never grafted on to this sector in the way that occurred elsewhere. Linen simply faded from the regional scene in the early decades of the nineteenth century. Cotton was probably the shortest-lived of the textile industries, but it had an equal impact on the economy of Galloway in the period 1790–1820 as the tweed trade had later, 1860–1900. Cotton spinning was established in Galloway largely because of the similarity of the environment to that of central Scotland and Lancashire. South-west Scotland had long-standing commercial links with the latter region and it was natural that a district with good water-power resources and ease of access by sea to the markets of north-west England and elsewhere should attract entrepreneurs already familiar with its natural advantages. It was no coincidence that the earliest and largest cotton mills in Galloway were financed by Yorkshire businessmen already in the cattle trade, encouraged by a far-seeing local nobleman.

WOOL

'Galloway for wool' was for centuries a truism, the province being famed even in late medieval times for the quality of its wool. Symson, writing in 1684, describes it as one of the chief products of the region, both wool and woollen cloth finding their way to markets in central Scotland and England.[1] Certainly sheep were already of considerable economic importance in Galloway at this period, especially in the upland interior. Three main types of wool were produced—laid, deal and moor wools—the latter being the best in quality. The key production areas were Penninghame, Kirkcowan, Mochrum and Glenluce in Wigtownshire and Minnigaff and the valley of the Fleet in the Stewartry.[2]

Domestic woollen-cloth production was of ancient origin in Galloway and in the early eighteenth century the industry was carried on in widely scattered, small-scale units. The main product was coarse cloth for local markets, though Patrick Lindsey in his *Interest of Scotland Considered* (1733) mentions the importance of blanket and plaiding manufacture in Kirkcudbright and Minnigaff.[3] General Roy's map of c 1750 indicates the locations of at least eight 'wauk' or fulling mills, where waterwheels provided the power for wool-finishing machinery—such as the wooden hammers that beat the cloth in the fulling processes.[4] The majority were situated in the parishes mentioned above and served surrounding districts. Some were of earlier origin, such as that mentioned in the Hay of Park estate papers, where a tack dated 1711 records the lease of the 'walk mill' and lands at Stocking Hill to William Ker, 'walker in Glenluce'.[5] This mill had previously been let to John Baillye in 1681, but this particular tenant had gone by default of £33 10s (Scots) rent.[6] Remains of these early wauk mills are naturally few, but the walls of one very old mill (marked on Timothy Pont's *Gallovidia* map of 1654) can be seen on the Penkiln Burn above Minnigaff, immediately adjacent to its eighteenth-century successor.

Although spinning, carding and weaving remained important cottage industries during much of the eighteenth century, there is evidence of growing mechanisation in the regional woollen industry as contemporary technological improvements made small-scale factory organisation possible. This applied particularly to the carding and spinning processes, for weaving on handlooms remained important in Galloway—as in most parts of rural Scotland—for a much longer period than in the highly industrialised central lowlands. Indeed hand-loom weaving survived in south-west Scotland until the latter half of the nineteenth century.

A large number of small, water-powered carding and spinning mills were built in Galloway towards the end of the eighteenth century and many of the older 'wauk' mills were refurbished and equipped with new machinery. A 'wool manufactury', for example, was established in Wigtown parish on the River Bladnoch at Waukmill, which by 1792 had 40 workers making 'plaiding and flannel' for export to England; another at Kirkpatrick-Durham, started c 1785, was operated by a co-partnery encouraged by the local minister and landowner, the Rev David Lamont, who was a driving force of 'improvement' and in-dustrialisation in the Stewartry; and yet another near Twynholm (c 1798), once a distillery and then a cotton mill, had 'greater demands for yarn than others in the trade'.[7] The latter mill, it was recorded, had been equipped with 'improved machinery, water-powered from a small stream', including 'teasing or scribling and carding machines' as well as 'several hand jeanies'. It too was run by a co-partnership, a chief member being Lord Daer, another active 'improver'.

Typical of the smaller wool mills erected in the late eighteenth century is Bar Mill in the parish of Mochrum. The remains of this old wool-carding and spinning mill are situated on the raised beach near West Barr (itself a very old farmstead site marked on Pont's *Gallovidia*) in the valley of the Elrig Burn overlooking Luce Bay. The structure (see page 69) of whinstone and granite rubble is 45ft long and 18ft wide on walls 2ft thick. The mill has been two-storied with numerous windows (some blocked up) and access doors at ground and first-floor levels. Probably the carding machinery was located on the ground floor and the spinning jennies above. The former wheelpit (partially in-filled) indicates that the wheel was breastshot (of wood and cast iron) about 13ft in diameter by 4½ft wide, and was driven from a lade off the nearby burn. The mill is now roofless and overgrown. Numerous other examples of small wauk mills scattered throughout Galloway and Dumfriesshire, which have survived in one form or other, are described in Section Two.

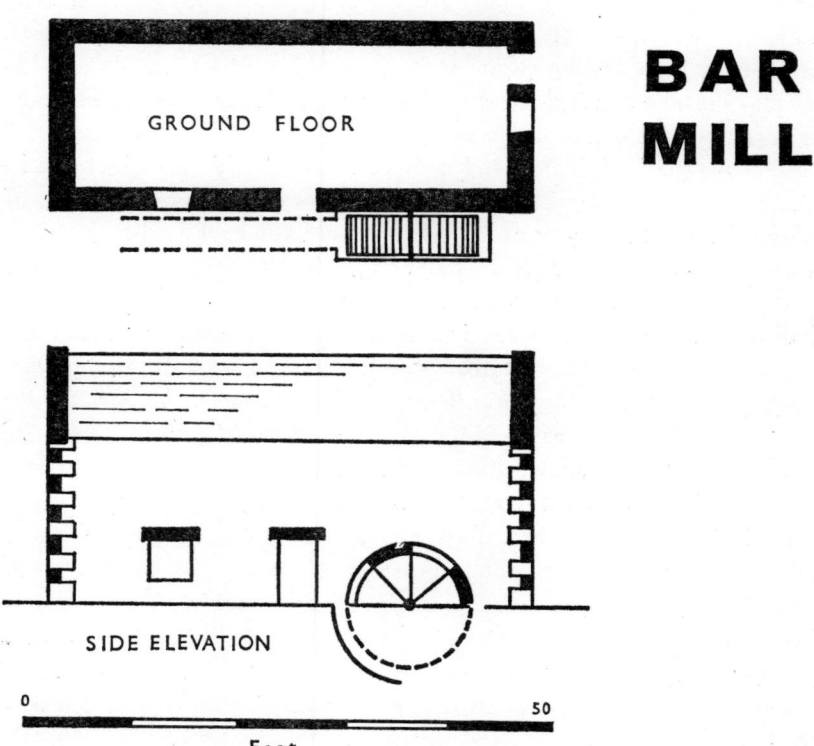

The growing importance of woollen textiles in the rural economy of the province is reflected in the numerous references which appear throughout the *Statistical Account*. In the parish of Minnigaff—long an important district of wool production—there were said to be over 30,000 sheep; from Glasserton sheep were exported by sea to markets in Liverpool and Whitehaven, while wool was sold to Ayrshire and merchants even came from England to buy the local product; and from Stranraer, Galloway plaiding valued at £3,000 per annum was sold to Virginia.[8] Handloom weaving, a textile craft of long-standing domestic importance, was already beginning to assume considerable significance in Galloway—not only wool, but also cotton and linen. This craft industry was a direct antecedent of the large-scale factory tweed industry which developed in Dumfries and Langholm after the mid-1830s. Because of its close affinities with general textile manufacture it is considered in a separate sub-section.

During the period 1790–1850 there was a considerable increase in the number of wool mills throughout Galloway, the majority being of larger scale than earlier mills. Cumloden Waulkmill, Old Minnigaff, was started about 1800 (plate, page 53). It is probably one of the most complete and best-preserved textile sites in Galloway. Built on the banks of the Penkiln Burn, it replaced an even earlier wauk mill, famous for its wool cloth in the seventeenth century. Cumloden (see page 73) is a three-storey granite and whinstone structure with a slate roof, the interior being lit by large cast-iron multi-pane windows at each level and by fanlights in the attic. In the basement is a fine, wood and cast-iron overshot waterwheel 13ft in diameter by 5ft wide, ingeniously constructed to allow the maximum power effect of water falling from the trough, which enters from the lade on the west side of the mill (plate, page 53). The main driving machinery was located in the basement, power being transmitted by vertical and horizontal gearing to the upper floors directly from the wheel. The spinning machinery was located on the first floor, while in the attic above was the loom-shop, the latter originally housing handlooms and later small power looms. In a lean-to was a dye-house, where two large, cast-iron dyeing vats still lie as they were left. Cumloden employed twelve workers in 1842 and continued to operate until the early 1920s, manufacturing its traditional product, blankets and plaiding. The continuity of many craft activities in Galloway until fairly recent times is well illustrated by the history of Cumloden Waulkmill.[9]

Kirkcowan, a moorland parish where the main economic activity

Page 71   (above) *Print of Gatehouse cotton mills by the edge of the River Fleet c 1847. Note the arrangement of waterwheels;* (below) *workers' housing in Gatehouse, late eighteenth century*

Page 72 (above) *Ruined workers' housing at the Woodhead lead mines, Carsphairn;* (below) *entrance to abandoned level at Wood o' Cree lead mines, near Newton Stewart*

was sheep-rearing, attracted Robert Milroy as a suitable location for a wool mill and there in 1814 he built a carding mill. Milroy, who had served his time with John Falconer, a dyer in nearby Mochrum, was by this time getting on in years (he was born in 1751), and the business was taken over by his son, also named Robert.[10] In partnership with other brothers (who were merchants in Canada, Jamaica and Trinidad) Robert Jnr built a larger mill by the Tarff Water on the site of his father's original plant.[11] The mill was considerably enlarged in 1835 by William and Thomas Milroy (Robert Jnr's sons) and by 1839 employed 39 workfolk (26 men and 13 women), having a 12hp water-wheel to drive the spinning machinery.[12] About the same period Wauk Mill was described as 'a thriving establishment' manufacturing 'blankets, plain and pilot cloths, plaidings and flannels', the local water

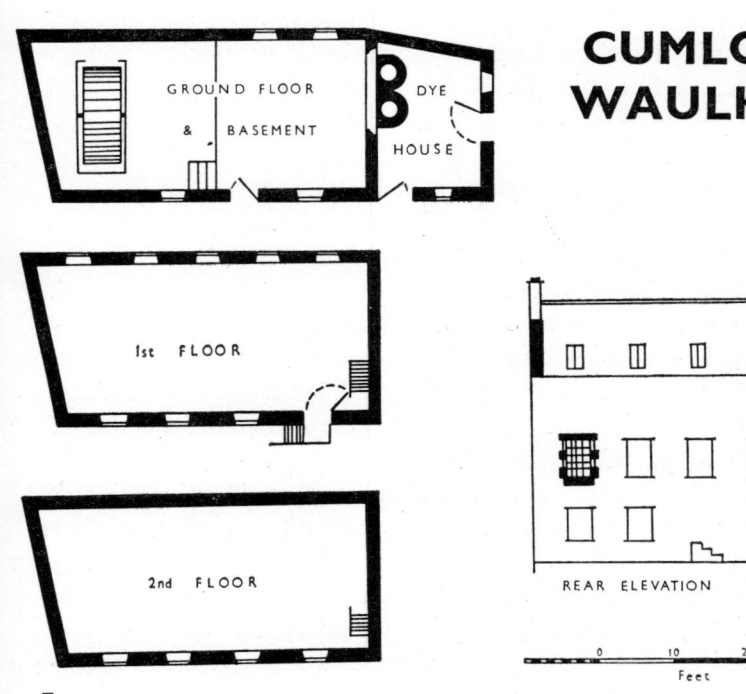

CUMLODEN WAULKMILL

GROUND FLOOR & BASEMENT

DYE HOUSE

1st FLOOR

2nd FLOOR

REAR ELEVATION

0   10   20   30   40
Feet

E

'being well adapted for the purposes of dyeing and milling'.[13] Much of the original building survives, although there were substantial additions made later in the nineteenth century (plate, page 54).

There were numerous other wool mills, like Milroy's at Kirkcowan, widely distributed throughout Dumfries and Galloway, 'the woollen manufacture', as one contemporary put it, 'being rendered much cheaper and easier by means of machinery for teazing, carding and roving of wool'.[14] At Twynholm the carding and wool-spinning mill mentioned above was still active c 1840, while Newbank Mill in the parish of Kirkpatrick-Durham (which still survives) was using the full 16hp generated by its twin waterwheels and employed 10 workers.[15] Somewhat larger in size was the Dumfries wauk mill on the River Nith, which in 1824 was rented at £31 10s per annum.[16] Like cotton mills, wool mills attracted the attention of improving gentry, who saw in them a means of diversifying their interests from the agrarian sector, and of establishing a settled population in planned villages on their estates. A fine example of this is provided by the village of Brydekirk (begun 1800) on the estate of Major-General Alexander Dirom of Mount Annan. What Gatehouse in the Stewartry was to the regional cotton industry, Brydekirk in Dumfriesshire was to wool, though on a much reduced scale. Brydekirk was laid out on a classic grid-iron and crescent plan by the edge of the River Annan. In ten years it had 250 inhabitants, all mostly employed in the local wool, flax and corn mills, a freestone and limestone quarry, or on the estate lands. One of the first buildings to be erected was the wool mill 'upon a large scale and on the most improved plan', located at a point where the river 'being large and rapid affords falls and power capable of turning any weight of machinery'.[17]

These brief case-studies serve to illustrate the wide dispersion of woollen-textile manufacturing throughout south-west Scotland (see page 75). Yet despite the scattered nature of the industry in relatively small units, specialisation in various branches of wool manufacture and finishing developed relatively early in the region. The importance of plaiding and blankets in Wigtownshire and western Kirkcudbrightshire has already been stressed, but other districts and towns also developed specialist textile working. By the closing decades of the eighteenth century the manufacture of carpets was well underway in the Nithsdale town of Sanquhar, and was also carried on in Newton Douglas and nearby Creetown. Stocking-making and hosiery were important in Dumfries and Langholm, and in both of these centres the tweed trade began to assume a new importance after the 1840s, when the popularity of this cloth led to the growth of the textile industry in neighbouring Border towns.[18]

Carpet-making was a natural development in Galloway, as it had been earlier farther north in Kilmarnock, for abundant supplies of coarse wool from moorland sheep were readily obtainable. The earliest reference (c 1792) is that to a 'small manufactory of coarse carpets' in Newton Douglas, which had been 'attempted by a Mr Tannahill under the patronage of Mr [William] Douglas'.[19] Shortly afterwards, two small carpet mills were started at Crawick near Sanquhar, where there

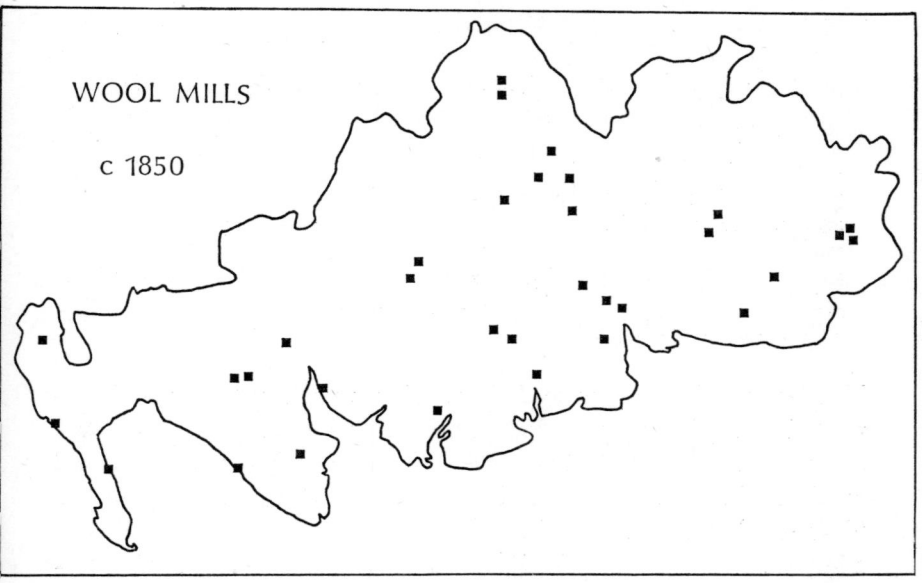

WOOL MILLS

c 1850

was 'plenty of water and descent to drive weighty machinery'. A carding and spinning mill prepared the wool, and in each of the two weaving-shops 'five weavers, two draw boys, a pirn winder, two yarn twisters and a bobbiner' manufactured 12,000yd of carpeting worth nearly £1,500 per annum.[20] An interesting example of business integration was provided by this plant, for another eight weavers working on the spot made 'stuffs, serges, plaids and flannels'. Some considerable expansion took place during the French Wars, for by 1812 the wool mill employed 100 workers. In that year a detailed description of the works was written by a contemporary, which outlines the day-to-day activities there.

When the wool arrived at the factory it was first washed in vats with urine and warm water, 'which by aid of the yolk purge it of extraneous matter'. Women were employed to trample it in the vats and thereafter it was carried to the mill-lade to be rinsed and washed. When dry, the long wool strands were sorted out 'and the best set aside for wheeling warps; the refuse is taken for waft and the whole employed in the manufacture of carpets'. Afterwards,

> the wheeling warps are all spun on jacks, and likewise all the wafts; but the worsted warps on another set of machinery. Houses and machinery are to be seen there for teazing, carding and roving coarse wool; and for spinning it by jacks with spindles, thirty in each, into carpet yarn. These machines can prepare and rove a pack [12 stones] of wool per day; and one jenny spins 24 lbs. One man and two boys attend the roving machinery; and one man and two women attend a jack. In the worsted spinning machine, five persons prepare, rove and twist 24 spindles or 80 lbs of long wool per day; and one spindle answers for ten yards of carpeting. The threads appeared very evenly and perfectly spun.[21]

Nearby was the dye-house, 'where colours were put on, which appeared beautiful and were said to be all durable'. At this time the carpet-weaving shop contained nine looms on which a weaver could produce six yards per day. The weaving was carried out on the 'draw-boy' system, so called because while the weaver drove the loom a boy worked in the required pattern by drawing certain cords overhead.[22] Crawick carpets were famed for fine patterns and found their way to continental as well as home markets.

The original proprietor of Crawick Mill was Archibald McNab of Holm, a member of the local gentry who also had interests in coal mining in the Sanquhar district.[23] Later a partnership of farmers and gentry (known as the Crawick Mill Carpet Co) was formed to work the mill. More loomshops were erected and in 1837 'the big Shop' was built to accommodate 32 looms, sixteen on each of its two floors. According to the *Reports from the Assistant Handloom Weavers' Commissioners* there were 36 'factory looms' at the carpet factory in 1839, which by this date had a new dye-house and a gasworks, the latter lighting not only the mill but also the nearby workers' village at Crawick Old Bridge.[24] In spite of several partnership changes the company prospered for some years, but by the mid-1850s lack of capital to replace outdated machinery, management troubles, and above all the rise of large-scale, highly mechanised carpet mills in Kilmarnock and Glasgow brought about the close of the works. Many of the Crawick carpet weavers found alternative jobs in the mills of Ayr and Kilmarnock. In 1876 the Crawick mill was converted into a woollen factory. The old buildings were rebuilt and a new waterwheel (generating four times the power of the old one) and steam engine fitted. There were 1,000 spindles and nineteen power looms producing 50–60 blankets per day.[25]

Another carpet factory operated in Creetown, housed in a building which had previously been a cotton mill.[26] By 1839 it employed 38 workers in a two-storey mill range, where an 8hp waterwheel provided power for the machinery.[27] This factory seems to have ceased operations about the same time as that at Sanquhar, for by 1870 it was rated at only £13 and clearly could not have been operational.[28] The building—which still survives in a ruined condition—is described in the inventory in Section Two.

Hosiery manufacture—like many other branches of textiles—began as a domestic craft, but following the introduction of the stocking frame c 1770 it became an industry of some importance in south-west

Scotland, particularly in Dumfries and Langholm. Stocking and hat making had 'succeeded pretty well' in Dumfries by the mid-1790s and later, c 1800, there were about thirty stocking frames at work in Maxwelltown and Dumfries.[29] The industry remained relatively small-scale until 1810, when Robert Scott (later founder of the Dumfries tweed industry) entered in partnership with William Dinwiddie and developed stocking and hosiery making 'by opening up an extensive and profitable connection with the London and other English markets'.[30] Others followed and by 1832 McDiarmid noted that hosiery had become 'a staple article of trade and gives employment to upwards of 300 hands located in Dumfries and the surrounding villages'. 'Of stockings, socks, drawers and flannel shirts', he recorded, 'from 350 to 400 dozen are fabricated weekly, the value of which may be averaged at the same number of pounds; and it would thus appear that the capital turned over in this branch falls little short of £20,000 yearly.'[31]

Hosiery continued to expand at a considerable rate, for by 1869 there were more than 500 frames or stocking looms in Dumfries and district, compared with 279 in 1833.[32] At this period there were five leading firms—R. Scott & Sons, Milligan & Co, James Dinwiddie & Co, all of Dumfries, and William Halliday and Robert McGeorge, both of Maxwelltown on the other side of the Nith. The continuous family connection of the Scotts and Dinwiddies was still apparent and this certainly seems to have been common in the Dumfries woollen industry. Bremner, writing in 1869, estimated that the hosiery sector represented an invested capital of £40,000, with an annual turnover 'as nearly as possible represented by the capital'. The industry employed 500 workers, including weavers, winders, seamers, trimmers, finishers and warehouse men, whose earnings ranged from 10–25s per week. An estimated 120,000lb of yarn was required each year, obtained mainly from Hawick, Peebles, Alloa and Kinross. Yet the Dumfries hosiery industry appears to have been fairly typical of Scottish woollens in its failure to mechanise until fairly late, for only one mill—that of Milligan & Co—used power looms.[33]

After a period of amalgamations and partnership changes, James

McGeorge emerged as the largest firm in the Dumfries hosiery trade, following his take-over of R. Scott & Sons in 1881. From 1885 this firm specialised in the production of gloves on knitting machines developed in their own works. Further expansion took place from 1888, and when Walter Scott & Sons retired from the large St Michael's Mills, McGeorge transferred business to the weaving sheds there. By 1902 the firm had part of the Nithsdale Mills (a large, mid-Victorian structure), where 700–800 workers (mostly young women) were employed. The firm 'had a very large trade with home, colonial, and foreign houses in Woollen gloves, knicker stockings and ties of silk and cotton'.[34] In spite of fierce competition, changing fashion and economic circumstances, and above all the complete disappearance of the Dumfries tweed trade, hosiery is still an important industry and employer in the town, while old-established ancillary industries like dyeing and finishing are also significant. Several of the original firms are still in business, notably James Robertson & Sons and J. & D. McGeorge.

The origins of the tweed industry in Dumfriesshire are to be found in the old-established domestic wool trade, notably in handloom weaving of coarse cloth and plaiding. Clearly the existence of textile skills among a substantial sector of the adult labour force in the towns of Dumfries and Langholm and the success of firms in the hosiery trade in both of these places were as important growth factors as 'the coincidence in time of the power loom, the exploitation of fashionable demand, and the availability of supplies of wool from Australia, New Zealand and South America'.[35] Yet, as an historian of Langholm wrote—'the coming of steam power brought about a fundamental change: the advent of the first engine marked a new era in the town's industrial history'.[36] A multitude of circumstances, together with undoubted entrepreneurial energy on the part of local wool-masters, combined to initiate this fundamental change and to create in Dumfries and Langholm an industry, which in sheer scale rivalled that of Border towns like Hawick, Galashiels and Selkirk.

The development of tweed weaving in Dumfries dates from 1846, when Robert Scott & Sons took over a large plant (formerly a sawmill) at Kingholm Quay on the Nith, about a mile south of Dumfries. At the outset fine-yarn spinning for the hosiery trade was the main activity, but shortly after the opening of the factory John M'Keachie, a damask weaver in Maxwelltown (long the centre of this craft), joined the firm and supervised the experimental weaving of tweed. By this time the brand name of 'tweed' was already well known and the long traditional designs had become popular 'with rich and poor'.[37] Commercial success was virtually ensured. The firm of Scott 'with characteristic shrewdness, saw at once that the germ of the new business thus inadvertently hit upon was worthy of being fully developed', and invested substantial capital in tweed production.[38] Development was most rapid after 1851 when Robert Scott Snr retired, leaving one of his sons, John, to manage Kingholm Mills, where considerable expansion took place. John's brother, Robert Jnr, in partnership with another son, Walter (a textile merchant in Manchester), built a second tweed factory, Nithsdale Mills, in 1857. Nithsdale Mills, the smallest of the nineteenth-century tweed factories in Dumfries, still survives in a dominating position overlooking Dock Park. It is a gaunt, four-storey, Italianate structure in brick with sandstone facings, which with its 174ft high chimney was described by one contemporary as 'almost palatial in aspect'. In 1866 Walter Scott dissolved the partnership and erected an enormous plant, Troqueer Mills, on the Maxwelltown side of the Nith. By 1872 the firm of Walter Scott & Sons owned all three mills in Dumfries and employed 1,400 workers on 35,000 spindles and 400 looms, producing 10,000yd of tweed each month, most of the raw wool being imported from Australia and New Zealand. At this period the firm was the largest manufacturer of tweeds in Scotland.[39]

Another big development took place in the mid-1880s when Samuel Charteries (whose background was the commercial side of the tweed industry) and Robert Spence (a former designer) became partners in St Michael's Mills, a smaller tweed factory built c 1868. In 1885 they purchased Rosefield estate, adjacent to Troqueer Mills and built Rosefield Mills, one of the largest tweed factories in Scotland. The mills were designed by Alan Crombie on a frontage to the Nith of 130yd and ultimately housed 180 power looms. By 1906 this huge, highly integrated plant employed over 700 people. The entire Dumfries tweed industry had shifted its centre of gravity to the Galloway bank of the Nith and was concentrated in the two firms of Walter Scott & Sons and Charteries, Spence & Co.[40]

There was a similar history of growth from the late 1830s in the Eskdale town of Langholm, where old-established woollen manufacturers (mostly family concerns) branched into tweed production. The 'Muckle Toon' quickly established a reputation for its 'shepherds' checks', which were originally woven on handlooms in the many weavers' dwellings in the New Town of Langholm. As late as 1839 there were no fewer than 250 handloom weavers at work in Langholm.[41] Tweed manufacture developed on a large scale after 1851, Reid & Taylor being the first firm to erect an integrated mill, described by one observer in 1869 as 'one of the most extensive tweed manufactories in the trade'. Several other large mills followed. At that time the annual turnover of the Langholm tweed industry was estimated at £200,000 and the invested capital at £130,000.[42] One of the largest mills, Waverley (still operated by James Scott & Sons), was erected by Alexander Scott in 1866 and extended in 1871. It is one of the finest mid-Victorian factory ranges in the town. Buccleuch Mills, built by Scott & Erskine in 1878, was taken over by Arthur Bell ten years later and is still worked by that firm.[43]

The key developments of the latter half of the nineteenth century in towns like Dumfries and Langholm radically altered the pattern and mode of production in the regional woollen industry. Many of the small, water-driven mills disappeared, although a few survived until the present century and some were extensively altered and enlarged to assimilate the technical changes which the introduction of steam power demanded. Cumloden is a good example of a mill which continued in the traditional way, while Waulkmill, Kirkcowan, is perhaps the best illustration of a plant that was enlarged in the mid-1880s. The majority of the small mills closed before 1914 and even the important tweed mills of Dumfries were forced out of business before 1930. Langholm was more fortunate and today many of the old-established firms are still operating. Fortunately for the industrial archaeologist many of the small, rural mills survive unmolested and even the large factory ranges in Dumfries have so far escaped re-development.

LINEN

The terse remark of the Drysdale minister in his report to Sir John Sinclair's *Statistical Account* that 'every family is a small factory for linen cloth' is at once as appropriate as it is misleading.[44] For in Galloway—as in most of rural Scotland—flax growing for domestic purposes was as common in the 1790s as it had been for much of the preceding century. At the time of the Union in 1707 the Scottish linen industry was almost entirely domestic, although some cloth was produced for export.[45] A fresh incentive to the industry was the provision by the Board of Trustees for Fisheries, Manufactures and Improvements (established by the Union Parliament in 1727) of an annual budget for the development of techniques. These efforts at technical improvement took several paths, including the introduction of foreign knowledge and skills (eg, Dutch bleachers and French cambric weavers), the dispatching abroad of 'young men of genius' to pirate secrets, and the improvement of flax-processing machinery. The meticulous records of the Board of Trustees provide a detailed analysis of the development of the linen industry during the eighteenth and early nineteenth centuries. The indications are that the contribution of south-west Scotland throughout most of the period was relatively insignificant (see stamped linen figures on page 85). Even at its height c 1800 regional production represented no more than 0·2 per cent of national output of stamped linen cloth. Quantitatively, then, the commercial linen manufacture of Galloway was unimportant.

There is considerable evidence of the local importance of flax growing and processing in Galloway's countryside until well into the nineteenth century. Small plots of flax were cultivated on most farms, on an acre or so of fairly fertile ground called the 'hemp rig'. When ripe the flax was harvested by hand, tied up in sheaves and stooked in the field for several days. It was then steeped in a pool (often called a 'lint well'), weighted down with boards and stones until the 'souring' process was completed—in ten days to a fortnight. It was dried by spreading it out in rows and was then sent to the 'lint mill' for further processing.[46] Often the mill was situated at a considerable distance and there were many complaints about 'the uncertainty of the time of dressing flax in the mills, the expense and operation and the imperfection in the performance in some of them'.[47] After dressing, flax was spun at home on the 'wee wheel' by women and girls and then sent to weavers to be worked into cloth on handlooms. Domestic linen making was still practised in the early decades of the nineteenth century and in isolated districts was still carried on as late as 1840. In 1835, for example, there was a total of 45 acres devoted to flax growing in seven parishes of Lower Annandale.[48]

Evidence of the development of a more commercial sector of linen production less oriented to local needs and more towards markets beyond Galloway is provided from a variety of contemporary sources including the records of the Board of Trustees and the reports to the *Statistical Account*. The Returns of the Stampmasters of Linen Cloth (a total of 50 were appointed to stations throughout Scotland) during the first half of the eighteenth century indicate that only in Dumfriesshire was linen produced for sale—and even this amounted to less than 12,000 yd worth £640 in 1747–8. Most of this probably originated from the Lochmaben district, later to become one of the main centres of the small regional industry.[49] General Roy's map (1747–55) indicates the location of a large number of 'wauk' mills and it is quite likely that some housed lint-scutching machinery and processed flax as well as wool.

The first process to be mechanised was flax or lint scutching and the typical lint mill housed simple machinery for this purpose. It consisted of a fly-wheel with sharp-edged scutchers of hard wood fixed to the end of the spokes, or a series of toothed horizontal rollers, which either beat or rubbed the outer covering of the flax stalk and so released the fibre.[50] The machinery was water-powered and the mill itself single or at most two-storeyed. The earliest detailed documentation relating to the linen industry in south-west Scotland (apart from the stamped linen returns) is a report by John Dickson 'Stampmaster at Moffat' on a lint mill in Lochmaben in 1772, which is worth quoting fully.

The Lochmaben lint mill, he wrote,

> lies in Annandale about a mile North-West of the Burgh of Lochmaben. It is supplied with water from a neighbouring Loch 9 months in the year. Its method of breaking flax is with Rollers—Its method of scutching is in the horizontal way—Five people can scutch at a time. The Mill houses are capable of containing a considerable quantity if flax, but indeed proper housing is the only defect wanting.
>
> The Machinery is very good and its work gives general satisfaction. Lint is brought to it 14 and 15 miles distance. The Miller keeps skilful hands which he hath never changed. The Mill broke and completely scutched of crop 1770, 365 stones 6 lbs. and Scutched 30 stones 7 lbs. all Scots weight. The rate charged for breaking and completely scutching is 2/– per stone—for Scutching only from 1/8d to 1/–. The Miller pays neither rent nor feu-duty. He is a heckler himself, but hath exceeding bad heckles. There are hecklers in the neighbourhood who charge from 10d to 1/– per stone. The mill is insured against Fire.[51]

Clearly there was considerable expansion of the industry during the last few decades of the eighteenth century, especially in Annandale and the Rhins district of Wigtownshire. The stamped linen returns for the three counties indicate substantial growth after 1770, although it seems likely that considerable quantities of unstamped material were sold both locally and outside Galloway.[52] When the reports of the stampmasters of lint mills in their own districts were submitted to the Board of Trustees there were clearly no mills in Wigtownshire or the Stewartry, so that the phase of expansion must have come between 1772 and c 1795, when evidence from parish accounts indicates the existence of many lint mills in these areas. By 1793 Lochmaben had two lint mills 'which are insufficient to perform the work that would come to them'; in Applegarth a mill was 'now building' on the Water of Annan; in Dunscore, where Robert Burns rented a farm, a flax mill was about to be erected on the River Cairn; and in Morton the mill 'for dressing lint' serviced a wide area up to sixteen miles distant.[53]

Linen Cloth Stamped in South-West Scotland 1727–1822

	1727–8		1737–8		1747–8	
	Yd	Value	Yd	Value	Yd	Value
Dumfries	3,022	152	5,416	210	11,984	640
Kirkcudbright	—		—		—	
Wigtown	67	3	—		—	

	1757–8		1767–8		1777–8	
	Yd	Value	Yd	Value	Yd	Value
Dumfries	18,872	392	243,189	17,424	127,575	8,683
Kirkcudbright	—		604	78	3,901	310
Wigtown	968	82	15,737	655	16,844	724

	1787–8		1821–2	
	Yd	Value	Yd	Value
Dumfries	112,492	8,229	1,577	179
Kirkcudbright	—		7,686	611
Wigtown	28,391	1,268	3,723	177

(Value in £)

Source: A. J. Warden, *The Linen Trade* (London 1864), 477–9

Heron noted that 'quantities of linen cloths have been manufactured to sufficient advantage' in districts round Dumfries, and also remarked that flax 'had become a favorite crop' in the neighbourhood of Stranraer, particularly in the parish of Stoneykirk.[54] In the nearby parish of Kirkmaiden 'more flax was raised than formerly' (1791) and it was 'growing important' in Stranraer and Inch.[55] Although Chalmers remarked that 'linen fabrics have never taken very deep root in Wigtownshire'[56] there were at least six lint mills in the greater-Stranraer area c 1795, and locally grown flax was 'worked up into coarse linens', the yarn being spun by old women.[57] There was a bleachfield in Stoneykirk, but linen was brought into the Stranraer market 'both green and bleached', which with coarse yarns was mostly bought by

Glasgow and Kilmarnock merchants. Local yarns were woven into coarse Osnaburghs for export to 'the West Indian Market'—probably by handloom weavers scattered throughout the district.[58] Some measure of the growth of the industry in the Rhins area is provided by the stamped linen returns (see p 85), for production rose from 968yd (worth £82) in 1758 to 28,391yd (worth £1,268) in 1788 and reached a maximum of over 30,000yd in 1802.[59]

Production in the Stewartry was never very great (3,900yd worth £310 in 1778), although there are records of at least eight mills—notably in Dalbeattie, Kelton and New Abbey. The majority were relatively small units whose main function was flax-dressing for the country folk of the surrounding district. A number of lint mills appear on Ainslie's map of the county (1797) and several survived well into the nineteenth century (see below). In Tynholm, Lochrutton and Urr flax mills were still active in the 1840s but most had other machinery for wool carding or sawing.[60]

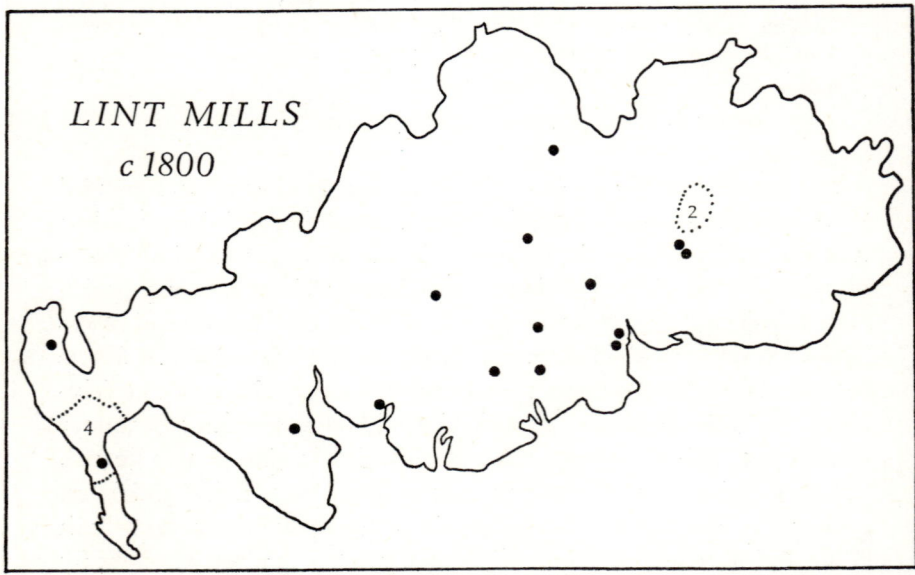

LINT MILLS
c 1800

Throughout the whole of the eighteenth and the early decades of the nineteenth century the most important area of linen manufacture was Lower Annandale, production being centred on the neighbouring towns of Lochmaben and Lockerbie. In the 1760s, when output was greatest, nearly 250,000yd of linen were annually stamped for sale in Dumfriesshire, the majority from Annandale. During the later decades of the eighteenth century annual production averaged around 100,000yd, a good deal more than half coming from Lochmaben. Local conditions suited flax growing, particularly the rich, fertile haughs of the River Annan and the Water of Ae. Here in the 1790s local flax 'and a good deal of foreign flax also' was spun by women and woven by men into coarse linens. At this period the output was 60,000yd per annum 'which is all sold into England, mostly unbleached at from 6d to 1/- or 13d per yard'.[61] In the nearby parish of Tinwald, at Trailflat, was located 'one of the most extensive bleachfields in Scotland', operated by Cruickshank & Son, and there were several other bleachers in Dumfries and Maxwelltown.[62] Despite the existence of these works, much of the annual output of Drysdale parish (a total of 50,000yd including locally woven woollen cloth) was sold unbleached at the Lammas and Michaelmas fairs in Lockerbie during the 1790s.[63]

During the Napoleonic Wars the Galloway linen industry declined and by the early 1820s had virtually succumbed to the overwhelming competition of the large-scale factory industry in eastern Scotland and nearby Ulster. Always a domestic activity in the south-west it survived as a country craft till at least mid-century in isolated parts of Galloway. The ruins of a lint mill (still active c 1850) on Shirmer's Burn, high on the moors near Balmaclellan, are sufficient testimony of this. Like the regional cotton-spinning industry, linen engendered several important associated activities, notably handloom weaving and damask manufacture, which are considered in a later sub-section.

COTTON

'The establishment of the cotton industry', wrote one recent historian of Scottish economic growth, 'required men with capital, with commercial experience, and with an ability to organize their workers in new places and with new techniques.'[64] Entrepreneurs with such abilities emerged in central Scotland to create from the old-established textile crafts a highly integrated industry, the impact of which was of vital significance during the period of industrial growth. The cotton industry, with its large-scale application of technical improvements, introduced into the Scottish landscape the most tangible element of the early phase of industrial revolution, the water-powered, cotton-spinning mill with its associated workers' village or housing. The Scottish cotton industry presents a classic instance of an industrial revolution without steam (which Mantoux noticed elsewhere) and even by the mid-nineteenth century (despite the rise of steam-powered mills in Glasgow) many of the largest Scottish cotton mills were primarily water-driven.[65] South-west Scotland was amply endowed with power resources; it had men of capital with unlimited commercial experience, like William Douglas (who had strong connections with the Galloway Banking Co), or sympathetic gentry like James Murray; and, above all, it had long-established connections with Lancashire, Ulster and the west of Scotland, the key centres of linen and cotton-textile production.

The earliest development in the regional cotton industry of Galloway was in the handloom weaving of cotton yarns and the sewing of muslins, supplied through agents based on local market centres. This domestic sector remained important for many years—power weaving was never important in Galloway (except at Gatehouse) and, indeed, the cotton industry there did not survive long enough for such a change to take place. During the period 1790–1840, despite severe and continued depression after the close of the Napoleonic Wars, handloom weaving of cotton was widespread in the towns and villages of Gallo-

Page 89   (above) *Wanlockhead village, a former centre of the Dumfriesshire lead-mining industry;* (below) *water-pressure beam engine at Wanlockhead, probably built and installed c 1770*

Page 90 (above) *Bank of limekilns, Closeburn, Dumfriesshire;* (below) *original brick lining of one of the three kilns viewed from the top*

way. Locally spun yarn, as well as materials distributed by agents (for firms in Glasgow or Carlisle) were worked into cotton cloth of every description. Handloom weaving is discussed later in this chapter.

If David Dale was the key driving force of the cotton industry in the west of Scotland, William Douglas (his partner in at least one cotton venture) exhibited similar entrepreneurial enthusiasm in the creation of cotton mills in Galloway. Douglas and Dale were remarkably alike in many ways, being self-made men of humble rural origins, who made fortunes for themselves by engaging in business and commerce during the maelstrom of the early industrial revolution. Douglas was born in 1745 and, following elementary schooling, began life as a country pedlar.[66] In 1766 he began business in Glasgow in company with his brother, James Douglas (of Orchardton) and later moved to London 'and entered extensively into the American trade'.[67] His family connections clearly were an advantage for several of his uncles and brothers had settled and made their fortunes in the Colonies, notably in New York, Virginia and Jamaica. Little is known of Douglas's early business career, but he was obviously successful, for by the mid-1780s he began 'to make extensive purchases of land in Scotland', mainly large estates in his native Galloway. Among these were Newton Stewart and Carlingwark.[68]

So early as 1785 Douglas seems 'to have resolved to retire from business and to reside on his Estates in Galloway', and during the following years spent an increasing amount of time away from London. In 1783 the co-partnery with his brother terminated and Douglas continued in business on his own until 1790, when with a young relative of his father, Sir James Shaw, he formed the firm of Douglas & Shaw. Active management was committed to Shaw and to Samuel Douglas, William's younger brother. This new partnership prospered, for some years later the business was stated 'to be on as great an extent as ever' and 'consists principally in the exportation of the manufactures of this country to the extent annually of nearly £100,000 and in the importation in return of the produce of America'.[69] Sir James Shaw estimated the fortune of William Douglas and his three brothers

F

to be in the region of £400,000.[70] After 1790 William, having time to devote to his own interests, invested a substantial part of his large fortune 'in promoting manufactures of different kinds' in Newton Stewart and Carlingwark, in building and endowing with burgh charters planned villages at these two locations, and in obtaining for himself a baronetcy and the prestige which accompanied it.

Galloway Cotton Mills Valuations

Mill	Owners	Date of Valuation	Valuation Breakdown		Total
Gatehouse	Birtwhistle & Murray	1788	Mills & Offices Stock	£1,200	
			Machinery	£2,400	£3,600
Wigtown (Kirkcowan?)	Milroy	1793	Mill Stock	£110	
			Machinery	£450	£550
Newton Douglas	Douglas, Dale & McCaul	1797 (a)	Mill	£2,500	
			Machinery & Millwright work	£3,500	
			Houses & Smithy	£700	£6,700

(a) adjusted valuation

Source: *Sun Fire Insurance Office Register* (by kind permission Dr S. Chapman, University of Nottingham, and Dr J. Butt, University of Strathclyde)

When Robert Heron visited Newton Douglas (as it became when Douglas had its burgh charter renewed) in 1792 he found 'a thriving village of late origin' with a population of over 1,000, where 'an enlightened and spirited landholder' had developed the cotton-textile industry. 'Since its having succeeded so happily at Gatehouse', he wrote, 'machines for carding cotton wool have been introduced . . . and several mules for spinning cotton have been set up.'[71] The partnership of Douglas, Dale & McCall planned to erect 'a large work for the spinning of cotton by mill machinery' on the River Cree upstream from the village. The mill was built on the west bank c 1793 and according to Sir James Shaw cost £10,000, although later commentators put the capital cost at nearly £20,000. Shaw's estimate was probably nearer the mark, for the Sun Fire Office with which the mill was insured had it valued at £8,200 in 1795, though even this valuation was later adjusted (see table on page 92). Although little is known about operations at Newton Douglas, a spinning and reeling book of 1800 indicates that 'when the work stood for want of water' the mill had advances to 172 spinners and reelers. The workers were paid on piece rates. By 1809–10 the weekly wage bill was a mere £10 and one room in the mill housed fewer than thirty spinners and thirteen reelers.[72] The site of this mill was where the present Cree Woollen Mills now stand and the large horseshoe weir on the river just above this point is probably that built to supply the wheels of the cotton mill.

Carlingwark, a small estate and village situated on the military road beside Carlingwark Loch, was purchased by William Douglas in 1789, probably because it was immediately adjacent to the large property of Gelston which he had acquired some years earlier.[73] The year following he obtained a charter erecting Carlingwark into a burgh of barony called Castle Douglas and began the creation of a classical planned-village with widely spaced streets on a perfect grid-pattern.[74] This led Burns to scorn Douglas for 'christening towns far and near'. Heron, on the other hand, remarked that 'this village every day becomes more thriving and respectable; flax dressers, weavers, tanners, saddlers, masons and carpenters are now established', the last two trades no doubt being employed in building the new houses of Castle Douglas.[75] Sometime prior to 1795 Douglas erected a 'cottonworks' (in the vicinity of Cotton Street), which was described as being 'on a smaller scale' than that at Newton Douglas.[76] This mill, like several others in the south-west, probably did not survive the crisis of 1812. It was badly sited, both from the point of view of transport and of water-power, which were certainly less of a problem at Gatehouse and Newton Douglas. Sir William Douglas (he was knighted in 1796) died in 1809, and it is likely that the mills at Castle and Newton Douglas, in the face of oncoming, general depression in the cotton trade, succumbed shortly afterwards. The mill at Newton Douglas stood idle till 1826, when it was purchased by Lord Garlies 'for about five per cent of the original cost'. The machinery was sold and the fabric removed for building purposes.[77] William Douglas's greatest monument was probably not the splendid marble tomb he willed himself (at a cost of £1,000), but rather the town of Castle Douglas itself, with its fine period buildings, shops and old coaching inns.

Although Sir James Shaw remarked in a letter to Henry Dundas that William Douglas had upset the old-established nobility of Galloway in his schemes for improvement, there was certainly no lack of enthusiasm among some for cotton textiles.[78] Heron noted that the success of Gatehouse had 'roused a passion for the cotton manufacture through this whole country' and in the mid-1790s numerous small mills (see below) were built in different locations.[79] Rerrick in the Stewartry had no less than three mills: one at Dundrennan was started in 1793 'by a few spirited young men' with a capital of £1,200; a second

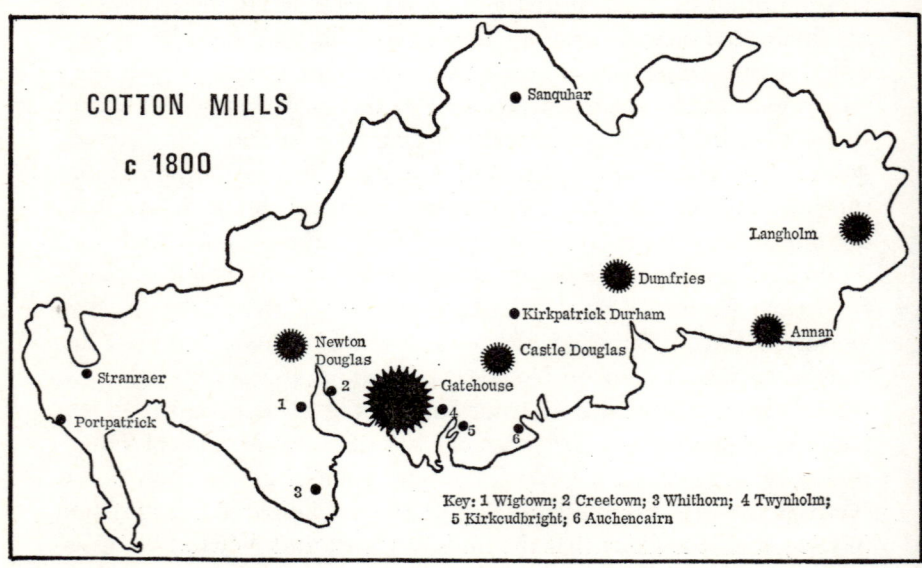

COTTON MILLS

c 1800

Key: 1 Wigtown; 2 Creetown; 3 Whithorn; 4 Twynholm; 5 Kirkcudbright; 6 Auchencairn (water-powered) was launched by a co-partnery of farmers headed by 'a patriotic gentleman'; and yet another was planned 'on the lands of Mr Cairns of Dundrennan'.[80] One mill at Wigtown (probably that of John Milroy, a relative of the Milroys of Kirkcowan wauk mill) was less successful, for 'it was soon hurt after its commencement and is now [1795] almost entirely ruined by the iniquities of the times'.[81] Lord Daer converted his cotton mill at Twynholm (a former distillery) into a wool mill, and the mill at Creetown, which employed thirty workfolk in 1795 afterwards became a carpet factory.[82] The latter was established in 1790, one partner being James Murray Denniston, a militia captain educated in Gatehouse, and another J. McCulloch of Barholm, the local landowner, who had Creetown raised to burgh status in 1791.[83] The Creetown mill is a most interesting survival, described in Section Two.

Farther east in Dumfriesshire cotton spinning developed in Annan and Langholm, both of which had good water-power sites on large rivers and good access to Carlisle, the centre of a widespread system of weavers' agencies which covered most of lower Dumfriesshire. Carlisle merchants were involved in the establishment of one Langholm mill, which began production in 1790. Known as Meikleholm Mill (later to become a corn mill) it was located on the Wauchope Water in New Langholm. A photograph taken before its demolition c 1880 shows a long, three-storey and attic range with blocked-up windows and a large wheel-house at the side.[84] The company which started the mill soon employed 80–100 workers, 'but by the late shock of commercial credit [1794] it has been at a stand since July last'. Most of the workers made idle by this bankruptcy found employment in weaving 'checks' for Forrester & Fergusson, 'two respectable manufacturers in Carlisle'.[85] The mill recovered and continued to operate during the Napoleonic Wars, after which it was converted to a corn mill, but by 1812 another 'considerable house', known as Whitshiels or High Mill, was operating on the Ewes Water a mile north-west of Langholm. The capital cost of this mill was £2,600 and it was managed by a Mr Cross for its owner, a Mr Cliffe of Carlisle. There were 3,552 mule spindles 'with suitable apparatus' and 50–60 employees, 'who work in summer from 6 am to 8 at night, and in winter from daylight to 8 in the evening, having one hour to dine, and their breakfast before work or taken at the house, as the mill does not stop for this meal'. A fine yarn was produced and marketed in Carlisle or Glasgow, where it was manufactured into 'superfine calicoes'. The wage bill c 1812 was £30–35 per week and the workers were said to enjoy good health.[86] By about 1830 cotton spinning had ceased in Langholm, and Whit-shiels Mill was worked by T. & A. Renwick in 1836. At that time the 50hp waterwheel and forty workers were employed in wool spinning, the forerunner of Langholm's tweed trade.[87]

Cotton spinning in Annan began in 1785 in a mill on the west side of the town by the bank of the River Annan, across which a weir was built to supply the waterwheel. Ten years later it employed 100–130 workers, men, women and children.[88] The mill was owned and operated by a Mr Hurst in 1812 and the weekly wage bill then was just over £50. Twenty or thirty women were occasionally employed in 'picking cotton' and the workers in general were said to be pale 'but not unhealthy'.[89] By 1825 the mill had been taken over by William Douglas & Co of Manchester and was considerably enlarged, for in 1839 it had two steam engines generating 30hp in addition to its original 28hp waterwheel.[90] About this time it employed 140 workers and spun 4,000lb of cotton into yarn per week.[91] The Annan mill continued to operate until about 1850 and much of it still survives as an animal feeding-stuffs mill and store.

It was Gatehouse-of-Fleet, a small village on the estate of the far-seeing James Murray of Cally, which became the real focus of the Galloway cotton industry. Today Gatehouse presents 'a rare and beautiful example of an arrested industrial village and a source of satisfaction for the industrial archaeologist'.[92] Gatehouse acquired this industrial history by quirk of fate for Messrs Birtwhistle & Sons of Yorkshire, who were an old-established firm of cattle dealers and merchants, originally intended to build a cotton mill near Kirkcud-bright, probably on the River Dee. The Earl of Selkirk, proprietor of the town and neighbourhood, refused permission for fear his 'mansion might be disgraced by the vicinity of an establishement of manufacturing industry'.[93] James Murray, who had planned and directed the building of Gatehouse and successfully established craft industries there, in 1785 granted the Birtwhistles a lease of land on the banks of the Fleet. A joint-stock company in which Murray held shares was formed and soon after Birtwhistles built 'a large fabric at Great expense' on land immediately upstream of Fleet Bridge. They followed this with a second mill. The first building and its contents were valued at £3,600 in 1788 by the Sun Fire Office. A Mr McWilliam established a third mill in the same complex.[94] Thomas Scott & Co (an Ulster concern based on Belfast and Bangor) built a fourth mill on the northeast side of the village adjacent to the entrance to Cally Park.

Of the four cotton mills in Gatehouse (plate, page 71), the two largest were twist mills, one being four storeys high (120ft by 30ft) and the other three storeys high (84ft by 32ft). Together they employed more than 300 workfolk c 1794. The remaining two were mule mills, three storeys high (70ft by 20ft) employing one hundred each. A weaving shed, containing handlooms, produced muslins 'of neat pattern and good fabric'.[95] Water to drive these mills—and the several other industries of Gatehouse—was brought to the village by an extensive system of lades from Loch Whinyeon, located four miles away in the hills above the Fleet valley. The main lade was part rock-cut at a cost of over £1,200 and supplied dams at the head of the village 'with a copious stream of water'.[96] From these dams two lades carried water to the various mills. One passed through the centre of the village serving a brass foundry (which had been established to service spinning and weaving machinery), a brewery, and the two large wheels of the Birtwhistle mills, which according to the *Factory Return* of 1839 produced 55hp between them. The other lade followed the east side of the village, powering Scott's mill and one of Gatehouse's two tanneries.

In the early days, when Heron visited Gatehouse, three hundred workers were employed and the total weekly wage bill was £50. The yarn produced in the mills was sold in Glasgow and locally, for handloom weaving of cotton became a common occupation in the district and remained highly profitable for some years. Little is known of the subsequent history of the mills. Scott's mill succumbed fairly early and the Birtwhistle mills went out of production c 1810. The latter were leased in 1832 to James Davidson & Co, the buildings repaired and new machinery installed including 74 power looms. In 1840 a factory inspector found everything in order at Gatehouse mills, where 174 workers (including 64 under 18 years of age) were still employed in cotton spinning. 'None are employed under 13 years of age', he noted, 'but found one working for his father and sent him home'.[97] The production of cotton cloth in 1844 was no less than 1½ million yards.

The Gatehouse mills finally closed about mid-century and some-time later were acquired by Thomas & William Helme, who ran a large timber business from their headquarters in Dalbeattie. They converted one of the mills into a bobbin mill and another was used as a bark mill (stressing the importance of tan-bark export and tanning in Galloway even at this date) and as a store.[98] The 'bobbin mill', by which name it is still known locally, operated until the early 1930s manufacturing pirns or bobbins for other textile mills far beyond Galloway. All three mills in the Birtwhistle complex soon fell derelict, in which condition they still survive, roofless but picturesque ruins by the edge of the quiet flowing Fleet. Scott's mill was more fortunate and after serving as a timber mill for some years was converted to a private house. It has a permanent memorial of its days as a cotton mill on the face of the Gatehouse halfpenny (1793), which holds the unique position of being the only trade-token issued in south-west Scotland. Birtwhistle Street, though less imposing than the main thoroughfare, is a fine example of eighteenth-century workers' housing, where hand-loom weavers once produced cotton cloth from locally spun yarns (plate, page 71). Although Gatehouse had many other trades and indust-ries, cotton textiles were unquestionably most significant and created perhaps the most interesting aspect of its industrial archaeology.

HANDLOOM WEAVING AND TEXTILE CRAFTS

Weaving, perhaps the oldest domestic craft, became a vital link between all three sectors of the regional textile industry during the latter half of the eighteenth century and much of the early nineteenth century. In the early period handloom weavers merely serviced the local textile industry, but later when the linen and cotton industry of the west of Scotland expanded, the agency system developed in many parts of the south-west. The development of both cotton and woollen industries in Galloway also led to a substantial increase in the numbers of weavers, particularly in the period 1790–1830, and weaving survived much longer in Galloway than in many parts of rural Scotland, where the rise of the power loom in the integrated textile mills of central Scotland was decisively felt early in the nineteenth century. A number of ancillary textile crafts were practised in Galloway on the domestic or agency system, notably damask manufacture and muslin sewing, both of which were at their height around 1830.

Numerous contemporary references in the *Statistical Account* point to the importance of weaving during the 1790s. Wigtown had a wool mill, where forty handloom weavers manufactured plaiding for export to England, while by contrast five weavers in the Stewartry parish of Crossmichael were engaged simply in domestic work for the local population of 700. In Dumfriesshire there were nearly 600 weavers, the largest concentrations being in the Dumfries, Langholm, Moffat and Gretna districts. In these areas the system of working through agents (who provided the materials and collected the finished cloth) was already well established and had even penetrated as far as the isolated parish of Westerkirk.[99]

With the rise of wool and cotton-spinning mills in Galloway, the number of weavers increased considerably. This was particularly so in villages and parishes adjacent to cotton-spinning mills, for example Newton Douglas, Castle Douglas, Gatehouse and Annan. One of Sir William Douglas's aims in developing the cotton mill at Newton

Douglas was to provide employment opportunities as weavers for the rapidly expanding population of his new village. The idea of self-supporting communities, later expounded by Robert Owen and others, was much in vogue at the time, and planned communities where agrarian activities and rural industries could be combined were held in high esteem by improving landlords.[100] Many villages in south-west Scotland had a high proportion of handloom weavers among their inhabitants and the weaver's cottage with its wide 'lights' and attic dormers is a common sight throughout the region.

The evidence of the 1790 parish accounts is conclusive enough in its indication of a rapid growth in handloom weaving, although there is much supporting evidence from parliamentary inquiries and other contemporary sources. Certainly the development of the agency system was a feature characteristic of the textile industry throughout western Scotland, but it seems to have been particularly common in Galloway. Weavers' agents based in the main centres penetrated the most isolated districts, though weaving was generally concentrated in the towns and villages, which had a tradition of textile manufacturing and hence a skilled labour force. One such agent was David Laird, who acted for James McGowan & Co, cotton manufacturers in Glasgow. Laird, a former foreman with McGowans, became their 'country agent' in Newton Stewart sometime before 1814. Laird supplied the handloom weavers around the town with yarns, shuttles and other necessities of the trade and his 'Account Books' 1814–16 give some hint of his activities. At regular fortnightly intervals the number of 'pieces' of cloth are entered with their cost, presumably before dispatch north to Glasgow. The following are selected entries from one of Laird's books:

20 June 1814	144 pieces	£75	19s	9d
4 July „	91 „	£45	6s	0d
17 July „	151 „	£66	11s	5d

Little else is disclosed in the account books and the only pattern which emerges is the fall in production about harvest time and an average payment of 8s per 'piece'. James McGowan was bankrupt by 1816 and

Laird's prosecution followed a year later. His crime—probably a common one among many in his position—was feathering his own nest at the expense of his head office.[101]

The numbers employed in handloom weaving in the period 1820–30 are given in data from the *Report from the Assistant Hand-loom Weavers' Commissioners* (1839), which is reproduced in the table below. The marked concentration of the craft around the lower Dumfriesshire parishes is a notable feature, particularly in Dumfries, Annan, Langholm and Gretna. The distress among weavers caused by low wages and long working hours at this period is nowhere better illustrated than in a contemporary account of Gretna, where 120 families (600 persons) worked at looms for 12–14 hours per day, earning an average wage of 7s per family a week. 'By diligent labour and punctual payments', wrote the local minister, 'they are thus able barely to support their families.'[102] The majority of weavers 'subsist entirely by the loom and engage in no other pursuits' and as a result had to work long hours to produce more cloth. Although by 1839 the industry still had a substantial labour force in south-west Scotland, many weavers had given up their formerly profitable craft and had 'fallen into the class of farm labourers'.[103]

Handloom Weavers in South-West Scotland 1828–38

Location	Factory Looms	Domestic Looms	Totals 1838	1828
Newton Stewart	–	100	100	311
Stranraer	9	105	114	–
Whithorn	–	20	20	–
Wigtown	–	13	13	–
Kirkcudbright	–	60	60	–
Dumfries	–	450	450	550
Ecclefechan	–	265	265	130
Annan	–	260	260	360
Gretna	–	250	250	150
Langholm	–	250	250	300
Sanquhar	36	146	182	182
Moffat	–	38	38	–
Scattered places	–	50	50	–

Some indication of the standard of living of the weaver and of wage rates in Dumfriesshire at this time is given in the table below. The conditions in some parts of the Duke of Buccleuch's estates were so bad that the duke himself had to provide relief. In Langholm 'the expense of maintaining poor weavers' amounted to £830 in 1840–1, while over £1,448 was spent in Sanquhar the following year.[104] In the latter district 276 cotton weavers and families were dependent on the craft and practically all were as badly off as the 'poor weaver' whose weekly family income is indicated in section (a) of the table below. [105] Even the skilled weaver relied heavily on the constant help of wife and children, as section (b) of the table clearly indicates. The 'best embroidery' was 'very badly paid' and agents often cheated weaver and employer alike.[106]

(a)   *Family Income of 'a Poor Weaver' in Sanquhar 1842*

John Brown weaver, aged 30	4s	2d
Isabella, his wife 28		9d
John, son 13, apprentice	1s	6d
Christine, 15		9d
4 other children		
	7s	2d

(b)   *Family Income of a Skilled Weaver in Dumfriesshire 1838*

Father weaving, son 12 years old drawing for him	12s	6d
Wife, winding pirns	2s	2d
Son 14 years old, weaving	3s	10d
Son 9 years old at school		
Daughter 17 years old, embroidering	4s	6d
£1	3s	0d

(c)   *Weekly Wage Rates in Southern Dumfriesshire 1830–8*

	Average Weaver		Skilled Weaver	
1830	7s		8s	1d
1	6s	4d	7s	6d
2	6s	4d	7s	6d
3	6s	4d	7s	4d
4	7s	9d	9s	6d
5	6s	3d	8s	9d
6	5s	6d	7s	5d
7	4s	3d	6s	2d
8	4s	6d	7s	6d

Sources: PP, 1839, XLII, *Reports from the Asst Handloom Weavers' Comm*, 521, 529
SRO, *Buccleuch Mun* GD 224/511 Letters re the State of Manufactures at
Canonbie & Sanquhar 1842

Handloom weaving was a dying craft by the middle of the nineteenth century, although it did survive later in country districts and in small, local woollen mills, like Minnigaff. Other textile crafts, such as muslin sewing and embroidering, were practised by women and often operated on the agency system. Damask making was a speciality of Sorbie parish, employing 91 workers in 1838. The district was 'much famed for the superiority of its fabrics and patterns of double damask' and it is not surprising that the weavers' cottages with their wide windows are a notable feature of this district.[107]

PAPER MANUFACTURE

Paper making, an old-established Scottish industry, is traditionally associated with the east of the country, especially the Lothians, Fife and Aberdeenshire. Scottish paper manufacture, however, was much more widely dispersed than at present, particularly in the late eighteenth century, when the industry expanded rapidly. One region of the west of Scotland where such an expansion took place was Galloway. In at least four locations small, water-powered mills were operating after 1790 (see page 104) representing a substantially larger sector of the Scottish paper-manufacturing industry than has previously been

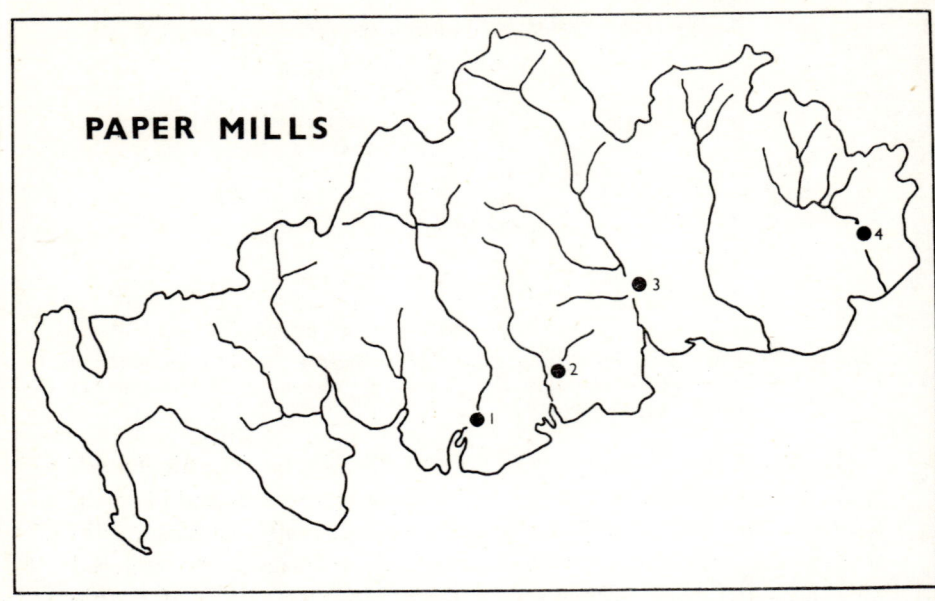

Paper mills in south-west Scotland c 1800

Key:
1 Tongland   2 Dalbeattie   3 Dumfries   4 Langholm

realised. An even stranger anomaly is that despite the rapid demise of three of the four mills early in the nineteenth century, the remaining mill (probably the oldest) survived into the present century.[108]

The earliest paper mills in Galloway were those at Dalbeattie and Tongland, both of which are mentioned in the *Statistical Account*. Alexander Wilson obtained a feu c 1790 from Alexander Copland, co-founder of the town of Dalbeattie, for ground on the King's Grange estate to build his mill. The spot Wilson chose, known as Mount Pleasant, was an ideal water-power site located half-way down the twin lade from Barrbridge to the Dalbeattie corn and wauk mills in the town itself. By 1793 the Dalbeattie mill was said to have 'prospered abundantly'. According to *Pigot's Scottish Directory 1825–6* there were two paper mills in the town, both owned by Alexander Wilson 'paper manufacturer', but this may have been a compiler's oversight. By 1835 Wilson had retired, having sold out to an individual named Cochtrie and according to the *Return of Paper Mills* (1851) the Dalbeattie mill had only one beating engine—a further indication of its small scale. Later owners included William Lewis and John Forsyth, the latter operating Mount Pleasant for over 37 years. In the early 1900s the business was acquired by Andrew Wright, who later sold out to Henry Marshall. In 1919 William Thyne & Co, the Edinburgh paper and cardboard manufacturers, acquired the Dalbeattie mill and operated it for a few years. Mount Pleasant did not survive the 'Depression', although the ruins of the building remain to provide the industrial archaeologist with a unique and interesting site (plate, page 54).[109]

Tongland paper mill stood near the church beside the much older corn mills on the River Dee. A lease of 1788 granted the mills of Tongland to William McWhinnie, a Kirkcudbright merchant, and it was probably he who erected the paper mill. In 1801 a partnership of William Chalmers, bookseller in Dumfries, and Anthony McKenzie, another Kirkcudbright merchant, operated the mill, but little else is known about the mill's history. A plan of the Tongland mill feus dated 1846 shows the layout and dimensions of an 'old paper mill', obviously long disused (see page 106). It stood on a complex power site, where water from the Dee drove corn, saw, farina and paper mills.[110]

A third paper works at Langholm was also short-lived. It was in operation before 1812, employing 20 workers with two vats, manufacturing 80 reams of paper each per week, with a total production valued at over £4,000 per annum. This mill was located on the banks of the Esk, near the old distillery. The fourth mill was in production about the same time, carried on by the same William Chalmers who was a partner in the Tongland mill. It was located in Maxwelltown and had probably ceased activity by the 1820s.[111]

Paper making probably developed in Galloway because of the region's traditional associations with older forms of textile processing and because of the excellent water-power resources. The rapid de-

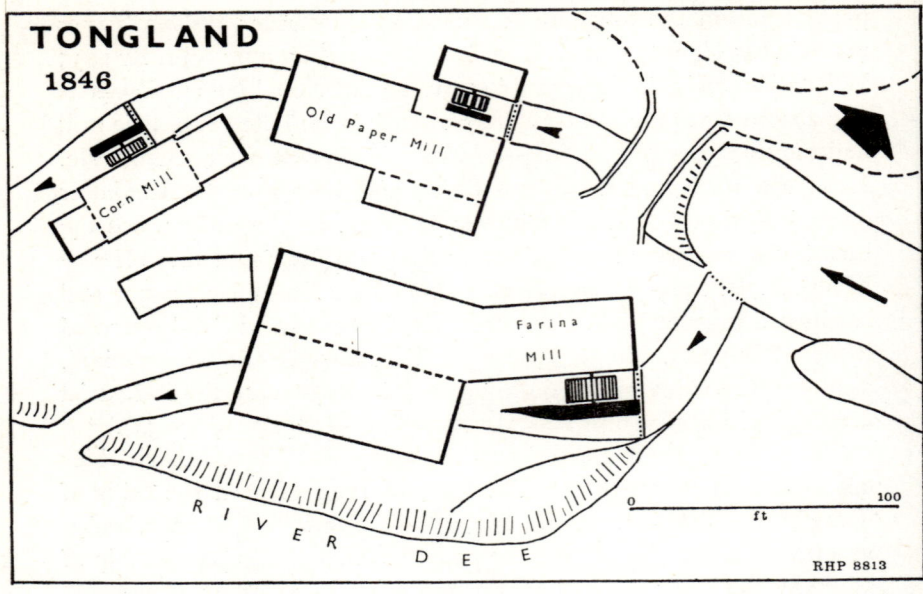

velopment of the regional woollen and cotton industries no doubt made available large quantities of textile waste, which paper mills could put to profitable use. The relatively high cost of capital equipment probably prohibited the growth of the industry, restricting it to small units of production and—as in other sectors of the Galloway industrial economy—quickly giving the cost advantage to other paper-manufacturing districts, such as the Lothians. Although paper making was the most unusual of the industries to develop in Galloway during the industrial revolution, in one way it was quite typical—its use of water power as a prime mover.

(*See pages 246–8 for notes*)

Page 107 (left) *Range of conical kilns at Buccleuch brickworks, Sanquhar; (right) ruined brick kilns at Terally in the Rhins of Galloway, typical of many supplying the needs of local agriculture*

Page 108 (above) *Kelton toll-house, near Castle Douglas. Note the 'gothic' style windows;* (below) *Cree Bridge, Newton Stewart, built to a design by John Rennie in 1813*

CHAPTER FOUR

Mining and Quarrying

MINING and quarrying were of great significance in the nineteenth-century economy of south-west Scotland. Quarrying became an important activity in the Stewartry and Dumfriesshire and, as the following section seeks to show, provided the region with an important source of employment and a significant export trade in building stone to the urban districts of Britain. Metal mining was more widely dispersed and although of less economic consequence, affords some remarkable examples of business acumen and persistence in the face of challenging environmental factors. The section devoted to metal mining illustrates, by means of several detailed case-studies, the commercial organisation and technical activities which the pursuit of minerals engendered in south-west Scotland. Coal mining was more limited by natural circumstance, but both colliery districts were located on the vast estates of the dukes of Buccleuch and the aim of this section will be to introduce new documentary material relating to the Sanquhar and Canonbie mines during the eighteenth and nineteenth centuries. An associated agrarian activity, limestone quarrying and lime burning is only now receiving the attention it deserves from industrial archaeologists, and here documentary material is used to illustrate day-to-day activities in two notable Nithsdale limeworks. Tile drainage grew naturally from the era of agrarian improvement and a number of small brick and tile works developed to serve local needs in Galloway.

QUARRYING

Quarrying for building stone and slate was probably of little more than local significance in Dumfries and Galloway during the eighteenth century. Undoubtedly, stimulus to the industry derived from the improving movement—to meet the demand for materials for the famous Galloway dry-stane dykes engendered by enclosure and for building stone and slate for new, planned estate villages and country seats. An enormous number of quarries (mostly very small businesses) must have been working during the latter half of the eighteenth century, operating as season permitted and local demand warranted. The mark of this activity is stamped on period buildings in town and countryside.

Local granites and whinstones were widely worked in Galloway, notably in Kirkmaiden, Kirkmabreck and Colvend near Dalbeattie. In Dumfriesshire the red sandstones of Nithsdale and Annandale were in great demand for local building purposes and the genesis of an export trade was already evident. In 1794, for example, 125 tons of sandstone from Cove estate in Kirkpatrick Fleming parish was exported annually through the port of Annan, which a few years later had a significant shipping trade in building stone. From Caerlaverock, red sandstone flags went via the Nith port of Glencaple to form the pavements of the rapidly developing cities of Dublin and Liverpool.[1]

Associated with the harder rocks was slate, worked very widely at this time throughout the south-west. One of the most important slate quarries was Cairnryan, where according to Heron the commodity had been 'wrought for these many years'. Slate was also quarried in Kirkmaiden and Kells, while at Castlewigg in the parish of Whithorn it was worked with marble. A quarry near Parton had ceased production by 1791 as a result of 'unskillful management', yet later reopened to employ 8–10 men, working good-quality slate for many years. An equally strong and durable slate was quarried near Moffat, only one of many locations in the hills of Dumfriesshire. In spite of the widespread quarrying, Galloway slate was generally of inferior quality to that of Wales and the Scottish Highlands, and local slate was soon displaced by the superior import.[2]

The granite of the Dalbeattie mass was worked at a number of quarries for local needs during the latter half of the eighteenth century.

Perhaps only one quarry, Glenstocking, near Urr Waterfoot, was of any importance, for it was widely famed beyond Galloway for the quality of its millstones. In 1796 Glenstocking was said to produce 15–20 sets of stones per annum, valued at £3 each, even exporting them to Ireland. As early as 1800 a small firm operated by Andrew Newall of Dalbeattie was carrying on a successful trade in granite hewing throughout the neighbourhood.[3]

When Robert Heron passed through the small village of Dalbeattie in 1792 he thought it 'rather surprising that a situation so favourable has not before this time been occupied by a town or village of considerable magnitude'.[4] He could not have imagined that this planned village with its mills and busy port would owe its continued development to the granite by which it is encircled. In 1826 began the first large-scale exploitation of Craignair granite when the Liverpool Dock Trustees leased a section of Craignair Hill from John Maxwell of Munches, the local laird. Massive granite blocks of 7–8 tons were quarried and operations were so successful 'that within a few weeks the skilled manager shipped to Liverpool the first quantity of stones'.[5] For a time over 200 workmen and labourers were employed and thousands of tons of granite shipped to Liverpool, where dock engineers were so pleased with the quality of the stone that a second quarry was opened. Operations continued until 1832, when the increasing difficulty of finding blocks of sufficient size and high costs forced the Dock Trustees to look elsewhere for building stone.[6]

Another series of quarries were opened in Kirkmabreck (see page 112), where good granite was available and transport by sea easy. Work began in this location in 1830 and by 1834 450 workers were employed and annual outlay ran at around £15,000.[7] Granite was quarried without blasting and transported in schooners to Liverpool. The initial impetus over, production fell and by 1844 only 160 men were employed. During the height of activity, eleven vessels chartered by the Dock Trustees were in constant use, not without danger, for three vessels were lost 'two with all hands' between 1830 and 1844. On one occasion when the quay at Kirkmabreck was transferred from one

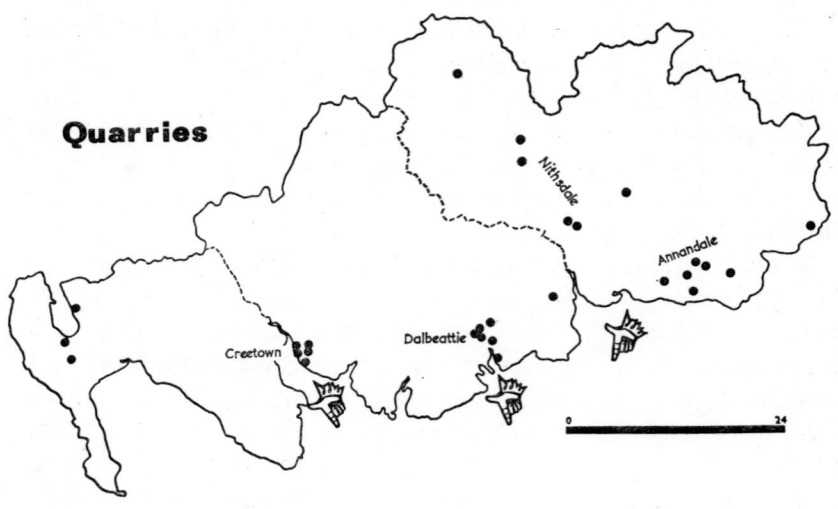

proprietor's land to that of another, no fewer than nineteen vessels spent six months transporting stone from the abandoned wharf to the Mersey.[8]

Following the opening of the Dumfries & Castle Douglas Railway in 1859 there was a considerable revival of large-scale quarrying around Dalbeattie. West of the town, three enormous quarries were worked on Craignair, the most important being that of D. H. & J. Newall, an old-established granite-working business. Other quarries were worked at Craigrowan and Old Lands, about two miles south on the opposite side of the Urr, and at Howlett and Spycraig on the east side of the town. The industry concentrated on dressed and polished granite, but after 1870 the granite-crushing industry became important, with growing demand for rail-track bedding and road metalling. By 1896 there were six crushing plants in Dalbeattie, all steam-powered. Of the four at Craignair, two were worked by Stuart's Granolithic Paving Co, and this product found its way to the pavements of cities all over the world. Fraser & Young, another old-established quarrying company, had two crushing mills, one at

Dalbeattie station (connected to the quarry by an aerial rope-way) and the other at their Old Land quarry, where there was a wharf for direct shipment of granite.[9]

The Creetown quarries continued to supply the Mersey docks, but during the 1860s and 1870s several new quarries were opened in the district, notably Fell Hill, Bagbie and Silver Grey, which were all linked by tramroad to a quay on Kirkmabreck shore. The Bagbie quarry on Kirkdale estate was leased to Forrest, Wise & Templeton, who began operations in 1864. The granite here was of especially high quality, being worked without blasting. Creetown, like Dalbeattie, was originally a planned village, which grew rapidly after 1860. Both towns have some particularly good examples of solid, granite-built workers' housing of the mid-Victorian era, which contrast markedly with earlier period buildings. The population of Kirkmabreck parish reached 1,834 in 1881, the majority of workers being engaged in quarrying and ancillary occupations.[10]

Stewartry granite found its way all over the world for use on city pavements, in docks and harbours, lighthouses, civic or public buildings and in numerous other spheres. 'Many thousands of tons of material' were transported by rail to form the Thames Embankment from Shearer, Smith & Co's Dalbeattie quarry, and paving stones were exported to areas as far apart as Russia and South America. Galloway granite was used in the construction of docks at Greenock, Leith, Liverpool, Birkenhead, Newport and Swansea. It provided much of the material for the great Glasgow Corporation Waterworks, opened in the 1850s at Loch Katrine, and for an enormous range of pretentious Victorian buildings—from the Prudential Assurance Offices in London to the Midland Hotel in Manchester. On a humbler and more utilitarian level, granite was used in making heavy rollers for grinding plant (eg in the flour-milling, paint or dye industries), railway ballast, tarmacadam and artificial slabs, and for setts and general building work in millwrighting and engineering. It was also in great demand for monumental work.[11]

The sandstone quarries of Nithsdale and Annandale were among

the most important Scottish sources of New Red or Permian sandstone, which from its variety of colour and fine grain has always been
in demand for building purposes. Many quarries were opened in and
around Dumfries, Thornhill and Annan after 1840 (see page 112). The
coming of the railway and a succession of urban building booms,
brought about the rapid development of quarrying (there were over
25 quarries by 1860). At the time of the *New Statistical Account*
(1835–45) sandstone quarrying was beginning to assume some significance in the local economy. Four sandstone quarries in the Dumfries
district were valued at £1,000 per annum in 1833, while there were
several quarries near Closeburn, one of which was drained by pumps
'put in motion by a water-wheel'. From six quarries in Kirkpatrick
Fleming 'many shiploads' of stone were sent to Ireland through the
port of Annan.[12] The most spectacular period of expansion took place
in the last decade of the nineteenth century and by 1900 the quarries
employed nearly 1,000 workers producing over 190,000 tons of stone
per annum.[13] Much of this was used in building tenement flats for
middle-class citizens in the western and southern districts of Glasgow.

(a)   *Employment in Quarries 1881 and 1891*

	Stone		Limestone		Slate		Clay	
	1881	*1891*	*1881*	*1891*	*1881*	*1891*	*1881*	*1891*
Dumfries	169	374	30	4	–	–	19	36
Kirkcudbright	318	259	–	–	4	–	21	10
Wigtown	12	26	–	–	–	–	31	24
Total	499	659	30	4	4	–	71	70

(b)   *Quarries and Workforce 1904*

	No of Quarries	Inside Workers	Outside Workers	Total Workforce
Dumfries	23	437	590	1,027
Kirkcudbright	39	308	345	653
Wigtown	7	40	–	40
Total	69	785	935	1,720

(c)   *Quarry Output 1900–1920 (tons)*

	1900	1910	1920
Granite	62,497	42,425	32,181
Sandstone	190,612	102,497	30,007
Whinstone	3,454	30,771	52,075*
Limestone	13,600	16,614	13,814

* Increase due to use as road metal.

Sources: *Report on the Condition of Labour in Open Quarries* (1893); List of Quarries 1904; Mines and Quarries Reports 1900–20

Sandstones from Corsehill, Cove, Annanheath and Kirtlebridge quarries were used in public buildings in Europe and North America, notably the Great Eastern Railway Hotel, London, the University of Edinburgh and the State Capital, Albany, New York.[14]

Undoubtedly the period of greatest activity was in the late Victorian and Edwardian eras, particularly the period 1895–1910, when rapid urban expansion brought about demand for building stone.[15] Some indication of the trends in the quarrying industry are provided by employment and production statistics for the period. Table (a) on page 114 provides a breakdown of employment by county and types of quarry and shows that although granite was fairly static, and indeed declining, sandstone quarrying expanded. Employment rose from over 600 in 1880 to about 1,750 in the peak year of 1902, and table (b) shows the distribution and job allocation of the workforce two years later in 1904. Granite quarrying in the Stewartry clearly expanded in the initial phase of demand for building stone, but the effect of the boom was most dramatically felt in the sandstone quarries of Dumfriesshire. Table (c) shows clearly how rapid was the decline in sandstone production after 1910, while granite fell at a slower rate.[16] The introduction of cheaper methods of building after 1914–18 led to further decline in production and by 1939 only four sandstone quarries were working and few granite quarries survived.

Clearly the archaeology of quarrying is less exciting than an examination of the business history of the industry, but it is only by inspection of the actual site itself that one can appreciate at first hand the sheer scale of past quarrying activities in Galloway. One only needs to stand on the shore of Wigtown Bay opposite the yawning gap in the Kirkmabreck massif, to realise the scale of operations which were involved in quarrying and transporting half a mountainside from Galloway to the Mersey.

METAL MINING

The Ordovician and Silurian rocks of south-west Scotland are endowed with a wide range of metalliferous ores which have been worked in many localities during the last two hundred years. Most significant were ores of lead, zinc, copper and iron, associated with intrusive rocks throughout Galloway, but particularly on the edges of the Criffell, Cairnsmore and Merrick granite masses. In the Lowther Hills, on the Lanarkshire border, there existed an important concentration of minerals, notably lead and precious metals, providing a unique Scottish example of almost continuous exploitation from medieval times. The period of greatest activity in the search for and working of native ores in Galloway was 1760–1850, an era of widespread metal mining throughout the British Isles. Lead was the most important mineral worked in Galloway—most attempts to mine other ores being short-lived. A recent study of the lead industry has emphasised its relative unimportance, for according to contemporary estimates, Scotland accounted for less than 5 per cent of total British output in 1830 (around 3,000 tons), and certainly far less at an earlier date and later in the nineteenth century. Yet a handful of mines in south-west Scotland (see page 117) probably produced 75 per cent of Scottish output between 1780 and 1820.[17] Although quantitatively unimportant, metal mining was of some significance locally within Galloway and provides many features of interest for the industrial historian.

Undoubtedly the earliest mining activity took place at Leadhills and Wanlockhead (plate, page 89) on the edge of the region. Both were important during the latter half of the seventeenth century and by the

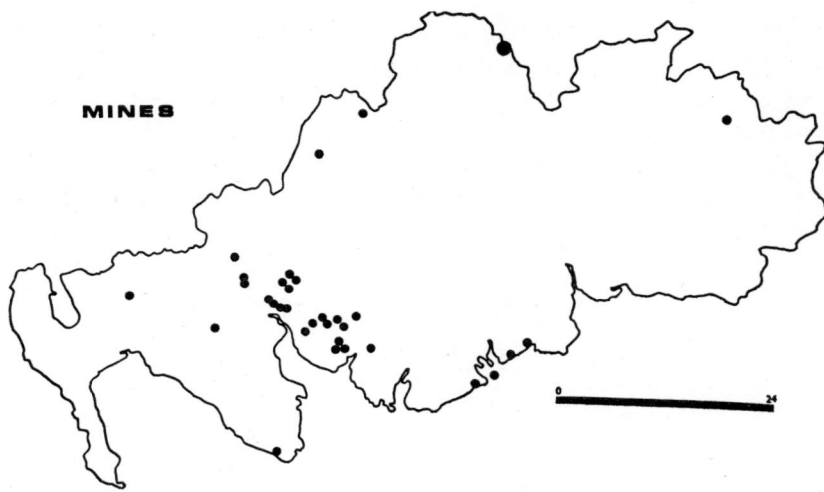

MINES

Metal mines

1720s had become the centre of Scottish lead mining.[18] The long history of mineral exploitation at these two places has been narrated elsewhere, but consideration is given below to activities after 1760 and the industrial archaeology which this engendered.[19] Wanlockhead and its long-standing rival, Leadhills, are classic examples of the isolated mining communities which metal mining in areas like Galloway engendered, and it is remarkable that these long-established villages should outlive later settlements, like Woodhead near Carsphairn, a growth of the nineteenth-century revival in lead prices colonised from the twin villages after 1840.[20]

The years 1760–1815 were an era of mounting prosperity at Wanlockhead, when the mining lease was held by Ronald Crauford & Co, a partnership combining Ronald Crauford, an Edinburgh lawyer, his brother John, an emigré lead merchant in Rotterdam and Gilbert Meason, whose family had long associations with the working and management of the lead mines.[21] Rising lead prices in response to increased demand as a result of the American and French wars not only encouraged great activity at Wanlockhead, but also brought into being many mines in other parts of the south-west. In 1809 lead prices reached £32 per ton and despite a general slump after 1812, lead was still fetching £24 per ton on the Leith market in 1813, and as much as £27 in 1818.[22] Some indication of output during this period is provided in the table below compiled from documents in the Buccleuch Muniments:

Lead Output at Wanlockhead 1811–23[23]

Year	Tons	Bars
1811	1,196	22,687
1812	804	15,316
1813	1,050	20,000
1814	1,081	20,615
1815	1,220	23,274
1816	751	14,153
1817	384	7,336
1818	703	13,375
1819	940	17,773
1820	930	17,667
1821	754	14,250
1822	701	13,211
1823	529	9,967

Much of the industrial archaeology of this period has been obliterated by later activity and although numerous early adit-mouths and wagonways can still be traced in the valleys around Wanlockhead, perhaps the most remarkable survival of all is the water-pressure beam engine at the foot of the village, which was probably in use c 1770 before the company purchased Boulton & Watt engines (plate, page 89). The stone base of a second engine can be seen farther down the valley of the Wanlock Water.[24]

The Duke of Buccleuch undertook the working of the Wanlockhead mines on his own account after 1842. A period of more buoyant lead prices after 1860 led to a revival of activity during the last decades of the nineteenth century and created much of the surface evidence which survives today. Paradoxically, had the industry declined sooner, much of the early plant might have survived, but as circumstances would have it the lead trade revived dramatically in 1906 after a decade of depression. Much of the plant was installed after 1870 and renewed from time to time. The ore-dressing plant and smelting mills, now badly ruined, are of this date, and continued in use until final closure in 1928.[25]

Amongst the earliest and best documented of the Galloway mines were those developed at Blackcraig and Machermore in Minnigaff, in a district where lead had been accidentally discovered in 1763 by a soldier engaged on building the military road.[26] Some years before this chance discovery Cuthbert Readshaw of Richmond, a merchant already actively engaged in lead mining and the lead trade in Scotland, had established contacts in Galloway. As early as 1755 he had exchanged letters with William Carruthers, a merchant in Dumfries, and George Clerk of Dumcrief about lead and copper prospecting in Dumfriesshire, the securing of leases and the creation of a mining company.[27] By 1758 these individuals had (with others) formed a company and, no doubt through Carruther's local knowledge of Galloway, decided to try their luck in Minnigaff.

Readshaw, Carruthers and partners obtained a mining lease from Patrick Heron of Heron in 1764 'of all mines and minerals in the Lands of Dallammie and the Path in the parish of Monigaff for the space of 31 years', with the traditional lordship of every sixth bar or part of lead mined. The company was

> ... given full power of searching for and taking out from the Grounds all ores, metalls, minerals, fossills of every kind, and of smelting and other ways dressing and manufacturing the said ores etc; and of erecting houses, smelting milns, furnaces, fire and water engines, putting up bingsteads and knocking places; digging and sinking pits, pitt shafts, sumps, driving insetts and drifts, and by raising and conveying by water-courses above and below ground all water necessary for the said works.[28]

In addition, the workmen were to be allowed to build houses adjacent to the mine.

By articles of agreement dated May 1764, Cuthbert Readshaw,

Joshua Readshaw of London, merchants, Philip Jackson of London, Joshua Readshaw Jr, George Clerk of Edinburgh, William Carruthers of Dumfries and others became partners in the Craigtown Mining Co. Patrick Heron was himself described as 'joint-adventurer with them'.[29] Clearly work did not begin immediately, for a rough plan of Blackcraig (see page 121) dated 1768, preserved in the Clerk of Penicuik Muniments, merely indicates the location of the 'proposed lead mine'.[30] Yet the Craigtown Mining Co had a head-start on another firm with newly acquired rights on the adjacent property of Machermore, belonging to Patrick Heron's neighbour, Patrick Dunbar. In April 1764, Thomas Paton and Richard Richardson (a banker in Chester) with others were granted a lease 'to mine and open the grounds of Machermore', and with this object formed the Blackcraig Company.[31] According to later evidence, the company 'made some triffling Tryals upon the lands of Blackcraig which was afterwards abandoned and given up'. The company persisted in its efforts, however, with some success.[32]

Activities at the Craigtown mine are particularly well documented during the period 1770–90, when operations were at their height. The manager, William Mure, sent regular reports to (Sir) George Clerk from 1778 to 1787 and these, supplemented by other reports and records of output, form an invaluable source of data on day-to-day affairs at Blackcraig.[33] Several rough plans (mostly drawn by Mure) indicate the location of the Craigtown mine and that of the Blackcraig Co (near the military road by the edge of the Cree), together with various shafts, levels and cross-cuts underground and the location of smelting and washing plant (see page 121).[34] The Blackcraig site derived some advantage from its coastal location because coal for the furnaces could be imported from Cumberland by sea, though supplies were often unreliable in winter.[35] Peat and oak-wood were available in plenty and water-supply (an indispensable feature of every lead works) was readily provided for washing galena and driving the water-powered bellows of the furnaces. Sea transport not only provided the means of smelting the ore, but also provided the vital link in the export of bar lead and lead shot to the London market.[36]

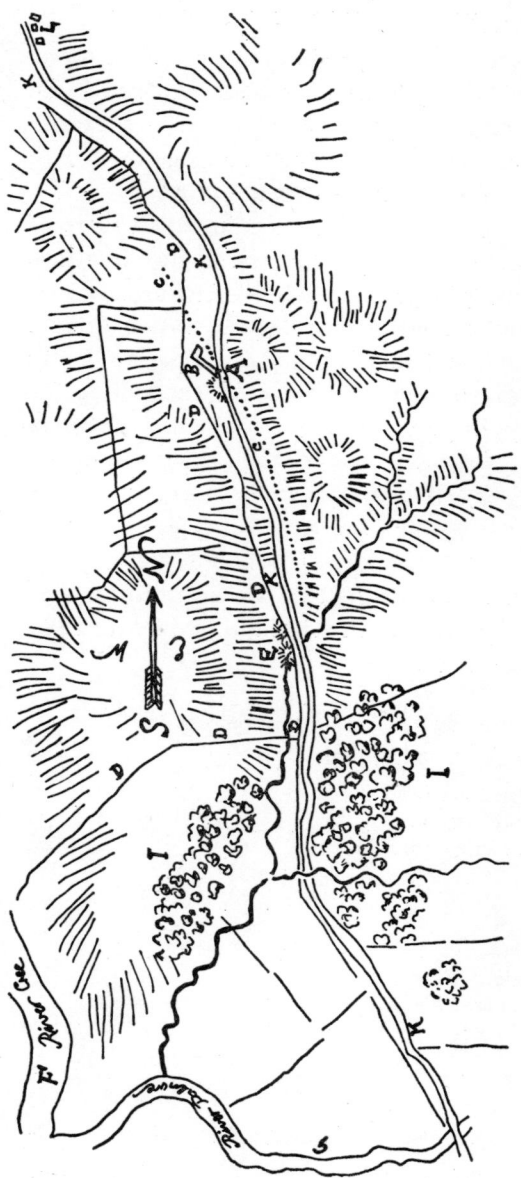

Rough plan of Blackcraig Lead Mine c 1760—this interesting sketch shows the location of lead-working activity in the Blackcraig area. The original key is reproduced below:

A Here the Mine was first discovered
B Here a Cast made to gain Level
C The supposed Course of the Vein
D March betwixt Mr Herron & Machremore
E Old working by Machremore, where a strong vein of spar mixed to metal was said to point directly into Mr Herron's Liberties and may be the south end of our vein
F The river of Cree, navigable
G The river Palnure likewise navigable near the bridge for vessels of 60 or 70 ton
H The bridge distant from our Tryal about one measured mile
I Oak wood fit for all kinds of work under ground, the property of Mr Herron
K The Turnpike road lately made from Newton Stewart to Ferry town of Cree, Dumfries
L Houses where some of the miners are to lodge

By 1780 there were 44 workmen employed at the Craigtown mine, including 25 pickmen, 7 smelters, 3 drawers of water, a smith and a wright, all engaged in working and processing galena.[37] In nearby Creetown, the process of manufacture was carried a stage further in a shot mill, erected c 1780 and also driven by water power.[38]

A series of accounts covering 1783–6 indicate the small scale of activities at Craigtown, a scale more typical of the Galloway mines (and of the Scottish lead industry in general) than Wanlockhead, which was very much the exception to the rule. In the year ending August 1783, the company sustained a loss of £150 4s, expenses being £903 14s 5½d and output of 761 bars (50 tons) of lead selling for £753 10s 5½d at the current price of £15 per ton.[39] William Carruthers had earlier written to Clerk of Penicuik expressing anxiety about the state of the company and suggesting that William Mure should be ordered to 'withdraw and dismiss the Men from every dead tryal'.[40] Later years saw an improvement, although production in the best year for which figures are available was only 65 tons and profit little over £150. One fairly profitable feature was the shot mill, which in 1783 showed the following balance sheet:

Transactions of the Shotmiln at Creetown belonging to the Craigtown Mining Company 1783

Sale of Patent & Common Shot including Casks and Bags	£333	14	½
Patent Shot shipped to London in 221 Casks	710	14	6
	£1,044	8	6½
To Bar Lead 49 Tons	701	13	10
Expences of Working, Oversears wages, casks, Bags and Miln rent	93	6	3
	£795		3
Profit	£249	8	3½

Average sales over three years indicate a profit of about £200 per annum, which probably gave the company a narrow profit margin even

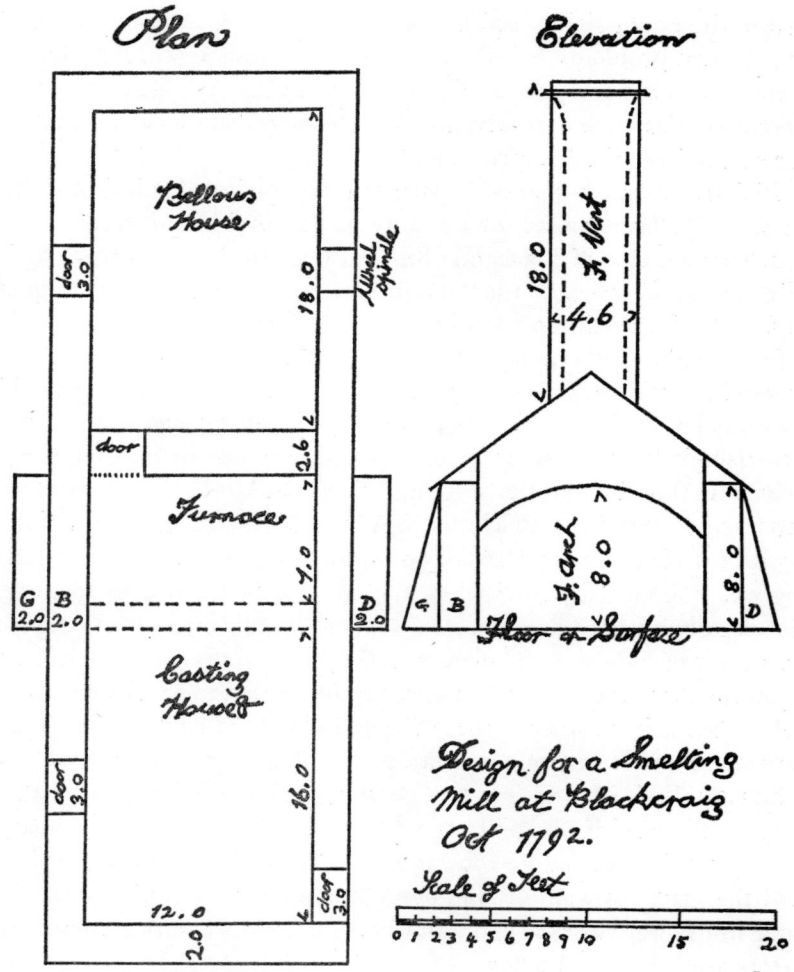

Design for a smelting mill 1792—A careful scale drawing by Robert Scott,
showing the plan and layout of a typical eighteenth-century lead-smelting
plant (from SRO, GD 46/17/5)

before the era of rising lead prices in the late 1780s.[41] The shot mill had its own problems, for Thomas Adamson, shot agent, reported to a meeting of the company at Newton Stewart on 23 August 1783 that urgent repairs were necessary to the waterwheel and lade and that an access road required improvement.[42]

Richard Richardson and his partners, who included Admiral Keith Stewart of Glasserton, met with more success in the short term on the Machermore side of Blackcraig hill and for a time output from their mine averaged over 400 tons per annum, the majority being shipped to Chester for smelting.[43] Letters in the Seaforth Muniments provide a few details of operations at Machermore. In 1792 over 100 men worked the mine in seventeen groups on a contract system, being paid by tonnage of ore raised. The majority of labourers and miners, not surprisingly have Welsh or Quaker names. Drainage levels were being driven at this time and a 'fire engine' was at work. According to a report by Robert Scott in a letter to Admiral Stewart, the depth of the lowest working was 115yd, 65yd below the lowest level.[44] Some smelting was undoubtedly carried on, though 'not in the proper manner, the slags being thrown out before all lead is extracted'.[45] The figure on page 123 indicates the plan of 'a Smelt Mill' designed by Robert Scott for Blackcraig, though it seems unlikely that this was ever built. John Taylor in another report of 1792 indicated that the mine 'may be carried on as at present quite profitably, but the resources will gradually diminish and in a few years the mine will be reduced to a very small scale'.[46] Certainly the *Statistical Account* reports a sharp drop in production before 1793 and Scott noted that many miners had 'left the place for want of employment' after 1791.[47] Both the Blackcraig mines were worked sporadically in later years and these developments are considered below.

The era of steady and rising lead prices after the 1780s brought about increased activity on the part of Galloway landowners anxious to pursue prospecting or re-open earlier workings. In New Luce parish the Earl of Stair had a survey carried out of the isolated Knockibae mines c 1785, when 'several hundred-weight of ore was found' and

Page 125   (right) *Milestone on the former Carlisle–Portpatrick turnpike, typical of many in Galloway;* (below) *Port Logan harbour and light in the Rhins of Galloway*

LONDON
415.
P. PATRICK
1.
STRANRAER
7.
DUMFRIES
83.

Page 126   (above) *Fleet canal, near Gatehouse, showing granite piers of derelict swing bridge;* (below) *South Pier and inner harbour, Portpatrick*

made a second attempt there in 1792, this time clearing out old workings only to abandon them after unsuccessful trials.[48] Hugh Stewart of Tonderghie, who improved large areas in Whithorn, discovered veins of lead and copper on the rocky coastline of his estate about two miles north-west of Burrow Head and sometime before 1790 leased the mining rights to a company for the low lordship of one-eighth of profits and damage compensation. This was also short-lived, for Stewart died and the company withdrew.[49] The upland Stewartry parish of Kells witnessed several abortive trials: on the estate of Sir William Millar a lead mine had 'never been worked to any extent'; while copper, discovered by miners going from Leadhills to Minnigaff, was worked for an equally short period.[50]

There are numerous examples of short-lived mining ventures in Galloway. The typical life cycle of those developed in the late eighteenth-century and early nineteenth-century booms is that of chance discovery followed by rapid exploitation and exhaustion of readily worked ores. Few survived the drop in prices after the end of the Napoleonic Wars and the later removal of protective tariffs which permitted import of cheap Spanish lead in the late 1820s.[51] The partial recovery of the Scottish lead industry after the mid-1830s was reflected in the opening of several new mines in Galloway and a revival of earlier workings.

Woodhead mines in the remote hills above Carsphairn were discovered in 1838 and in the years following 'this upland solitude was converted into a stirring scene of operative industry and a village rose to have a population of three hundred'.[52] The development of the mine excited the interest of the writer of the *Statistical Account* in 1844 and he remarked that the population of the parish had almost doubled during five years and 'a large village', with the traditional library and schoolhouse had been established (plate, page 72).[53] The situation at Woodhead certainly compared favourably with that described by Joseph Fletcher, visiting Leadhills in 1841:

At the time of my visit there were a number of families remaining in the village, the heads of which, to the number of perhaps 80 had gone to work

H

at the newly opened mine at Carsphairn in Galloway about 60 miles distant, where there is as yet no permanent home for those dependent on them.[54]

Unlike Fletcher, Lord Cockburn, that arch-dilettante and traveller, seems at least to have visited Woodhead, penetrating its mountain fastness to record that 'it looks like a colony of solitary strangers who were trying to discover subterranean treasures in a remote land'.

The proprietor of the mines, Colonel McAdam Cathcart, appointed 'skilful and steady overseers' (mostly Cornishmen and 'all followers of Wesley') and secured his workforce from Wanlockhead and Leadhills.[55] Two veins were worked—Woodhead and Garryhorn—and a complex series of adits and levels created for working and drainage. Crushing, washing and smelting plant was installed, a waterwheel 30ft in diameter providing power for the crushing mill.[56] The furnaces processed most of the ore raised and as the table below indicates, output rose to a maximum within a few years of opening, then dwindled steadily:

Output of Woodhead Lead Mine 1840–73

Year	Lead (tons)	Year	Lead (tons)
1840	340	1857	72
1	495	8	63
2	905	9	45
3	850	1860	59
4	638	1	61
5	416	2	51
6	362	3	42
7	354	4	41
8	301	5	35
9	263	6	29
1850	290	7	20
1	302	8	—
2	194	9	30
3	93	1870	61
4	50	1	63
5	56	2	34
6	85	3	12

Total tonnage raised 6,712

Lead was transported overland to Ayr by Dalmellington and shipped to Liverpool.[57] After 1852 the amount of ore raised could hardly have repaid costs, but even as late as 1876, Malcolm Harper saw nearly 100 workers 'all busily engaged at work on the surface'. Optimism, as T. C. Smout recently remarked, died hard in the Scottish lead industry!

Cairnsmore lead mines on the estate of the same name were worked on a small scale before 1845. In that year a lease was granted to the Kirkcudbrightshire Mining Company who started work near Strathmadie. A mine was opened and it produced 3,280 tons of ore before 1855, the majority being shipped from Palnure to be smelted elsewhere.[58] Annual output 1847–59 is indicated in the table below and shows the drop in production after the early years when rich veins were worked out:

Output of Cairnsmore Mine 1847–59

Year	Lead (tons)
1847	317·5
8	477
9	320
1850	360
1	322
2	307
3	247
4	248
5	193
6	–
7	19
8	–
1859	3
Total tonnage	2,813·5

The total value of ore raised in these years was £36,000, an average price of £11 per ton. The Kirkcudbrightshire Mining Company conducted other operations locally and secured copper-mining leases on the lands of the Broughton & Cally estates, which they worked sporadically in a variety of locations at this time.[59] The development

of Cairnsmore in an era of more buoyant lead prices brought about
a revival of activity at the Blackcraig mines after 1853. The extensive
workings at the East and West mines continued to yield lead and zinc
ore until the early 1880s. As the table below indicates, amounts were
relatively insignificant, apart from a short period of frenzied activity
in the 1870s when East Blackcraig produced over 2,500 tons of lead
ore, over 1,500 tons of lead and nearly 1,000 tons of zinc.[60]

Output of West & East Blackcraig Lead Mines 1853–80

Year	West Blackcraig		East Blackcraig	
	Lead Ore (tons)	Lead (tons)	Lead Ore (tons)	Lead (tons)
1853	501	383		
4	25	18	137	106
5	25	18	137	106
6			20	15
7	17	13	97	73
8	109	83	45	24
9	74	65		
1860	24	18		
1	30	23		
2				
3				
4				
5	16	12		
6	103	82	99	66
7			131	98
8	184	138		
9	72	55	182	131
1870	52	39	32	24
1	37	28		
2			149	114
3			244	183
4			261	195
5			424	318
6			455	341
7			356	267
8			284	213
9			354	264
1880			197	147

Source: Memoir of the Geological Survey of Scotland, *Lead Ores*, 49

A wide variety of other minerals have been mined in south-west Scotland, notably copper and iron ores. Copper was mined as early as 1770 in Colvend; the old mines on Heston Island were worked by an English company before 1845 and ores shipped to Swansea, and a Welsh company made unsuccessful attempts about the same time at the Mary mine near Tonderghie.[61] The trustees of the Cally estate granted mineral rights to several companies and individuals during the 1840s and many small (and often short-lived) mines were developed in the hills above Gatehouse.[62] Perhaps the most important was the Enrick mine of the Cally Mining Company, developed after the discovery of copper ore by labourers in 1820. The mine produced quantities of good ore, which was regularly shipped to Swansea from Gatehouse until work was finally abandoned in 1857.[63] Iron ore was worked at Carsphairn in the 1790s, but the mines were abandoned as soon as wood for charcoal was exhausted.[64] Later in Rerrick, a mine was worked at Auchenleck by an English company, producing 50–70 tons of 'superior ore' per week which was shipped south to Birmingham.[65] Another writer records a local story that 'whenever the directors of the last company which worked the Auchenleck mine were expected it was regularly "salted" with haematite from Cumberland'.[66]

The Louisa mine in the Eskdale hills of Dumfriesshire was the only mine to produce antimony in workable quantities in Britain. It was located a mile upstream of the Meggat Water near the farm of Glendinning in Westerkirk. It was worked commercially for a short time (amounting in all to about 12 years), but despite this it is particularly well documented in contemporary sources.[67]

Antimony ore was discovered at Glendinning c 1788 after surveys had been carried out on behalf of the local laird, Sir James Johnstone of Westerhall. The Westerhall Mining Company (with Johnstone, a Captain Cochran and a Mr Tait as shareholders) began work in 1793. The mine was worked by three main levels and between 1793 and 1798 produced over 100 tons of antimony ore worth £8,400. Ore was smelted at the mine and evidence of this activity can be traced by the banks of the Meggat Water where water power was used to drive the bellows. Fuel was obtained locally from peat or by coal from Canonbie, which no doubt was the source of limestone used in the manufacture of pure antimony. The product was used for 'speculums, bell metal and types for printing'.[68]

Forty men were employed, working a six-hour day for wages of £23–£26 per annum, with the usual liberties of land for a garden and some grazing. The company built a village for the workers, called Jamestown, on the haugh by the Meggat Water. A granary was built to store meal for re-sale to miners in winter or times of dearth 'at the rate at which it was purchased'. A school followed and the miners, with the earnestness for self-improvement typical of most lead-mining communities, started a library. This was instituted in 1792 with a gift of £15 worth of books, quickly augmented by the miners' own purchases. The minute book of the Jamestown Library indicates the concern of the miners for poetry, philosophy, comparative religion, geology and political economy.[69]

The mine was re-opened after nearly a century in 1888 by Sir Frederick Johnstone, but closed again after 1892, by which time some 90 tons of antimony had been raised from the long-abandoned levels. In 1919 another attempt was made and new shafts sunk below the original workings. Mining finally ceased in 1922, the levels left to flood with water, the surface equipment dismantled and the rolling hills around Glendinning left to the sheep.[70]

The histories of mines like Glendinning, Blackcraig, Woodhead, Cairnsmore and Wanlockhead illustrate the remarkable persistence of a fated regional industry. Adam Smith's remark that 'the value of a metallic mine depends more upon its fertility than its situation' was clearly no less true of Galloway than any other area of Britain where metal mining was significant. The majority of Galloway mines, with the possible exception of Wanlockhead, were not only badly sited from the point of view of exploitation, but also relatively unproductive in the long term. Yet one marvels at the eternal optimism and persistence of landowners and entrepreneurs who ventured capital in such hostile and isolated environments. Isolation may have frustrated the mine masters, but to the industrial archaeologist—arriving at Woodhead lead mines after a three-mile walk over rough tracks—it has proved a blessing in disguise.

COAL MINING

Coal mining in south-west Scotland was almost entirely confined to the Sanquhar and Canonbie districts of Dumfriesshire, where workable measures were present. The Sanquhar coalfield extends along the valley of the Nith and is essentially a continuation of the Ayrshire field. It covers an area of about seventeen square miles and almost all of this is occupied by productive coal measures. At Canonbie the area of exposed measures is $1\frac{1}{2}$ square miles, though there are many outcrops elsewhere, especially in the valley of the Esk and the Liddel Water. Thin coal seams occur elsewhere throughout the carboniferous limestone series of Dumfriesshire and south-eastern Kirkcudbrightshire, and many attempts have been made to work these thin seams for local use.[71]

Mining has been carried on in the Sanquhar district for many centuries, probably since medieval times. Over the last 200 years, however, two distinct phases in the development of coal production are evident. The first occurred during the latter half of the eighteenth century and early part of the nineteenth century when coal was mined from shallow, readily accessible seams by means of day-levels driven into the hillsides. The map of the Sanquhar district (see page 134) shows how extensively the shallow parts of the coalfield have been probed by pits and mines, the majority sunk in the early nineteenth century. The period of shallow sinkings ended in 1848, when large-scale, systematic working began at Gateside. A pit 26 fathoms deep was sunk by the Buccleuch lessees, the Misses Whigham. An event which 'marked a new era in the coal trade' was the opening of the Glasgow & South-Western Railway in 1850 and this led to further developments.[72] A major sinking took place at Bankhead in 1857 and a second pit at Gateside reached the splint coal at 58 fathoms in 1891.

Mining operations in the Kirkconnel area have since concentrated on the deeper, northern parts of the field and the important Fauldhead colliery began production in 1895. Output in 1910 was 279,912 tons valued at £83,473, when the mines employed 676, although these (and all other) statistics include the small Argyllshire coalfield, which for administrative purposes was linked with the Sanquhar–Kirkconnel mines.

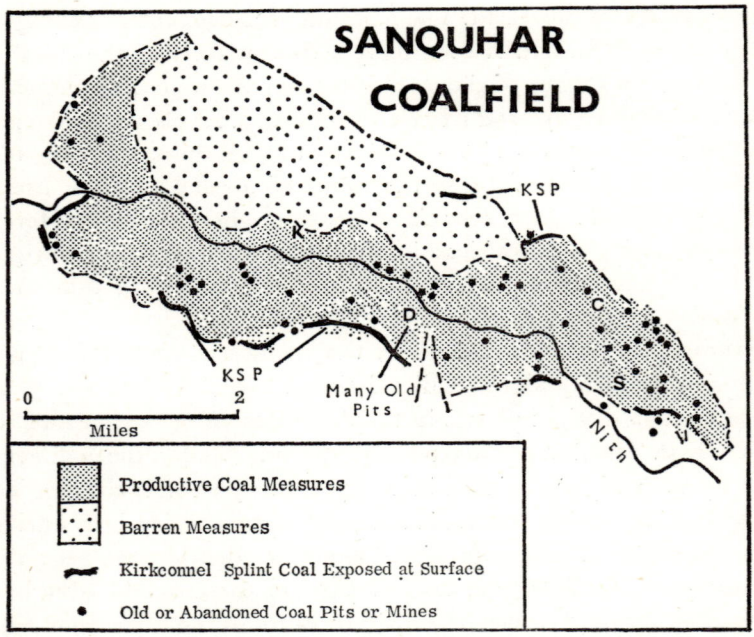

In the latter half of the eighteenth century most of the land around Sanquhar was held either by the burgh or by the Queensberry estate of the dukes of Buccleuch. Mining leases were a source of long-standing contention between the two. The earliest recorded tacksman of the duke's coal was Robert Barker, a mining engineer from Derby-shire who managed the mines at Leadhills, securing a lease in 1768.[73]

Several references to early coal-working occur in the burgh records. Robert Sandilands of Knowehead, for example, is mentioned in 1790 as the owner of a pit and another entry records the council's decision to open a pit of their own because of the local scarcity of coal. Sums of expenditure relating to the sinking of the pit are detailed: a James Henderson was paid £4 10s 'towards the pitt'; 14s 9d is entered for wood for the coal heugh; 2s 6d for blasting powder; and 24s in payment to a labourer for sixteen shifts at the coal pit.[74] Yet the small scale of operations is indicated by the fact that in 1793 there were only 40 colliers at work in Sanquhar.[75]

During the first decade of the nineteenth century the burgh increased its efforts to lease mineral rights in the town's lands. Archibald McNab of Holm, a local landowner, obtained a tack 'of the surface of Larsbraes and the coal within' for 999 years from 9 April 1805, with liberty 'to search for, work, raise and carry off coal of every kind'.[76] McNab obtained two further tacks in 1806 and 1808 of parts of the muir at Bricklands, Long Cleugh, and other locations. Coal was worked on a small scale at these places, but after McNab's death in 1812, the Duke of Buccleuch took over the leases and by 1821 held all three.[77] The burgh derived £2,069 from coal lordships between 1807 and 1822, but in later years income fell dramatically—an indication of the slow exhaustion of readily workable seams.[78]

Before 1822 Thomas Barker, Robert's son, was joint-lessee with a Mr Meason of coal on the Queensberry estates and also held leases in the burgh lands. He sunk pits in a variety of locations, including Hewksland, Quarrylands and Damhead. At the latter pumps were installed, powered by a waterwheel driven by the Nith. The weir was carried off by floods several times and the shaft was so near the river bank that during one heavy spate the entire workings were flooded and the pit had to be abandoned. Another lease of the burgh's coal at this period was the lead-mining company at Wanlockhead.[79]

George Whigham, landowner and lawyer, through his friendship with the Duke of Buccleuch obtained in 1822 the lease of the Kirkconnel and Sanquhar coalfield. By this date there were two main coalworks, at Burnfoot and at Drumbuie, south-east of Kirkconnel. Under the capable management of Christopher Anderson mining was extended to other locations and by 1841 four pits were working—two at Drumbuie, one at Crawick and one at Cairnsburn. Output was around 16,000 tons per annum.[80]

Old Gateside Pit (sunk in 1848) was the first to exploit the deeper seams of the coalfield. It was situated beside the Nithsdale line of the G & SWR (then under construction), which 'opened up a new era for coal mining in the district'. Gateside was the first to be sunk and equipped with steam power, reaching a depth of 100ft to work a 4ft seam. A beam engine provided power for winding and another engine combined haulage and pumping. The seams being so narrow, the former was done by wire rope. Coal for transit by rail was run down an incline to the line, the loaded hutches drawing the empty ones back—an arrangement known locally as a 'cuddy brae'.[81] The Misses Whigham, daughters of George Whigham, sank a second pit in 1857 nearby at Bankhead, where a seam of good splint coal was struck at a depth of 180ft. This was excellent steam coal and such was the demand from the G & SWR that production quickly reached 120 tons per day. J. I. McConnel, who leased the collieries after 1887, left an interesting description of the pits when he first came to Sanquhar and the following extract illustrates conditions among the Bankhead miners:

> The men were a very fine type of miners, bread and born in the place and who, or their parents, had worked for the Whigham family for many years. Strikes were unknown. A good miner made about 24s a week, provided his own lamp oil and explosives and paid for his picks being sharpened. They were paid on the larger coal only, except they got 2d a hutch of about 6 cwt for small coal sent up for the engine fires. Some ninety men were employed.[82]

When James Irving McConnel (who had been trained as an engineer) took over the Buccleuch leases in 1887 he was provided with working capital by his Whigham aunts and successfully applied his technical and business knowledge to the development of the collieries.

A new pit was sunk at Gateside in 1891, the old one being closed. The most up-to-date winding and pumping plant was installed. Fauldhead Nos 1 and 2 followed in 1896 and mechanical haulage and coal-cutting were introduced for the first time. Thereafter growth was so rapid that by 1903 McConnel had formed the Sanquhar & Kirkconnel Collieries Ltd.[83] Two more pits, Fauldhead Nos 3 and 4, were sunk near the others, reaching over 450ft in depth. Despite the onset of World War I and a reduction in the labour force there were over 780 miners employed in Gateside and Fauldhead pits in 1915, producing over a quarter of a million tons of coal per annum.[84]

Coal mining remained a vital industry to the twin towns of Kirkconnel and Sanquhar until the early 1960s when national policies for rationalisation of the coal industry began to take effect as they had earlier in the coal-mining districts of Ayrshire and Lanarkshire. The final link was broken in 1968 when Fauldhead colliery closed after a productive working life of over eighty years. It would be wrong to dismiss what is clearly industrial archaeology in the making, but the origins of what is now a lost industry have made a more permanent mark on the landscape in the form of the old levels and adits in coal outcrops, the overgrown bings and deserted wagonways, which can still be discovered in this interesting district of Upper Nithsdale.

The earliest reference to coal mining in the Canonbie district occurs in a Court of Session case of 1724. John Book and Thomas Dod, merchants in London, obtained a tack from the Duchess of Buccleuch 'of her Lands, Coalries and Ironworks' for 31 years from 1715. Book and Dod entered into a partnership with Obediah Sedgewick, also of London, who settled as business manager 'at the Iron-Forge of Canonbie'. Sedgewick held a fifth share and had a salary of £150 per annum, while each of his partners held two-fifths of the business. Sedgewick in 1717, unbeknown to his partners, arranged to let certain lands (containing coal) to Francis Hetherington of Astonbie in Cumberland, but later the partnership was dissolved, Sedgewick was ruined and Hetherington 'never got possession of the lands'.[85]

One of the most interesting documents in the Buccleuch Muniments (which contain a wealth of data on coal mining in Midlothian and Dumfriesshire) is 'The Journall & Charge in Carrying on the Coall of Cannonbie 1768–70', which was kept by Matthew Little, deputy chamberlain of the Duke of Buccleuch at Canonbie. During two years, operations to open up new pits were undertaken in the valley of the River Esk near Canonbie and Little's 'Journall' provides minute detail of activities there.[86]

A pit had been operating prior to the sinking which is recorded in this journal, but in May 1768 the duke himself 'entered on the works' with Little as overseer of operations. On the 27th of that month Messrs Fowler and Hunter (probably mining engineers from Midlothian), together with four 'of his Graces Coailiers from Dalkeith' arrived at Canonbie and began a survey on both sides of the Esk. When 'the Principal plan of Operations' had been evaluated it was resolved to sink a new level on the west side of the valley, work being carried out by the Canonbie colliers. The miners from Dalkeith agreed to 'carry on the present Going coall upon the East syde of the River for serving the Country'.[87] By June, a thin seam had been reached and it was found necessary to build up the sides of the level mouth. The duke himself visited the new pit in July, which by that date had reached $12\frac{1}{2}$ fathoms. In September the Lothian coal miners returned home and by November Little found the level 'doing very well'.[88]

By spring 1769 a good coal seam had been struck, though drainage was beginning to pose problems. To cope with this, ropes and buckets were ordered from Carlisle and the miners worked double shifts 'so that the Coall may be gott as soon as possible for serving the Country'. There was a substantial demand for coal locally, especially from nearby limekilns. The level was completed by the end of June and coal worked for sale from the west bank of the Esk. The following production figures indicate the small scale of activities in what were little more than drift mines:

Abstract of Coals Wrought from Byreburn 1768–9

Month	Loads
1	1,545
2	1,088
3	2,085½
4	1,083
5	529
6	706
7	840
8	868
9	960
10	900
11	938
12	856
13	668
	13,066½

Sales £190 11s ¼d   Charges £142 17s 9½d
Profits £47 13s 3d

Production during succeeding years ran at a similar level, although coal was also being produced from the new pit on the Hollhouse bank.[89]

A mineral lease was granted to an Englishman named Lomax in August 1770. He confined his operations to places where coal could be worked by adits in order to avoid the expenditure on drainage equipment. One of the conditions of Lomax's lease was that the supply of coal should 'be equal to the demands of the country', but clearly production was no greater than when the duke himself worked the collieries. The tacksman could have been held to conditions of his lease, but instead the duke let him continue as before and opened his own colliery again.[90]

After considerable outlay the new colliery was opened c 1790 at Byreburnfoot, located near the original pit. A 'water engine on a new construction' (the invention of William Keir, the duke's Canonbie factor) was used successfully for drainage:

The apparatus is operated by means of a bucket, suspended from the end of a lever, having a valve at the bottom in the centre, which by machinery, is made to shut and open in the instant of time the bucket should fill and empty itself. The other end of the lever is fixed to the pump or rod, and by the continued action of the bucket ascending and descending, filling and emptying the water it contains . . . pumping is carried on and the coal pit cleared of the water collected below.[91]

A bore made in 1792 revealed a seam 2ft thick at a depth of 68ft and at 146ft the main seam 5ft 8in thick. A more detailed survey in 1800 records that two seams were mined at 'Canoby coal-works' near Byreburnfoot, the top one 5ft 10in thick and a second 9ft below of 2ft 7in.[92]

No production data is available for this period, but in 1795 98 labourers were employed in Canonbie, including miners. Their earnings varied from 10s to 20s per week and they were described as being 'sober and attentive, bringing up their families in a decent manner'.[93]

By 1835 coal mining was solely the responsibility of the Buccleuch estates and the pits supplied the neighbourhood. A detailed record of the workforce and working conditions was drawn up a few years later in 1842, probably the result of the duke's anxiety about the state of affairs in his mines at a period of increasing activity on the part of royal commissions. This reveals a labour force of 81 at Canonbie:

Colliers drawing their own coals	56
Underground labourers	6
Above ground, including clerk, banksmen, smith, wrights, enginemen and labourers	19
	81

During busy spells up to 100 workers might be employed. The only children were eleven boys aged 14–18 years—'all colliers assisting their father, except one who works the winding engine'. Hours were 5 am to 10 am or 4 pm depending on 'the state of trade', with time for meals eaten at home. Colliers were on piece work, the average wage being 2s 6d and anything up to 4s was common. Boys earned a proportion of the full wage related to age, a sixteen-year-old being paid half a man's rate. The common labourer was less fortunate, working

6 am to 6 pm, 'allowing breakfast and dinner hours', for 2s per day.[94]

Other documentary fragments in the Buccleuch papers provide useful output data during 1856–61, by which time the older workings in the Esk valley were clearly exhausted and activities concentrated on a new pit at Rowanburn, where deeper but thicker seams were present. In one typical year 1860–1, output averaged 2,500 tons per month, total tonnage being 31,766 valued at £9,761 9s 4¼d. Costs were £6,301 19s 2½d, indicating a profit of £3,459 10s 1¾d. Bills of credit sales for the period show that Canonbie supplied customers as distant as Carlisle, as well as many local concerns including Langholm and Tarras distilleries, Tarras tileworks, Langholm gasworks, Reid & Taylor's tweed mill and the neighbouring limekilns of Harelawhill.[95]

During the latter half of the nineteenth century numerous shafts were sunk in the thickest seams around Rowanburn, and while reserves held out the small local industry prospered. A small miners' village grew up near the colliery—an alien feature in the rural landscape of lower Eskdale. So late as 1905 Canonbie provided work for 118 miners and in 1911 the colliery produced over 12,000 tons of coal. But the exposed measures were almost exhausted and by 1915 the labour force had dropped to 54. Mining continued at Rowanburn till 1922 when the colliery finally closed. Coal has since been mined locally on a small scale from time to time.[96]

LIMESTONE, BRICK AND TILES

Quarrying of limestone for agricultural and building purposes in Galloway was essentially an eighteenth-century development. Although lime had long been used for mortar throughout Scotland 'it was primarily the use of lime in agriculture which led to the multiplication of kilns in the countryside'.[97] South-west Scotland affords some particularly interesting examples of lime quarries and associated kilns which developed to supply the demand of local farmers and masons. Geological conditions were such that limestone was confined to a few districts in Upper and Mid-Nithsdale, Lower Annandale and the

Canonbie district. In Galloway itself a number of small quarries were worked where limestone existed—in small, isolated pockets in the Stewartry parish of Kirkbean and in the Rhins of Galloway. The figure below indicates the location of the main lime works. Lime was also a major import into Galloway from Cumberland, a trade dating from the late seventeenth century which became increasingly important during the period 1750–1850. An overland trade in lime from Douglas in Lanarkshire and from the coal-mining districts of Ayrshire supplied farmers in Upper Nithsdale and Annandale.

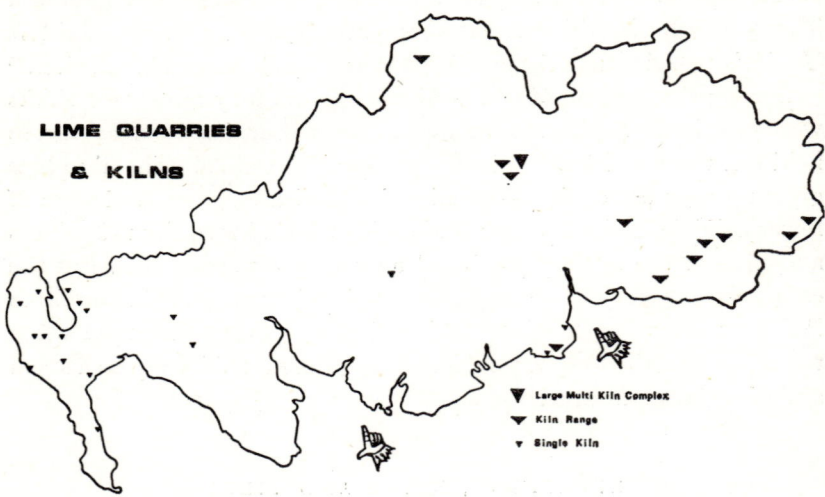

The earliest reference to the use of lime for mortar and fertiliser in Galloway occurs in Symson's *Description* of 1684. By the Baldoon shore of Wigtown Bay he observed that 'the sea casts in innumerable quantities of shells, which the whole shire makes use of for lime and it is the only lime which this countrey affoords'.[98] The shells were burnt with peats in primitive kilns (not unlike early corn kilns) and the process took as long as 24 hours, depending on the amount of lime required. Shell lime from Wigtown Bay was in use as late as the 1790s in parishes near the shore.[99]

Page 143   (above) *Deserted harbour at Garlieston. In the foreground is an early hand crane; (below) Dub o' Hass, the harbour of Dalbeattie photographed c 1880. Brigs reached the town at high tide and are seen unloading cargoes on to carts*

Page 144 (above) *Modern port use at Kirkcudbright on the River Dee;* (below) *Sorbie station on the former Wigtownshire Railway in LMS days. Milk churns from the nearby creamery await collection by the Whithorn train approaching the platform*

The first use of limestone deposits was in the coal-bearing districts of Sanquhar and Canonbie. In the mid-eighteenth century lime was burnt with local coal at Auchengruith, west of Sanquhar, and at Corsancone in the same neighbourhood kilns were supplied with coal worked from an ingaun-e'e in the Lagrae Burn, two miles west of Kirkconnel.[100] On the Duke of Buccleuch's Canonbie estates, a 'lyme quarry' was operating at Hollhouse in the valley of the Esk c 1768 and clearly the shortage of coal for these kilns was one of the reasons for sinking the new pit, described above.[101]

Sir James Kirkpatrick, an early improver, began the Closeburn limeworks c 1774 and this was the first of several in the district to use limestone deposits in mid-Nithsdale.[102] These works are not only well documented, but also preserve the finest bank of kilns in southern Scotland (plate, page 90). Sir James himself went bankrupt in 1780 and the following year his trustees entered into agreement with John Kellock Jr of Thornhill 'for the management of the limeworks in the lands of Kellock and Croal Chappel on the estate of Closeburn'. By a contract dated 17 January 1781, Kellock 'bound himself to use his utmost endeavours to bring forward the Works so as to have Lime ready for the Spring and thereby as much as possible prevent the loss which may arise from the Quarry having lately laid unwrought'. He undertook to employ the necessary workmen and 'to have a sufficient quantity of well burned Lime to answer the demands of the country' as well as to increase sales and 'keep regular books'. He was also responsible for work at the quarry and for keeping the limestone face there 'clear and open'.[103]

Kellock apparently did not keep to the letter of his contract, for by 1783 a new manager, Alexander Williamson of Dalton, was in charge of the limeworks at an annual salary of £45 with commission on each measure of lime sold. Drainage was becoming a problem and a level had been constructed 'to draw off water from the works'.[104] A valuation of tools at Closeburn in 1783 gives some idea of the equipment of a limeworks:

I

```
Iron tools including:
    18 Kiln bars and Pokers
    19 Napping hammers
    6 scrapers
    26 spades and shovels          £12   14s   7½d
Wooden tools including:
    24 earth Barrows
    17 buckets                     £42   16s   5½d
Coal 3,014½ loads                  £87   18s   2
Total valuation                    £133   9s   3d
```

A 'horse engine' or gin was valued in addition at £13 10s. This was used for drainage and haulage, though later replaced by a waterwheel. The same year James Stuart Menteith became proprietor of the Closeburn estates and the limeworks entered a period of renewed expansion.[105]

During 1778–91 the population of Closeburn parish rose from 1,000 to 1,490, an increase almost entirely due to the development of the lime industry, and the transformation of the landscape by the new agriculture was so noticeable that the acclaim given the proprietor and his limeworks by a contemporary is not at all surprising.[106] A second works was opened with its own quarry and kiln bank c 1787 and by 1794 output from the two works ranged from 60,000 to 70,000 measures per annum worth £2,250–£2,625. Production costs were high because coal was brought from Sanquhar, fourteen miles distant.[107]

The interest of the owners in their limeworks is clearly illustrated by the energy of Charles Menteith, who experimented with various types of kilns and invented fuel-saving methods. His description of the quarry and kilns at Closeburn in 1810 is most valuable.[108] The limestone seam was 18ft thick and it was quarried by mining, 'strong pillars to support the roof being left at 10 or 12 yards distance, the roof and floor worked into regular form, the latter accessible to horses and carts, and the kilns close at hand'.[109] 'The form of the lime-kilns', wrote Menteith, 'is oblong [and] having tried kilns of a variety of forms, the contractor and workmen are of the opinion that a kiln of this form produces a greater quantity of well-burnt lime in a given time, than the circular kilns of larger dimensions in common use; and that a less quantity of coal is necessary for burning a given quantity of lime-stone.'[110] The kilns were fitted with cast-iron grates (within arched entrances) and cast-iron tops or chimneys, the latter keeping heat in the kilns and aiding gravity loading. Output c 1812 was estimated at 100,000 Carlisle bushels (150,000 measures) and Menteith's profit was £2,000 per annum.[111]

Several notable developments had taken place by 1834, when the kilns were described as being 'of the most improved construction for burning lime with the smallest quantity of fuel'. Limestone was blasted and raised from the quarry to the kiln head by 'an iron railway' on an inclined plain 200yd long, 'up which loaded waggons ascend with the utmost facility, by means of a water wheel put in motion by a stream brought six miles for the purpose'. The water also turned a lower wheel which powered bellows to provide a blast in the kilns and drove drainage pumps as well as a sawmill. Annual output of lime was worth £3,500.[112] Much of the works, which continued in operation until the late nineteenth century, survives as it was in the 1830s, including the fine bank of three kilns and the track of its associated inclined railway.

On the opposite bank of the Nith another limeworks was begun in 1788 at Barjarg on the estate of the Hunters of Barjarg, an old-established landed family. Documentary fragments from the family muniments provide some detail of operations at this works during 1793–1811. According to the accounts, 1793 was a bad year, in which the loss on operations was £284:

To. Sir James Kirkpatrick for Iron & Wooden Quarry Tools, Smithy Tools Etc.	£338	To. Lime Sold	£694
To. Coals	£334		
To. Working Expences	£406		
	£978		

Clearly the loss was the result of the purchase of essential capital equipment from the Closeburn limeworks nearby.[113] The following year the works employed 30 to 40 labourers for seven or eight months each year, producing 20,000 to 30,000 measures of lime worth 9d per measure (two Winchester bushels), while accounts for 1794 indicate outstanding debts (mostly by local farmers) amounting to £129.[114] By 1802 the Barjarg quarry and kilns were let to David, John and William Kirkpatrick at a lordship of 2d on each measure sold. The output during the period 1803–9 was as follows:

	Measures	*Lordship*		
1803	35,793	£298	5	6d
1804	34,744	£289	10	8d
1805	39,076	£325	12	8d
1806	21,373	£222	12	8d
1807	25,013	£260	11	od
1808	28,112	£292	16	8d
1809	17,057	£177	13	6½d

An 'Abstract of Lime Burnt & Sold at Barjarg' details the destination of output during 1805. A great deal of lime was delivered to surrounding districts, but a large quantity found its way to more distant parishes in the Stewartry, notably Balmaclellan and Kirkpatrick-Durham. Rentals of 1810–11 indicate that the contractors leased Barjarg village for £9 per annum, paid £2 1s depreciation on quarry tools worth £40 and £4 1s interest on 'the expense of the Syphon'—a piece of drainage equipment at the quarry. Barjarg and a second works at Porterstown nearby were still operating in 1835 and lime produced there was still much in demand both for the land and for building purposes.[115]

Throughout lower Annandale a number of limeworks began production during the era of agrarian improvement in the latter half of the eighteenth century. South of Lockerbie, a quarry produced 'a course, dark-coloured lime for the land', while the Kelhead quarry in Cummertrees burnt limestone 'of exceeding fine quality', although burdened by the high price of coal imported from England.[116] Alexander Dirom of Mount Annan had a large limeworks at Quarry Park near Kirtlebridge, which supplied his own estate and surrounding parishes. As at Closeburn, experiments with various types of kilns were tried and the nearby quarries on Brownmoor were drained by water-powered machinery. Several works were active in the 1830s, supplying lime to inland districts of Dumfriesshire that could not derive the same advantage from imported English lime as the farmers on the Solway coast. Yet many of the works in Annandale had to rely on English coal for lime burning. Caldronlee, Kirkpatrick-Fleming, where there was a 30ft seam of limestone and four 'good draw kilns', either obtained its coal from Canonbie (nine miles away) or by sea from Cumberland, which involved eight miles cartage from Annan.[117]

Limestone existed in isolated pockets in the Stewartry and wherever discovered was eagerly quarried by 'improvers'. Only in the Kirkbean district were deposits large enough to merit more than local exploitation and three small limeworks were established within a few miles of each other. The earliest, Torrorie, was built by William Craik of Arbigland, the famous improver, and is marked on Ainslie's map of 1797. Another 'limekill', about a mile west of Arbigland, was working at the same time, deriving its raw material from a nearby 'marle pit'. The third kiln, located near Southerness, was built on the raised beach c 1830. Trials were made for coal and thin seams found, but the kilns were supplied from Cumberland. All three works were relatively short-lived, although Torrorie was still operating in 1855. The sites are not without interest to the geologist as well as the industrial archaeologist.[118]

Localised limestone deposits in Wigtownshire and particularly in the Rhins and Lochryan districts, led to the building of several small kilns serving one or more farms. The distribution of these unusual single kilns is indicated in the figure on page 142. Little is known of the origin of these kilns, though they probably date from the late eighteenth century, three being marked on Ainslie's map of 1782. Thirteen kilns survived long enough to be noted by the surveyors compiling the first OS map. The kilns were very primitive, roughly built of stones from the field (not unlike the older corn kilns) and fired with peats in the same way as shell-burning was pursued in Symson's time. A more orthodox kiln was built at Portpatrick to supply the harbour works, begun in 1821. Although infilled and partly obscured by a public convenience, it is an interesting construction with an unusual arched entrance.

During the last decades of the eighteenth and the first half of the nineteenth centuries the limeworks of south-west Scotland were a valuable asset to the agrarian economy of the region. But changes in farming methods, with consequent reduction in demand for lime, the rise of railways and technical problems (such as increasingly heavy overburden and flooding) brought about a decline in output. By 1881 only 30 workmen were employed in the limestone quarries of Dumfriesshire and ten years later their number had fallen to four.[119] Part-time labour certainly continued as season and demand warranted, but in 1895 after over a century's activity, the Closeburn works finally closed and Barjarg followed soon after. Workings at Kelhead, Kirtlebridge, Blackwoodridge and Caldronlee were also abandoned. All that remains of this once important industry is perhaps best seen at Closeburn, where the flooded quarry and overgrown but perfectly preserved kilns present a unique reminder of a past rural industry.

The traditional building materials in Galloway were the local whinstones and slates so readily worked throughout the region. The origins of the small brick and tile industry which developed during the nineteenth century lay in the demands of the agrarian sector for drainage tiles. In the few locations where suitable clay deposits could be worked, small tile works were established to fulfil the needs of 'improving' farmers and lairds. The smallest (mostly on estates) produced only drainage tiles, while the larger works in or adjacent to the market towns produced both bricks and tiles. The figure on page 151 indicates the location of the main brick and tile works in south-west Scotland c 1850. Those in Wigtownshire, with the exception of that at Stranraer, were fairly small, single or double kiln units, located on estates and serving local farmers and tenants. Those at Terrally (plate, page 107) and Monreith are good examples of this type, while that at Arbigland in Kirkbean (on the estate of William Craik, the improver) was probably among the first in Galloway. Little survives of the town works, such as those at Gatehouse and Dalbeattie, which succumbed to local

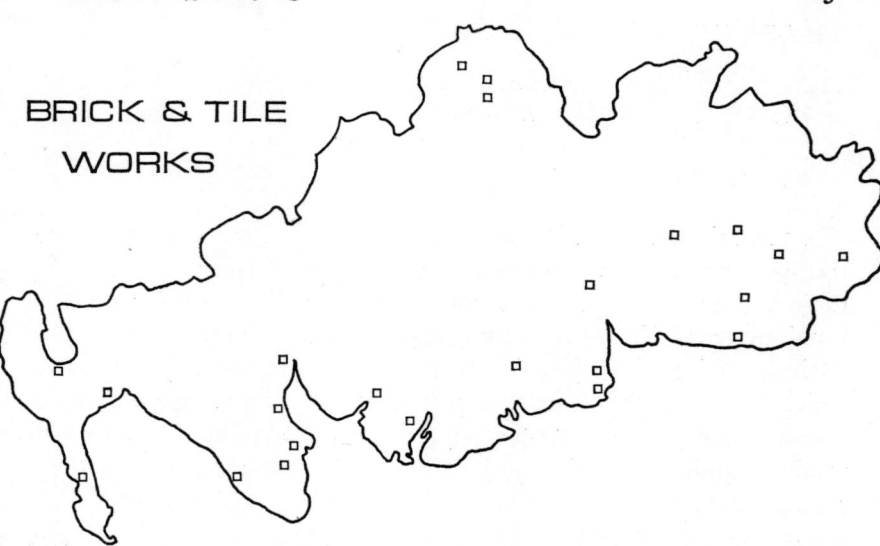

BRICK & TILE
WORKS

Brick and tile works c 1850

building stone and outside competition before the end of the nineteenth century. The handful of rural tile works which have survived
are described and illustrated in Section Two.

(See pages 248–51 for notes)

CHAPTER FIVE

Transport and Trade

'THE multiplicity of its linkages with the rest of the economy gave transport its key role in economic growth,' wrote Deane and Cole in their assessment of British economic growth during the last three hundred years. Undoubtedly the development of transport was vital to the growth of the regional economy of Galloway during the period which is the concern of this study. Transport improvements were essentially responses to better markets elsewhere and the stimulus of roads, shipping and railways on the agrarian economy was in turn considerable. Improved transport linked the regional economy with expanding markets in the industrial regions of Cumberland, Lancashire and the west of Scotland. Other sectors, such as agricultural processing, textiles, mining and quarrying, relied heavily on markets beyond the regional confines of Galloway.

This chapter opens with a history of road development during the eighteenth and nineteenth centuries, from the era of the drove and military highways to the demise of the turnpikes, examining briefly the archaeology which resulted. A short section on canals indicates the impracticability of this form of transport in south-west Scotland, outlining the developments which actually took place and others little more than speculation. Of vital importance, however, were shipping and trading links upon which Galloway so relied during the late eighteenth and early nineteenth centuries. The expansion of Solway coastal shipping and the Galloway ports is examined, with particular emphasis on the ports of the Nith and Urr. Portpatrick had a long and ultimately tragic history as a packet station on the shortest sea-crossing to Ireland, traced here in the light of contemporary parliamentary inquiries. Commodity trade and shipping between 1790 and 1850 is followed by an examination of the small regional shipbuilding industry. Railway development in the area is considered in the context of a detailed case-study of a locally financed enterprise—the Wigtownshire Railway—the last branch line built in Galloway. This is essentially concerned with the years of independent operation 1871–85, after which the line was amalgamated with the Portpatrick Railway as a joint committee of the Glasgow & South-Western Railway.

The industrial archaeology of transport has proved a most rewarding field in Galloway. The modern road system is virtually that created in the turnpike era and the heritage of bridges, toll-houses, wayside inns and milestones is particularly rich. Many Galloway ports are derelict though some survive as yachting and fishing harbours. Several have revived in recent years, notably Isle of Whithorn, Kirkcudbright, Palnackie, and Glencaple. The latter was recently revived when a coaster navigated the Nith to ship a cargo of drainage tiles to the Channel Islands—the first trading vessel to visit the harbour in twenty-one years. Railways are a more recent loss, becoming industrial archaeology as this work was being undertaken.

ROADS

Galloway shared with the Highlands an impenetrability which alarmed the military mind of the Hanoverians. The fact that this wild and inhospitable countryside had to be traversed to reach Ireland was an additional incentive to the strategists to press forward the improvement of communications between England and Ireland.[1] General Roy's map (itself an essentially military aid) surveyed by army engineers 1747–55 indicates the existence in Galloway of a pattern of route-ways following both coast and river valleys. These were clearly unmade roads, following long-accepted routes, like the earlier packways, drove roads and smugglers' trails. Such roads were maintained under the statute labour system by burgh or parish authorities as use or circumstance demanded. The Commissioners of Supply for the Stewartry of Kirkcudbright, for example, were responsible for the maintenance of many roads in that county and pressed forward a vigorous programme of reconstruction and bridge-building after 1728.[2]

While road-building under military direction proceeded apace in the unruly Highlands, the commissioners of supply for all three Galloway counties (consisting mainly of local landed gentry) applied to the government for a new road through south-west Scotland from Carlisle, or Sark Bridge to Portpatrick.[3] A survey of the proposed 'road from the River Sark to Portpatrick via Annan, Dumfries, Bridge of Urr, Gatehouse of Fleet, Ferrytown of Cree, Newton Stewart, Glenluce and Stranraer' was undertaken c 1757, when the cost of a direct route was estimated at £2,130.[4] This document, preserved in the Broughton & Cally Muniments because Murray was a commissioner, states that the 'intention of the proposed road is speedy and certain communication between Great Britain and Ireland, especially with regard to the passage of troops from one Kingdom to another'. No doubt the Galloway nobility and burghs also had sound economic arguments for supporting it. The route by Gatehouse was considered best for the area was 'more populous', nearer the coast and 'freer from floods and storms'. The total distance was in the region of 110 miles and the cost of construction varied from £16 to £25 per mile.[5]

The original proposals for the military road through Galloway as detailed in the survey of 1757 were implemented during 1763–4 by parties of troops under the direction of military engineers. Contrary to modern notions few stretches of new road were constructed, for the route followed existing roads and tracks, though many sections were straightened, widened, supplied with ditches, re-surfaced and in other ways improved.[6] In many places deviations from long-used tracks were made to straighten the line of the road, the stretch between Dumfries and Castle Douglas providing a particularly remarkable illustration of this. Several new sections were built, notably the Corse of Slakes road over the hills between Gatehouse and Ferrytown of Cree, as it was then known. Although contemporary roads were not without bridges, a large number were built along the course of the military road and many of the older ones widened or reconstructed.

The officer in charge of the military road-building programme in Galloway was Major William Rickson, who has left some penetrating descriptions of the difficulties encountered. Rickson was responsible for all aspects of the project, save the actual route, which followed that laid down in the 1757 survey. He was frustrated by lack of labour, supplies and finance, which hampered progress to such an extent that the programme of reconstruction would probably have never been completed without his constant badgering of those in higher authority. 'I will never trust in Treasury promises again', he wrote in 1764, 'and if disappointed a few times more I shall not even put my trust in Princes.'[7]

The route of the military road (as indicated on page 156) can still be followed on the ground, particularly along sections superseded by turnpikes. A few stretches survive as 'B' class and country roads, though the most interesting are those which have degenerated into mere tracks. The Corse of Slakes hill road from Anwoth Kirk to Creetown is perhaps the most fascinating length of military road outwith the Highlands, with a remarkable hair-pin bend on Ardwall Hill and a number of interesting old bridges.

Following the completion of the military road, a number of others were constructed, notably in the Stewartry, where the commissioners of supply pressed ahead with road-building after obtaining an Act of Parliament in 1780 to commute statute labour into money payments.[8] The most important roads built in Kirkcudbrightshire during this period were those from Rhonehouse to Twynholm by Tongland and Lower Bridge of Tarff (1768–72); Creetown to Gatehouse by the coast (1786–90); and Dalbeattie Port to Kirkpatrick-Durham (1772–7). Similar legislation was secured for Wigtownshire by an Act for Repairing Highways and Bridges of 1778, which introduced labour-money conversion and gave power to commissioners to widen and straighten roads, repair bridges and make roads to harbours and sea-ports.[9]

Road construction in Galloway, as elsewhere, was retarded by lack of finance from 'conversion money' and the landed and merchant

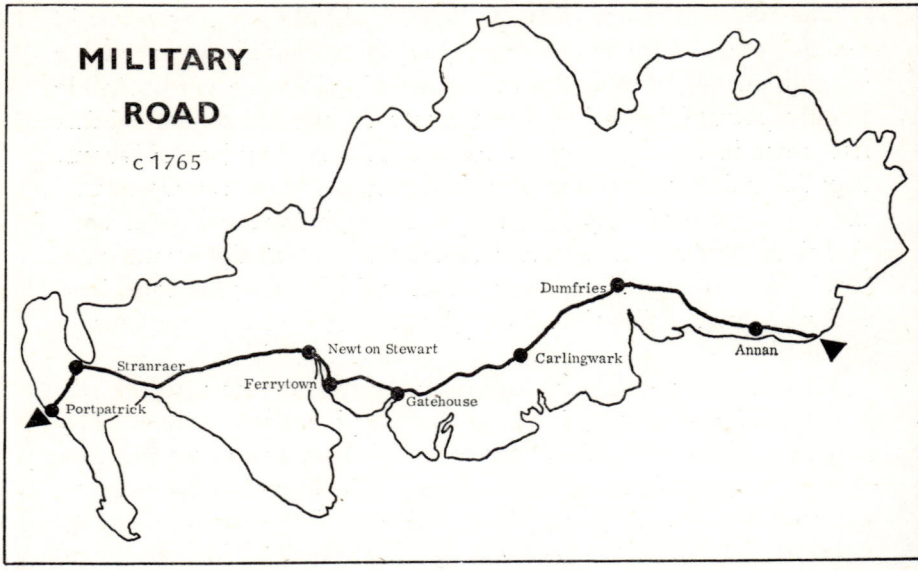

interest agitated for the introduction of turnpike trusts on the main highways. The parliamentary bill for the Stewartry, obtained in 1797, permitted trusts 'to make new lines of road and bridges' and 'supress useless roads'.[10] The responsibility for roads was transferred to road trustees and district trusts (composed mainly of the same landed gentry who constituted the commissioners of supply) and the construction or repair of eight toll roads was authorised. The most important was the Stewartry section of the old military road from Dumfries to Newton Douglas by Crocketford, Balmaclellan, Ken Bridge and New Galloway which involved reconstruction of part of the Old Edinburgh Road (see page 157). A continuation of the latter was to be incorporated in another road from Ken Bridge to Moniaive, linking up with the Dumfriesshire turnpikes. The road from Dumfries to Kirkcudbright by Dalbeattie was to extend to join the Portpatrick road near Gatehouse. Several important north–south roads were proposed: from Kirkcudbright to Dalmellington (as far as the Ayrshire boun-

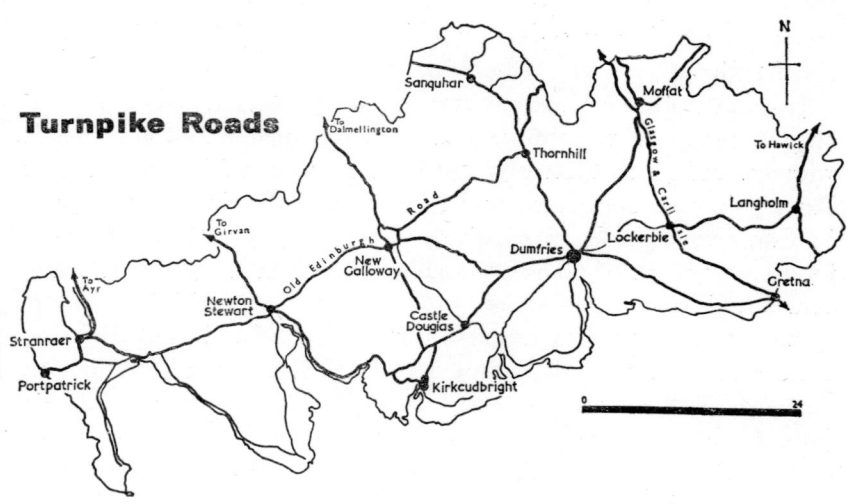

Turnpike Roads

dary); from Dub o' Hass to Moniaive turnpike by Old Bridge of Urr and Corsock; and from Castle Douglas to Palnackie.

Robert Heron described the roads of Galloway in 1792 as 'universally miry and unsolid', an observation reiterated by a statement in a draft bill for Wigtownshire to the effect that the 'roads require to be repaired and sundry bridges are necessary to be built and upheld thereon'.[11] The Act for Repairing Roads in Wigtownshire, passed in 1802, repealed the 1778 Act and appointed trustees to supervise the turnpiking of major highways in the county. Under the Act

> Gates and Turnpikes are to be erected across any part of the Road from the High Bridge of Cree by Newton Douglas, Glenluce and Stranraer to Portpatrick, and from Stranraer to the confines of the County of Ayr near the Cairn of Lochryan; and to erect such Number of Tollhouses as they shall think fit; to take and levy Tolls at each Gates before Passage is permitted.[12]

Hence only two main sections of roadway were turnpiked in Wigtownshire, the Newton Stewart to Portpatrick section of the old military road and the stretch of the Glasgow road within the county. The trustees were given powers to borrow money for initial financing of construction and repairs 'on credit of conversion money'.[13]

Just as the military highway through Galloway had been a concern of government in the 1760s, so the maintenance of communication with Ireland (accentuated by the Union) was a subject of constant inquiry in the early nineteenth century. As early as 1770 John Smeaton, reporting on the harbour at Portpatrick, stressed the need for improvement of Galloway roads, while Thomas Telford was a constant visitor to south-west Scotland after 1800.[14] Telford's report on his survey of communications between England and Ireland of 1809 emphasised many of the problems of roads and road-building in Galloway. Following an 'accurate survey of the different lines of Roads from Carlisle to Portpatrick', Telford favoured the direct route through Castle Douglas, Gatehouse and Newton Stewart, emphasising the great need for bridges over the rivers Dee, Ken and Cree.[15] John Spalding, a local MP, noted in evidence that the road to Newton Stewart from Dumfries by New Galloway was shorter than that by Gatehouse (41 to 52 miles), and though not finished would be completed that season. He thought it would 'be preferred by Mail coach travellers between England and Ireland' and 'though it goes through a Mountainous country it is in general level and seldom obstructed by snow during winter'.[16]

Another parliamentary inquiry on roads between Carlisle and Portpatrick of 1810 favoured the improvements suggested by Rennie and Telford and during two succeeding decades several notable bridges were built in Galloway under the auspices of the commissioners of supply and with the active encouragement of government.[17] The earliest and perhaps best known was Tongland Bridge over the River Dee built between 1804 and 1808 by country masons to a design of Telford. It consists of a high, single arch of 112ft span, with three narrow, pointed arches on either side, and an overall carriageway length of 166ft. Its interesting crenellated parapet and the bold sweep of its main arch over the swirling waters of the river make Tongland one of Telford's most interesting stone bridges.[18] Other bridges followed, most of them built jointly by government and public subscription. Cree Bridge (1812–14) followed the design of John Rennie (plate, page 108), though another of his works, Ken Bridge, was washed away by floods soon after construction and was not re-built until 1821–2. The fine granite bridge at Threave (1824) on the Dumfries–Portpatrick Turnpike replaced the Old Bridge of Dee, which was extremely narrow and difficult of approach.[19]

The toll roads of Wigtownshire came under scrutiny in a parliamentary report of 1823 into the state of roads between Glasgow and Portpatrick. The roads, it was recorded, 'would admit safe and convenient travelling', but part of it between Girvan and Stranraer was 'so bad, unsafe and unpracticable as totally to obstruct intercourse, which a good line of road would afford'.[20] Both Thomas Telford and John L. MacAdam ('whose local knowledge of the country enables him to speak with confidence') were agreed that despite many improvements the road from Girvan to Stranraer was still 'bad and dangerous', while William Mure, a trustee for Renfrewshire roads, said in evidence that 'the last time he travelled on the road [he] got out of the carriage and walked up and down the hills'.[21] The Stranraer–Portpatrick section had 'been all made of new', while another toll-road from Newton Stewart to the High Bridge of Cree had also recently been improved. The budget of Wigtownshire roads 1820–3 was as follows:

Revenue		Expenditure	
Toll rent	£2,008 – 19	Gravelling 18 mls.	
Mail Coach		New road to Ayr	
toll	£1,095	Repairs	£3,534 – 1
	£3,103 – 19		£3,534 – 1

This indicates a modest debt of just over £400, but the Wigtownshire road trustees had an added debt of £2,700, accumulated over the years in unpaid loans and interest.[22] Even before the creation of turnpike roads in Galloway, John Palmer, Surveyor & Comptroller General of the Post Office, had been astute enough to recognise the problems of profitability of coaches operating on the unfrequented routes through wild Galloway.[23]

The problems of turnpike trust administration were as obvious in Galloway as elsewhere. The small size of the Stewartry trusts was criticised in the *Report on Public Roads in Scotland* (1859), where about 250 miles of road were administered by nearly a dozen district trusts and had no fewer than 29 toll-houses along their length.[24] Yet the work of the Galloway turnpike trusts during the first half of the nineteenth century is clearly indicated in the table below, which shows road mileage in the three counties before the final demise of the turnpike system:

	Turnpike Roads	*Statute Labour Roads*
Dumfries	370	800
Kirkcudbright	249½	511
Wigtown	51	380
Total	670½	1,691
Three Counties	2,361½	

Turnpikes were clearly responsible for only about a third of all roads, a direct reflection of the insufficiency of internal trade. In Galloway the trusts created roads through inhospitable and unprofitable countryside, where local traffic was limited and the main link with other regions was by sea. By 1859 the effects of the railway were already obvious in Dumfriesshire (toll revenue fell on the Annan–Dumfries road from £2,000 to £400 in just under ten years) and during that year the Dumfries–Castle Douglas railway penetrated the Stewartry.[25] In evidence to the commissioners, the Earl of Selkirk could say with justification that the turnpike roads in the Stewartry were 'the best in Scotland'.[26] The road-engineering and bridge-building legacy of the trusts is perhaps more evident today in Galloway than in any other part of Scotland.

CANALS

In common with much of Scotland the landscape of Galloway did not encourage the development of canals and although numerous major schemes were suggested during the 'canal mania' and later, none came to fruition. Several of the proposed Galloway canals were quite practicable from the physical viewpoint, particularly those with tracts in Nithsdale and Annandale.[27] Like the Aberdeenshire Canal, which was built, those suggested for the valleys of the Nith and Annan might have serviced not only a rich farming hinterland but also have provided an important outlet for the sandstone quarries of Dumfriesshire. Both schemes reached the survey stage, but got no further as backers were not forthcoming. A third scheme, the Glenkens Canal, although least promising of all, actually got off the drawing board. Only two short sections were built, permitting navigation between Carlingwark Loch, the River Dee and Loch Ken. The fourth venture was less of a canal than a river improvement, for it merely served to straighten and deepen the River Fleet to provide navigation to the port of Gatehouse from the Solway Firth.

The Annandale Canal was proposed as early as 1794, the route being surveyed by a civil engineer named Jardine in 1810.[28] Its route from the Solway Firth at Annan 'where the tide rises to a considerable height at the Old Mill harbour', past Kelhead limeworks, and so 'along the hollow on the east side of the town of Lochmaben' near the Castle Loch.[29] Its depth was to be 7ft and its width 28ft at the surface, capable of taking vessels of 60–70 tons drawing a fathom of water. The cost of the scheme was estimated at £14,000, including two locks costing £2,000. Despite considerable local interest and a poem in praise of the proposed navigation in the columns of the *Dumfries Courier & Herald* the Annandale Canal never became a reality.[30]

The plan for a Nithsdale canal originated in the desire of the magistrates and merchants of Dumfries to improve navigation on the River Nith. Smeaton examined the channel and recorded that the only

K

way to improve access to the town was 'by cutting a canal with proper locks'.[31] About the same time he carried out a survey of Lochar Moss and suggested that the construction of a canal would greatly improve drainage there.[32] Consideration was also given to the possibility of making a canal from the Nith estuary near Caerlaverock Castle, by Lochar Moss, Torthorwald and Tinwald to join the Nith at Dalswinton, but this too was abandoned because of lack of funds.[33] Later, in 1810, when improvements in river navigation were being undertaken, the engineer, James Hollinsworth, suggested cutting a canal from Kelton to Dockfoot, the highest quay at the port of Dumfries. This plan, like the others, was never implemented. The cost was prohibitive and summer drought could only be overcome by 'taking water from the mills of Dumfries, which would render them useless'.[34]

The River Dee and Loch Ken form a natural waterway stretching nearly twenty miles inland from the Solway to the Glenkens and navigation of the tidal reaches of the river was of early origin. The Falls of Tongland and a series of rapids upstream prevented further navigation for a distance of eight miles and could only be resumed on the calmer waters of Loch Ken. As early as 1765, Sir Alexander Gordon of Culvennan cut a canal between Carlingwark Loch and the River Dee (see page 163). This not only reduced the level of the loch so that valuable marle could be worked, but also provided transport of this 'means of improvement' to upland parishes surrounding Loch Ken.[35] Sometime after 1780, when a clause for the regulation of navigation on Loch Ken was introduced into the Stewartry road Act, Gordon of Culvennan cut another short section of canal to improve navigation below Glenlochar Bridge (see page 164) and hence make possible passage from Castle Douglas to the Boatpool of Dalry near the head of Loch Ken.[36] Flat-bottomed barges carried marle from Carlingwark to the farmers of the Glenkens, returning south with timber and oak-bark.[37]

The initial success of these two simple schemes 'gave an additional stimulus to the wish so long entertained of extending navigable communication to the sea' and several surveys were afterwards carried out

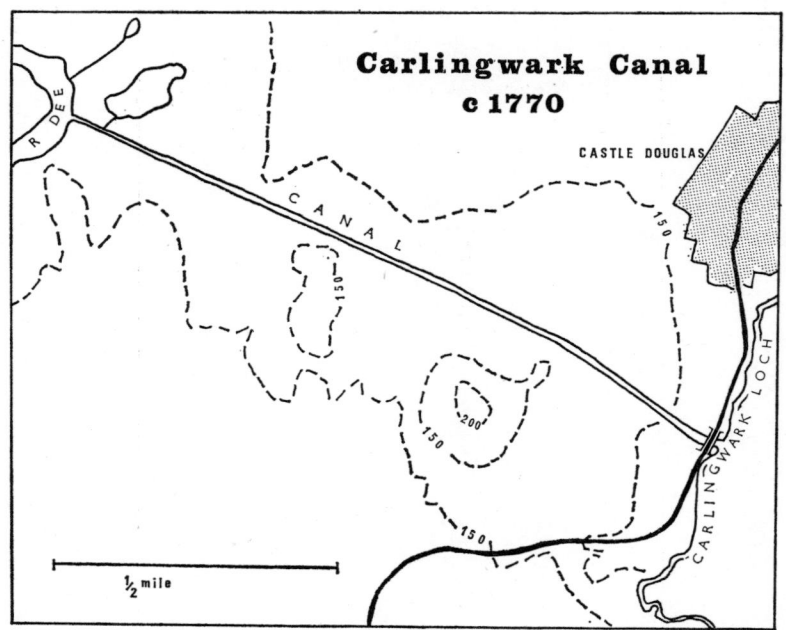

Carlingwark Canal
c 1770

CASTLE DOUGLAS

CARLINGWARK LOCH

½ mile

by different engineers.[38] So early as 1788, Sir William Douglas employed a civil engineer named Inglis who 'made a survey and estimate of completing the canal from Carlingwark to the sea at the mouth of the Urr in Orchardton Bay'.[39] A few years later 'skilful engineers' estimated that a canal to bypass the Tongland rapids could be built for £9,000, but this was never followed up.[40] The ground was again covered in 1796 when John Rennie, at the direction of Lord Selkirk and the magistrates of Kirkcudbright, prepared plans for a survey and 'gave directions how the survey was to be made'.[41] The work was carried out by a country land-surveyor, Gillone by name, 'a man of respectability in his line, who had never seen a rood of canal made in his lifetime' and in August 1796 Rennie himself inspected the route of the proposed canal.[42]

The Glenkens Canal was to begin at the 'tideway of the River Dee'

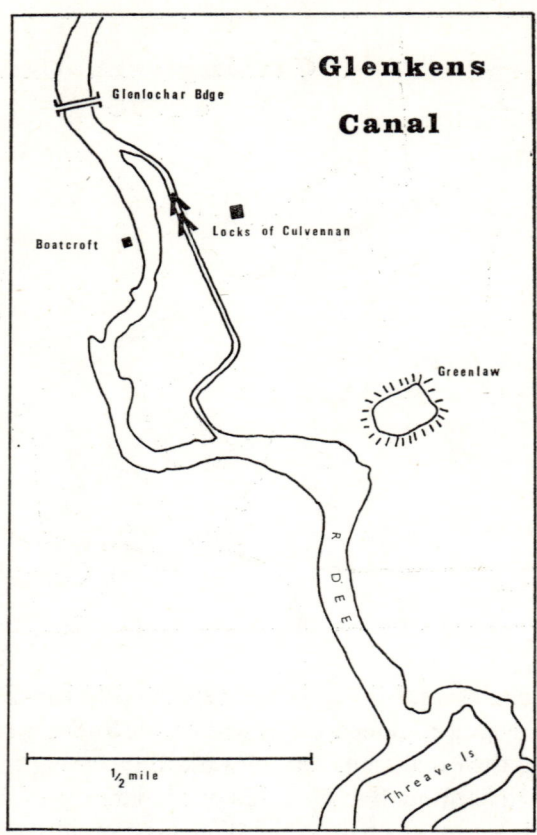

north of Kirkcudbright and running parallel with the east bank of the river for 10¼ miles, was to rise through ten locks to enter Loch Ken at Glenlochar Bridge. Beyond the head of the loch, a short three-mile stretch would bring the canal to Dalry 'where the navigation terminates'. The total length was almost 26 miles and the estimated cost £33,382.[43] Despite the hazardous nature of the enterprise it was considered that an extension of the canal northwards to Dalmellington 'would open a sort of traffic in coals and lime'.[44] It was estimated that the canal would carry at least 17,000 tons of freight per annum, including 10,000 tons of imported lime, 1,000 tons of Cumberland coal and 6,000 tons of grain for export through the port of Kirkcudbright. The revenue from tolls was expected to be at least £4,000 per annum.[45]

The Company of the Proprietors of the Glenkens Canal Navigation met for the first time in 1801. It consisted of an impressive assembly of local landowners and merchants including Sir William Douglas, Sir Alexander Gordon, the Rev David Lamont, Patrick Heron of Heron, Adam Maitland of Dundrennan, as well as the Galloway MPs and representatives of the various burghs. These and other gentry promised £15,000 in subscriptions and on 3 June 1802 the Glenkens Canal Bill was introduced in the House of Commons by John Spalding of Holm, the local member, and received the Royal Assent on 26 June 1802.[46] The Glenkens Canal Company, however, soon lost its support and the canal was never built, for 'the return [was] too remote and the risk too great for any prudent man to embark too deeply'. No one 'hardy enough to engage in it as an adventure' could be found and even as late as 1811 the lawyers who had drafted the parliamentary bill were forced to sue the trustees of Sir William Douglas and other gentry connected with the scheme to recover £775 costs.[47] Much later, Joseph Priestly described the non-existent canal in glowing terms, but the description given it by the frustrated lawyers was perhaps more appropriate. They referred to it as 'the ill digested fancy of a moment, wild in its conception, impractable in its execution, not desired by the country or thought of or talked of but in jest'.[48] Although the scheme was never implemented the two short sections built by Sir Alexander Gordon still survive and though little more than drainage ditches now, they are the more remarkable when it is remembered that both were abandoned as unnavigable before 1840.[49]

The canalisation of the River Fleet in 1824 improved navigation between the thriving industrial village of Gatehouse and Wigtown Bay, making it possible for vessels of up to 160 tons to sail up to Boatgreen just below Fleet Bridge. The canal (see page 166) was dug

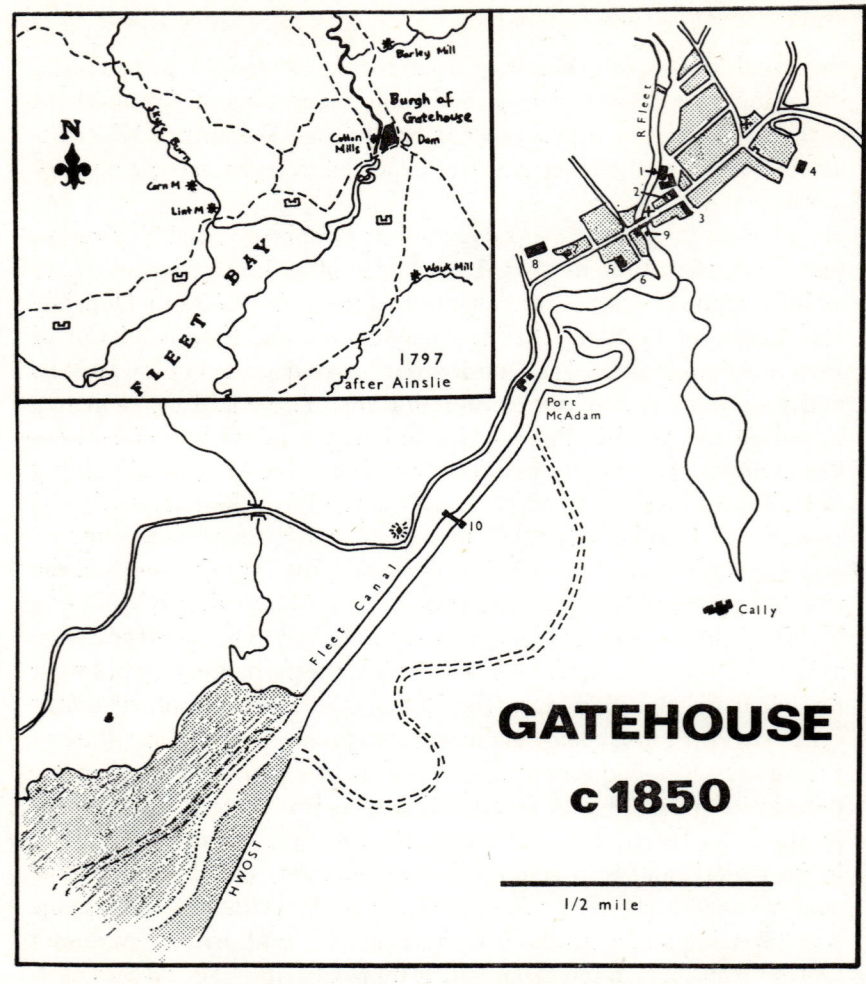

Gatehouse c 1850, showing the Fleet canal

Key to industrial sites:

1 Cotton mills		6 Boat yard
2 Brewery		7 Gasworks
3 Tannery		8 Brick kiln and field
4 Sawmill (former cotton mill)		9 Soap works
5 Tannery		10 Canal swing bridge

Inset map shows the environs c 1797

by 200 Irish peasants from Alexander Murray's Donegal estates, most of whom were in arrears of rent. The cut was 1,400yd long and straightened the river for over a mile, isolating several wide meanders on the Cally bank. Alexander Craig, Murray's factor, supervised the work of the navvies and, exhibiting considerable engineering acumen, directed them to dig a trench along the line of the canal and channel the river water along it to wash away the soil until a canal of the required width and depth had been scoured out by river and tide. In so doing, he reduced the cost of the canal from an engineer's estimate of £5,000 to an actual cost of £2,204 3s 5d.[50] Boatgreen, the harbour of Gatehouse, was greatly improved and later a new quay, known as Port McAdam, was built a quarter-mile downstream.[51] The canal itself still survives, and although badly silted up with sand and mud is still navigable. A few hundred yards from Cardoness Castle are the remains of a swing bridge supported on piers, which linked the re-claimed land on the Cally side with the turnpike road between Gate-house and Creetown (plate, page 126).

PORTS, HARBOURS AND SHIPPING

For centuries the uncertain navigation of the Solway provided Galloway's principal link with neighbouring areas of the British Isles. Its regional economy during the two centuries 1700–1900, with which we are concerned, was dependent on traditional links with north-west England, Lancashire, Merseyside, North Wales, the west of Scotland and Ireland, as well as regions beyond. During the period down to 1860, when the railway finally penetrated Galloway's landward fast-ness, ships and shipping through Solway ports provided the economic lifeline of farmers and businessmen. Maritime activity did not cease after the opening of the railway, though by 1900 the steamboats and sloops had all but disappeared from the Solway and the ports of Galloway slipped back into their medieval stagnation.

The isolation and backwardness of Galloway in the seventeenth and early eighteenth centuries is nowhere better illustrated than in contemporary descriptions of harbours and shipping. Thomas Tucker in his *Report Upon the Settlement of the Revenues of Excise & Customs in Scotland* (compiled in 1655) provides a striking pen-sketch of stagnation along the whole length of the Solway. Stranraer he describes as 'a pretty harbour for shelter of vessells', though he adds that 'there is not now nor ever was any trade to bee heard of'.[52] Portpatrick, 'a place much frequented by those who have any trade or affaires towards Ireland', was little more than a natural harbour which could shelter 'noe vessell of any burden'. Whithorn and Wigtown already had a limited trade with the Cumberland shore in 'salt or coales', but Kirkcudbright, despite its natural advantages as a port, was as moribund as Defoe found it over seventy years later. The drawbacks presented by the Nith to the port of Dumfries were already self-evident, for Tucker rightly remarks that 'the badnesse of comeing into the river [hinders] theyr commerce by sea'.[53]

Andrew Symson's *Large Description* (1684) is less concerned with the volume of trade of Galloway ports and more with detailing their worth as harbours. 'At the mouth of the Dee', he says, 'whole fleets mat safely ly at anchor,' while the Isle of Whithorn was 'an advantageous port to ships of a great burthen against all storms'.[54] He makes a most interesting reference to Port Nessock, where Robert McDowall of Logan 'hath been at great paines and expences to build a port for ships and barks cast in that way'.[55] Daniel Defoe, however, has a good deal to say about Scottish trade. Much of what he says about one port, Kirkcudbright, was applicable to all Galloway and indeed Scotland as a whole in the second decade of the eighteenth century. Of Kirkcudbright he wrote:

> Here is a pleasant situation, and yet nothing pleasant to be seen. Here is a harbour without ships, a port without trade, a people without business: and that which is worse than all, they do not seem to desire business, much less do they understand it. They have a fine river, navigable for the greatest ships to the town quay. But alas, there is not a vessel that deserves the name of a ship belongs to it. In a word . . . they have a gold mine on their doorstep, and will not use it.[56]

Defoe left Kirkcudbright 'with a sort of concern'.

The development of ports and harbours in the latter half of the eighteenth century was a direct consequence of agrarian improvement and the rise of a market-oriented, regional farming economy. The long-established maritime links with Cumberland, Lancashire, the west of Scotland and Ireland were vitalised by growing, bilateral regional trade. Natural harbours were improved by the erection of piers, quays or breastwork, in order to accommodate the sloops and larger sailing vessels engaged in the import-export trade. A typical harbour was that at Isle of Whithorn, where a new quay was built by the burgh authorities sometime before 1790. Nine ships were based on the harbour in 1795. The main imports were coal and lime, and the key exports fat cattle, sheep, pigs, grain and potatoes—the products of its agrarian hinterland, the Machars.[57] A similar picture could be found anywhere along the Solway coastline. Ships docked at harbours or beached at low tide provided the economic lifeline of Galloway during the late eighteenth and early nineteenth centuries. One commentator, describing shipping on the River Cree in the 1790s, remarked that it had been 'the source of all agricultural improvements which have been made in this part of the country'.[58]

Just as government strategy dictated the improvement of the Dumfries–Portpatrick road in the mid-eighteenth century, so it also influenced the construction of harbours at either end of the short sea route to Ireland. The improvement of communication with Ireland was a standing issue for over a hundred years (1760–1860), and the ports of the Rhins of Galloway, Portpatrick, Port Nessock (or Logan) and Stranraer in particular, were central to every inquiry.[59] The governments of the day were interested in the free and safe passage of troops, mail and passengers, but the support of county authorities and the landed gentry of Galloway had sound economic motivation, derived essentially from the growing cattle trade with Ireland and the outlets which improved harbours would provide for farm produce.

Wigtown, at the mouth of the River Bladnoch, was fairly typical of the small burgh port in Galloway. It has clear parallels in Kirkcudbright, Dumfries, Annan and Stranraer and much in common with the

smaller ports of the Cree, the Urr and the Nith. The town's earliest
harbour stood north of the castle, immediately below the kirk. Tucker
reported in 1655 that 'there comes sometimes a small boate from
England with salt or coales', while Symson said Wigtown had 'little
trading by sea'.[60]

During the latter half of the eighteenth century navigation was
improved and Wigtown's commercial links with other regions were
established on a firmer basis. The harbour was used in the 1790s for
the export (in sloops) of meal and other farm produce to ports like Ayr,
Irvine and Greenock on the Clyde, Whitehaven in Cumberland and
Preston in Lancashire. Imports included lime and coal from across the
Solway, manufactured goods from Liverpool and shells and lime from
the other side of Wigtown Bay.[61] The Customs Port of Wigtown
included every creek and harbour from the Mull of Galloway to the
mouth of the River Dee.

The course of the Bladnoch was diverted into a more southerly
channel in 1817 by the erection of breakwaters. A new harbour,
consisting of a pier, dock and associated breastwork was constructed
about a half-mile south-east of the town by the burgh authorities. It
was 'well adapted to the coasters that ship the agricultural produce of
the neighbourhood' and by the 1830s had a flourishing export trade
in grain and potatoes to Lancashire and the west of Scotland.[62] Steamboats made their appearance in 1825 and a regular service was established to Whitehaven and Liverpool soon after. Unlike other Galloway
ports, Wigtown did not decline rapidly after the tardy arrival of the
railway. The table below indicates the level of trade in 1869 and 1876,
before and after the opening of the Wigtownshire line. 'The railway
has not yet superceded the harbour', wrote a local commentator in
1877, 'for a mast or two denote the presence of a sloop or schooner.'[63]
The steamboat *Countess of Galloway* still provided a twice monthly
service to Liverpool and a smaller steamer maintained the link with
Glasgow. The railway slowly established itself as the medium of transport for goods as well as passengers and the harbour on the Bladnoch
was soon deserted, like so many others on the Solway (see page 172).

Trade of the Port of Wigtown 1869 and 1876

1869	Sailing Vessels	Tons	Steam Vessels	Tons
Imports				
Gt Britain	510	16,108	47	13,321
Ireland	11	815		
Foreign	3	763		
Exports				
Gt Britain	293	10,467	47	13,348
Ireland	2	76		
Foreign	2	533		
1876				
Imports				
Gt Britain	563	14,088	103	13,172
Ireland	10	654		
Ireland (ballast)	4	314		
Foreign	4	831		
Exports				
Gt Britain	332	16,391	93	13,290
,, (ballast)	601	9,992	24	2,098
Ireland	2	30		

Source: Gordon Fraser, *Wigtown and Whithorn: Historical and Descriptive Sketches* (Wigtown 1877), 195–6

    The economic progress of the town of Dumfries is mirrored in the history of its function as a port and in the efforts of its merchant-burgesses to improve navigation on the most fickle of all rivers, the Nith (see page 173). The increasing trading activities so carefully documented in customs and civic records of the late seventeenth and early eighteenth centuries afford evidence of the growing importance of the port of Dumfries.[64] Expansion was not confined merely to coastal shipping for by the early decades of the eighteenth century Dumfries had already established trade links with the North American colonies.[65]

About the beginning of the eighteenth century, buoys were placed

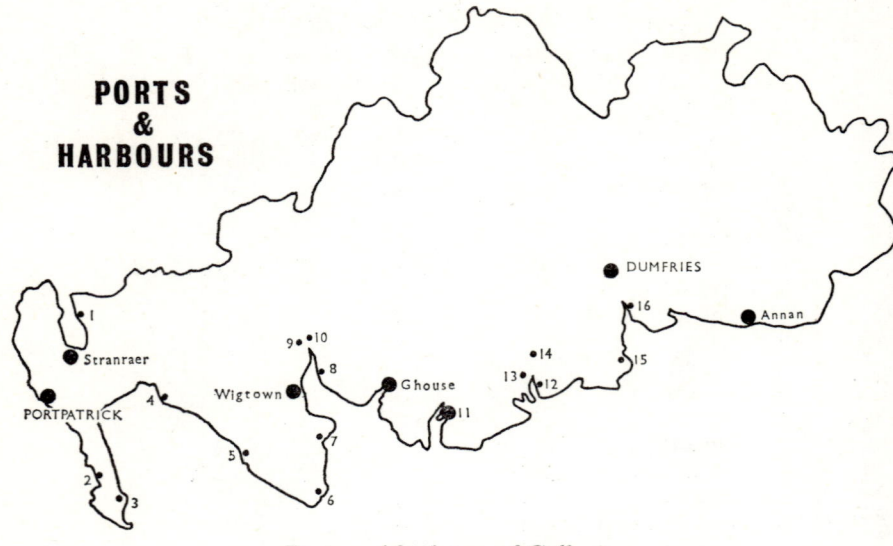

Ports and harbours of Galloway

Key:
1 Loch Ryan	5 Port William	9 Carty	13 Palnackie
2 Port Logan	6 Isle of Whithorn	10 Palnure	14 Dalbeattie
3 Drumore	7 Garlieston	11 Kirkcudbright	15 Carsethorn
4 Stair Haven	8 Creetown	12 Kippford	16 Glencaple

in the lower reaches of the Nith and attempts were made to remove obstructions from its channel. Yet it still had no harbour of any standing. In 1746, the Town Council of Dumfries in consultation with 'the chief merchants and shipmasters', decided that the best site for a harbour was at Glencaple burnfoot in the adjoining parish of Caerlaverock. An area of ground measuring six acres was made available by the local laird, William Maxwell, and a plan for the quay including 'warehouses and other conveniences' by a Mr Mercer was immediately implemented. Building material was obtained from a nearby quarry and the quay completed by the following year. Construction costs were carried by local merchants, shipowners and the civic authorities. Glencaple's first cargo is said to have been Maryland tobacco landed there

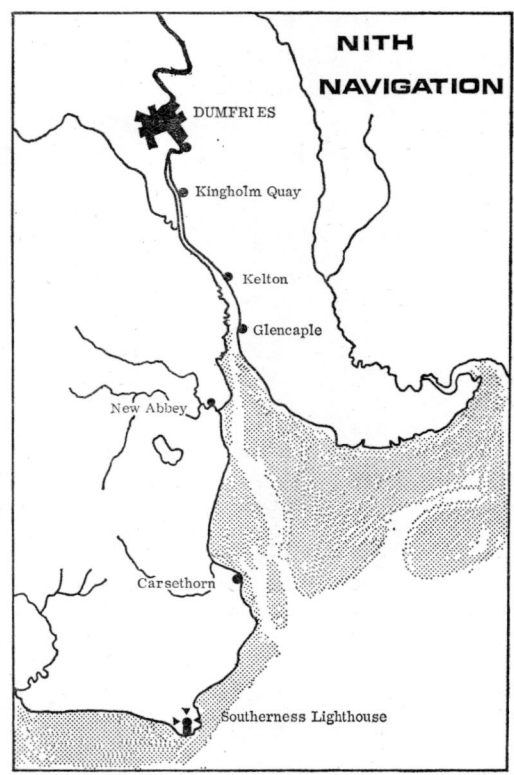

NITH NAVIGATION

DUMFRIES

Kingholm Quay

Kelton

Glencaple

New Abbey

Carsethorn

Southerness Lighthouse

by the ship *Success*, which belonged to a former provost of Dumfries.[66]

Another smaller quay at Kingholm, a mile below the town, was begun the same year as Glencaple, but could only be used by small vessels. Southerness lighthouse was erected in 1749 by the merchants of Dumfries to guide shipping entering the Nith from the Solway.[67] Despite these modest improvements navigation remained uncertain. Yet the trade and shipping of the port of Dumfries continued to grow during the latter half of the eighteenth century. Its coastal trade was considerable and it maintained links with the Baltic and North America. In 1793 ten coasting and three foreign-going vessels belonged to the town, although much of the port's trade was handled by ships from other ports. The imports coastwise at this period were lime, coal and merchant goods, and the key exports, grain, potatoes, sheep, cattle and pigs.[68] The growing import-export trade of Dumfries during the years 1790–1809 is indicated in the table below.[69]

Export/Import Trade of Dumfries 1790–1809

Year	Imports		Exports	
	Vessels	Tonnage	Vessels	Tonnage
1790	253	8,928	135	5,264
1791	265	8,783	183	7,099
1792	265	8,182	194	6,527
1793	293	8,563	174	6,064
1794	312	10,311	223	8,872
1795	353	10,305	294	10,984
1796	351	10,505	264	10,093
1797	380	11,320	206	7,622
1798	378	10,501	206	7,914
1799	382	10,402	259	9,521
1800	380	10,848	225	8,333
1801	393	12,574	242	9,510
1802	450	15,199	276	11,047
1803	409	14,792	228	9,387
1804	367	12,030	369	14,544
1805	391	14,306	344	14,298
1806	397	15,216	264	10,673
1807	516	20,232	251	10,521
1808	545	21,106	229	9,709
1809	493	18,985	287	12,090

Source: Singer, 430

Prior to 1810 navigation on the Nith had become 'very dangerous' even for small vessels and virtually impassable for vessels over 60 tons above Kelton, except at high tides.[70] Despite initial rivalries between the landed interest on the one hand (represented by local gentry serving as commissioners of supply for the Stewartry and for Dumfriesshire) and the town council, merchants and shipowners on the other, there was general agreement on the need for river improvement.[71] A survey of the Nith was undertaken by James Hollinsworth, a civil engineer, who drew up a plan for improvements in the course 'between the Jetty at Kirkconnel Banks by Glencaple Quay up to the Caul of Dumfries'.[72]

The 'Act for Improving the Harbour of Dumfries and the Navigation of the River Nith', passed in 1811, appointed commissioners to superintend improvements, with powers to borrow £16,000 'for the purpose of executing the work'.[73] The sponsors included a wide range of local interests—civic and mercantile. Among the landowners were Sir Alexander Gordon of Culvennan, John Maxwell of Munches, Douglas Craik of Arbigland, C. G. S. Monteath of Closeburn and the famous Patrick Millar of Dalswinton.[74] The act aimed to improve navigation on the river so that a depth of at least six feet would be available up to Dumfries 'for ships, vessels, Barges and Lighters to come and go'.

According to Hollinsworth's plan (see page 176) the course of the river was to be straightened and the channel deepened to improve access to jetties, quays and docks, particularly those at Glencaple, Kingholm or New Quay and Dockfoot—the latter being located just below the town.[75] Shifting sand and tides had forced the channel away from Glencaple, so that vessels had to land at Kelton 'on the bare beach', while at Kingholm 'few tides fill the dock' and silting was a continual problem.[76] Hollinsworth proposed an alternative scheme which involved the construction of a canal from Kelton to Dockfoot, at a cost of around £20,000. This was dismissed, not on the grounds of the capital cost alone, but because it would 'take water from the mills of Dumfries, which would render them useless'.[77]

The first course was followed and Walter Newall appointed as engineer to the Nith Navigation Commissioners to supervise improvements in August 1811. The month following, James Knox, a local contractor, submitted his estimate for 'cutting a New Channel for the River Nith thro' Nethertown Merse' to be 45yd wide and having slopes and sides 'well finished and embanked'.[78] On the Kingholm side another extensive cutting was made, thus straightening the river

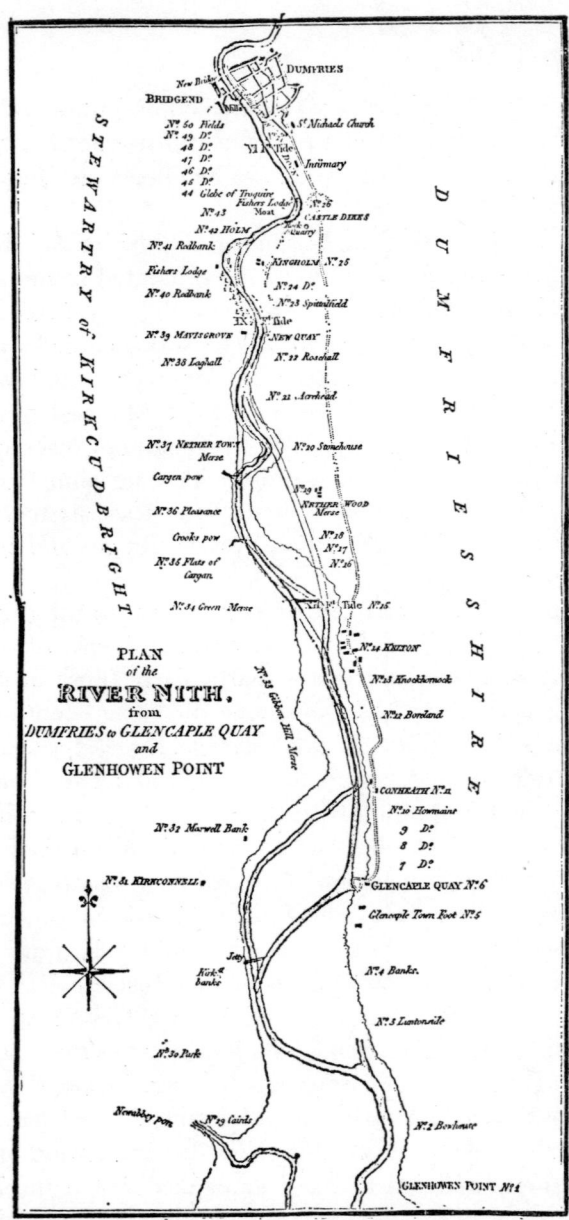

Plan of the River Nith from Dumfries to Glencaple Quay and Glenhowen
Point, 1811 (scale approximately ½in to 1 mile)

for over a mile. Embankments to fix the new channel and reduce the risk of flooding (always a problem on the Nith) were afterwards constructed. Finally the river was deepened by dredging and blasting at Castledykes and Glencaple. The whole operation cost over £7,000.[79]

Despite the efforts of the Nith Navigation Commissioners and their engineers, the river 'rambled from place to place to the great annoyance of shipping'.[80] More improvements were undertaken (1836–40), including deepening and the reconstruction of the main wharves and quays. By this date there was a total of 1,014yd of wharfage at five main harbours on the Nith—Glencaple, Laghall, Kingholm, Castledykes and Dumfries—though 230yd at Dockfoot, built in 1824, was virtually unusable.[81]

The coastal trade of the Nith ports reached its height in the mid-1840s. In 1846, 759 vessels (including steamers) with a total registered weight of 24,390 tons entered the port. The registered tonnage of the port itself totalled 8,669. The main imports were coal, slate, iron, timber and manufactured goods, while the key exports consisted of wool, freestone, grain and other farm produce.[82] Eighteen foreign vessels called regularly each year, mostly with cargoes of timber. Steamboats maintained long-established links with Whitehaven and Liverpool and were mostly involved in transporting passengers and livestock.[83]

Revenue in the 'annus mirabilis' of 1844 totalled £1,212, but by 1872 the commissioners' income had fallen to £589. Heavily indebted as a result of interest payments on the capital cost of £6,000 for a sea-dyke below Glencaple and by expenditure for maintenance of its harbours, the Nith Navigation Commissioners could do little more than witness the slow decline of seaborne trade in face of railway competition. The Glasgow & South-Western Railway reached Dumfries in 1850 and the opening of a wet-dock at Silloth in 1864 was another element contributing to the decline of the Nith ports.[84] Owing to mounting debt the lighthouse at Southerness was extinguished in 1867. Yet another misfortune befell the commission in 1875 following the grounding of the steam tug *Arabian*, for her owners successfully sued for damages

L

in the Court of Session. The Nith Navigation was virtually bankrupt and for some years ceased to function.[85] Despite a slight revival of activity in the late nineteenth century, which continued until 1914, the Nith ports never regained the position which they had battled to maintain in the early years of the century.

Navigation on the Urr and its estuary presents many interesting parallels with developments on the Nith. It had a similar tidal problem, although fairly large boats could navigate its twisting course as far as Dalbeattie (plate, page 143). Along its banks were small harbours, often little more than creeks even in the late eighteenth century, which served as outlets for the agricultural produce of surrounding parishes. When the local granite industry developed after 1820, it too relied heavily on shipping for transport. The figure on page 179 indicates the location of the main ports on the Urr, and also shows the position of the main granite quarries.

Originally known as Dub o' Hass, the port of Dalbeattie was improved in the late eighteenth century by the construction of a stone quay on the Urr about a half-mile south of the town.[86] It could be reached by vessels of 60 tons. Barlochan or Palnackie, three miles down-river, was the main harbour for larger vessels up to 350 tons. Here too the port facilities were improved and Palnackie became the centre of the Urr's seafaring community. Between Dalbeattie and Palnackie were two quays—at Oldland and Steadstone—which could take vessels of 250 tons, mostly involved in shipping granite from nearby quarries.[87] Near the mouth of the estuary was Kippford or The Scaur, a small fishing and shipbuilding village, the main port for the parish of Colvend.

The sea-going trade of the Urr was carried in small vessels, mostly barks and luggers sailing to the ports of Cumberland and Lancashire. Many Dalbeattie merchants, like their counterparts in Kirkcudbright and Dumfries, were also shipowners. Shipbuilding was important at Dalbeattie Port after the 1820s and many vessels built there sailed the waters of the Solway for many years.[88] The small vessels continued in use even after the steamers appeared on the Urr, and indeed survived

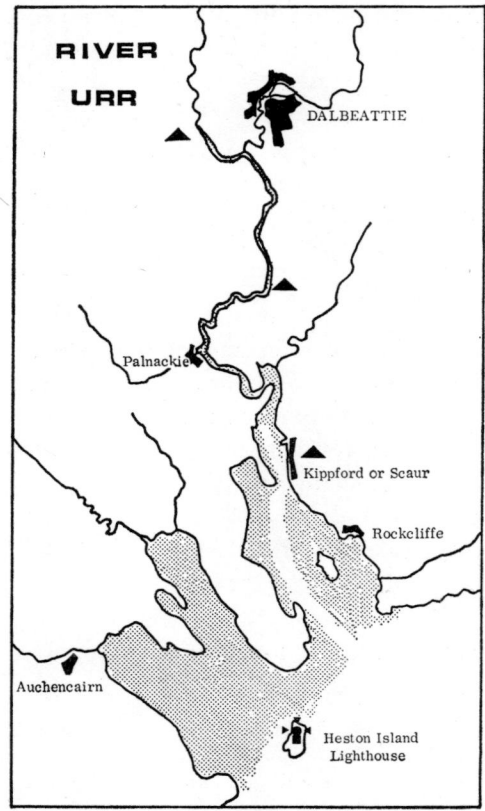

Ports of the River Urr

long after the demise of the steamship services. The Urr was served by two famous Galloway steamers, the *Countess of Selkirk* (built 1835) and the *Saint Andrew*, the latter providing a fortnightly service to Whitehaven and Liverpool for passengers and goods.[89]

Unlike the majority of ports, which declined very rapidly after the opening of the railway, those on the Urr maintained something of their former trade. The railway took its toll, but even so late as 1909 a local commentator could report that 'enough has been left to the steamers and sailing vessels that visit the Urr to maintain the sea trade of the town at something like its former consequence'.[90] Indeed, the Urr Navigation Trust (which took over responsibility for the management of the river from the Stewartry road trustees) was only instituted in 1901.

The long history of Galloway's connection with Ireland reaches back to medieval times. By the seventeenth century, as Tucker and Symson indicate, Portpatrick was the usual port for Irish-bound traffic. It had enormous disadvantages as a shipping port, especially for packets, boats which relied heavily on winds as well as tides. Yet it was one of the few natural harbours on the dangerous coastline of the Rhins of Galloway. Throughout its history as a packet station Portpatrick, like its Irish counterpart Donaghadee, was the subject of endless discussion as to whether it was the best terminal for the short sea route between Scotland and Ireland, at this point a mere 18 or 19 mile sail.[91] Its two rivals were Port Logan (plate, page 125), some ten miles farther south and Stranraer at the head of the relatively sheltered Loch Ryan.

As early as 1715 John Adair, a cartographer, reported favourably on Port Logan (or Nessock) in the following terms:

> I, John Adair, Geographer for the Kingdom of Scotland, having made a survey of the South and West coast of Galloway, and more particularly that part opposite to Donaghadee and the coast of Ireland, Do hereby declare that I did not see a fit and convenient place for making a Harbour to shelter ships, packet boats and other vessels, except the corner of the Bay of Nessock, which by building a good pier or head, they can lie safe and secure in all weather; the Bay also is fit and easy for turning in and out and for dropping an anchor upon occasion.[92]

Under favourable conditions, however, Portpatrick could also be described as an ideal harbour, but in fact neither could have made perfect havens for shipping. At Portpatrick a cortège of eminent civil engineers, including John Smeaton and the Rennies, father and son, battled against the waves of the Irish Sea for nearly a century, before their costly efforts were abandoned to the storms. Port Logan, for

which such a great future had been envisaged, earned the admiration
of Thomas Telford as a prospective packet station, was mentioned
in numerous parliamentary inquiries, but remained nonetheless a
crumbling little pier in a forgotten corner of Galloway.

The first step in the improvement of the packet route was taken
c 1766 following the completion of the Dumfries–Portpatrick military
road, when Lord Hillsborough, the Post-Master General, undertook
an investigation of the Irish routes. John Smeaton was appointed to
carry out a survey and visited Portpatrick in 1768. He found the
harbour 'almost in a state of nature', except for a small landing-place
for passengers. The major problem as Smeaton saw it, was to protect
the inner harbour from the heavy swell.[93] He proposed the construction of two piers across the mouth of the rocky inlet and the complete
rebuilding of the original harbour. Even with this modest plan,
Smeaton conceded, the harbour could only be used by packet boats
and 'small passage vessels'.[94] The work was completed according to
Smeaton's plan in 1778, having cost more than twice his original
estimate of £6,000. The ill-fated history of Portpatrick had begun.

Smeaton's North Pier, the outer half of which was not built on a
firm foundation, consisted of massive drystone blocks. The sea soon
washed through the joints, thus removing the sand on which the pier
rested, so that the stonework 'settled down on an unfirm bottom'. To
prevent the pier being completely undermined a bulwark was built
behind it in 1786 at a cost of £1,200. This also failed to withstand the
waves and had to be rebuilt in 1792, only to be destroyed again in 1801.
Thereafter 'a large quantity of stones' were used to strengthen the back
of the pier, but most of these were swept into the mouth of the harbour.[95] According to Joseph Whidbey, Master Attendant of His
Majesty's Dock Yard, Woolwich, the harbour at Portpatrick was
'small and inconvenient' and in 'a very decayed situation'.[96]

Pressure from the Irish side on the one hand and combined English
and Scottish interests on the other mounted continuously. At length
the government appointed Thomas Telford to carry out an investigation. Telford visited Portpatrick in 1802 and found it 'situated on a

bold, rocky shore surrounded by high land'. 'In viewing it from the
sea', he reported, 'it is destitute of any marked feature to distinguish
the precise situation of the harbour.' Winds from every direction
except the east caused a heavy swell and 'large reefs of rock' made
navigation into the harbour dangerous. Portpatrick, in Telford's own
words, 'was destitute of the advantages requisite for a perfect Harbour
for packets to ply from'.[97] A few years later a government inquiry was
held to investigate the whole problem but it produced no more definite
result than a recommendation that further surveys be made.

In consequence, John Rennie, one of the supporters of Portpatrick's
claims, was commissioned in 1814 to make detailed surveys of the
coast on each side of the channel. On Rennie's recommendation the
question was submitted to the arbitration of Trinity House, which
finally decided in favour of Portpatrick and Donaghadee in 1818.
Rennie produced a plan, modelled on Smeaton's, for two massive
piers and a lighthouse, estimated to cost about £120,000.[98] In 1820 the
government decided to go ahead with the project and under Acts of
that year construction began at Portpatrick with Rennie as engineer.
Shortly afterwards he died and was succeeded by his son, who supervised the building of the massive North and South piers.

John McDiarmid, a Dumfries journalist, wrote a vivid account of
building operations and the changes it brought to Portpatrick. He saw
700–800 labourers digging, quarrying, trundling barrows and building
by day and night in the light of 'blazing coals heaped up in cradle-
grates'. He saw too the thousands of tons of Dunbartonshire freestone,
Anglesey limestone, local whinstone and granite which was used in
constructing breakwaters and piers.[99] While work proceeded 'the din
of the ocean was stilled by the clang of hammers, the suction of pumps,
the hissing of boilers and the roar of bellows'.[100]

Work proceeded slowly, mainly because the government would
provide only small annual grants towards the cost of construction. The
South Pier, terminating in a circular sweep, with its 46ft high lighthouse was completed in 1836, though the North Pier remained un-
finished (see page 183). An unusually severe storm in January 1839

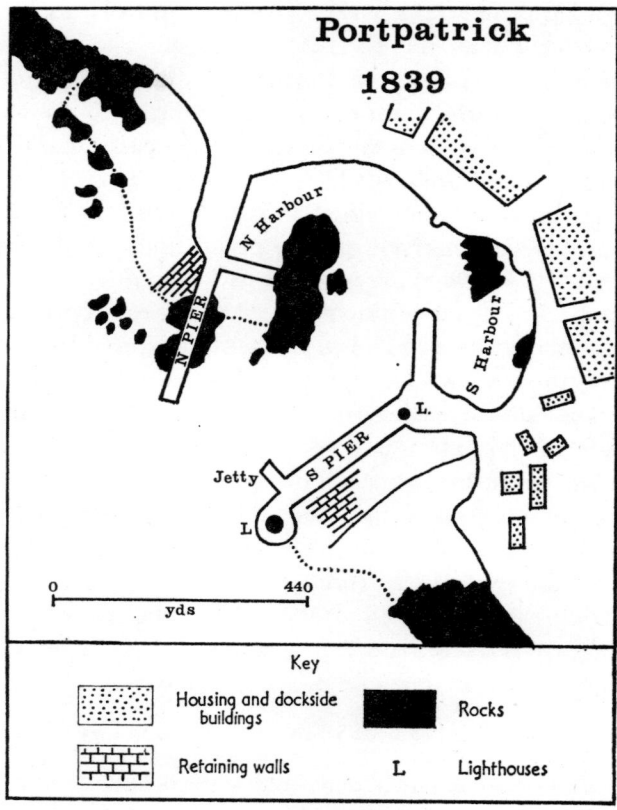

Portpatrick 1839

N Harbour

N PIER

S Harbour

S PIER

L.

Jetty

L

0   440
      yds

Key

Housing and dockside buildings

Rocks

Retaining walls

L   Lighthouses

undermined the end of the South Pier, endangering the lighthouse and causing £13,800 worth of damage. Construction costs had already soared to over £170,000 and it was estimated that another £35,000 would be needed to complete the harbour works.[101] 'Of all the harbours in Great Britain', recorded the *Report on Tidal Harbours* (1847), 'Portpatrick offers the minimum amount of shelter for the large amount of money that has been laid out upon it.'

Opposition to the Portpatrick–Donaghadee route continued to mount from all sides: in 1832 the Belfast Chamber of Commerce agitated for a transfer of the packet stations to Loch Ryan and Belfast; and a report on the affairs of the Post Office in 1836 was also highly critical of high expenditure at Portpatrick and Donaghadee. After continued agitation the Irish mails were diverted to the Stranraer–Larne route in 1849, but the future of Portpatrick and its Irish counterpart was still undecided.[102]

The harbours were maintained and some years later in 1857 the Portpatrick Railway received its Act, permitting it (with the Belfast & County Down Railway) to revive the packet stations at Donaghadee and Portpatrick. The government agreed to improve both harbours if the railway agreed to build lines to them and provide a steamboat service.[103] Improvements went ahead at Portpatrick with government sanction. The railway reached the town in 1861 and a half-mile branch to the ill-fated harbour was opened two years later. But the mail service was never fully resumed. The rival Stranraer–Larne route was seen to be far more satisfactory and the government finally backed down on the Portpatrick–Donaghadee packets in a flurry of compensation to the two railway companies.

Portpatrick was abandoned after 1873 and the harbour works left to the ravages of the sea (plate, page 126). Several years later Malcolm Harper, during one of his rambles, visited the scene and recorded:

> The destruction which has been wrought in the solid masonry of the piers is almost incredible. No description could give any idea of the havoc. The strong iron girders used in riveting together the ponderous stones forming the breastworks have been in many places snapped assunder like straws, and the great stones tossed about like peas.[104]

C. H. Dick, writing fifty years later, was more objective. 'They fell into ruin', he says of the harbour works, 'because no care was taken of them.'

Some indication of the nature of shipping and trading links between Galloway and surrounding regions of the British Isles has already been given in preceding sections. The prosperity of the regional economy clearly depended on trade with Cumberland, Lancashire, the ports of the Firth of Clyde and the west coast of Scotland, Ireland, and the

English and Welsh ports of the Irish Sea as far south as Bristol. These long-established links were of vital importance after the mid-eighteenth century when Galloway became a source of food supply for the rapidly industrialising urban areas to the north and south.

There is considerable evidence to indicate the level which trade had reached by the 1790s, and examination of a few specific ports will provide case-studies of what was general throughout the region. From the port of Garlieston in Sorbie parish (plate, page 143), the products of the central Machars, grain and potatoes, were shipped to London, Dublin, the Isle of Man and the west of Scotland; while sheep, wool, pigs and black cattle formed the main elements of trade from the nearby parishes of Glasserton and Mochrum.[105] The trade of Kirkcudbright in 1794 was more concerned with importing general merchandise and exporting grain, than the provision of agricultural supplies to neighbouring parishes. But the smaller Dee port of Tongland had an unusual export (to Manchester and even London) in salmon caught in the famous Dee fisheries below the Falls.[106] The trade of Rerrick, a nearby Stewartry parish with no formal harbour (where ships simply beached at Balcary, Port Mary or Mullock Bay) was fairly typical:

Imports 1794	*Exports 1794*	
10,000 bushels lime	15,280 stones meal	
General merchandise	880 bolls barley	
	231 ,, bear	
	198 ,, wheat	
	116 tons potatoes	

Barley export was important in Wigtownshire and also in Kirkbean and New Abbey, the most easterly parishes in the Stewartry. This latter district had an established potatoes export trade dating back to 1774.[107]

Little detailed information is available on the business activities of Galloway merchants in trading and shipping, but two short case-studies do serve to emphasise the importance of coastal links with Cumberland, the west of Scotland and regions much farther afield.

The sequestration in 1816–17 of William McClellan & Co, timber merchants in Kirkcudbright, illustrates well the interests of a small local trader in ships and shipping. This bankruptcy arose from a debt of £1,340 owed to Samuel McCaul, a merchant in Kirkcudbright (probably associated with the Newton Douglas cotton mill), for 'a cargo of American pine timber' imported in the brig *Port of Sunderland* to Kirkcudbright in December 1815.[108] The cargo consisted of 'timber deals and Lathwood from Marriamuchie [ie Boston] in British North America', which was consigned to the company yard in Castle Douglas.[109] William McClellan of Drumskelly was a partner in this company with John Caillie, grain and spirit merchant in Kirkcudbright and a list of the latter's debts shows business contacts in Dumfries, Leith, Glasgow, Whitehaven and Stafford.[110] McClellan and his partner were concerned in the building of a sloop, the *Countess of Selkirk* with Robert Erskine, Alexander Kirkpatrick, a ship's carpenter, John Telford, a mariner, and John Shaw, ropemaker in Garlieston.[111] The cost of this boat was more than £1,400 and its builders provide an interesting example of linked vested interest in navigation. The bankrupt partners had additional investments in coastal vessels, including a sloop of 110 tons built at Kippford for William Copeland, mariner of Palnackie and another named *Gordon* also built at The Scaur in the summer of 1815, whose home port was Kirkcudbright.[112] The assets of McClellan himself show that he owned an eighth share in a sloop *George & Jean*, registered at Kirkcudbright and described in February 1817 as 'on a voyage to the West of Scotland'.[113]

Samuel McKnight, also of Kirkcudbright, a merchant, shipowner and corn dealer was similarly engaged in a number of trading activities from Galloway. His main business was in grain and sometime prior to 1819 he entered into partnership with James Parker of Twynholm and James Broadfoot, miller in Dalbeattie, 'for speculations in the purchase of grain'. He also dealt in whisky, but when declared bankrupt in 1819 his assets were tied up in two vessels, *Bruce & Ann* and *Mary*, and also in 'considerable quantities of oatmeal lying in Store at Preston, Londonderry, Fort William, Oban, Inverary, Strachur and Greenock'. Perhaps no better illustration could be found of the main areas of demand for the products of Galloway.[114]

The commerce of Dumfries has already been described in detail, but that of Annan, its near neighbour on the upper Solway, is worth examination. Agricultural produce was of key importance, although c 1797 the Annandale quarries were exporting building stone to Ireland. The coastal trade was concerned with export of grain and potatoes to Liverpool, Whitehaven and the Firth of Clyde, as well as the import of 'merchant goods' from Liverpool. The cattle trade constituted an important element of the town's commerce but this was mostly confined to droving.[115]

The pattern of trade, shipping and commodity trade had altered very little over the half-century to 1830. Steamboats made their appearance in the Galloway ports and provided improved communication along the existing lines of coastal trade. Steamboats ran regular services after 1830 between the Galloway ports and Whitehaven and Liverpool, as well as to Glasgow and the Clyde. The small coastal sloops, however, still continued to carry the majority of regional trade. A famous steamer, the *Countess of Galloway*, provided transport between the main ports of the Cree and Dee and Liverpool, continuing in service until finally outpaced by the railway in the 1880s.[116] Steamer services were mostly confined to the larger ports, like Stranraer, Garlieston, Kirkcudbright, Dumfries and Annan, though small harbours like Carsethorn on the Nith estuary had a twice weekly connection with the Liverpool steam packet.[117] The main imports, whether by steam or sail, continued to concentrate on domestic and agricultural supplies, coal, merchant goods, lime and timber. An increasingly important element at this time—as shown in the section on quarrying in Chapter Four, was the export of building stone from Creetown, Dalbeattie and Annan.

The economic effects of steamboats on the Galloway economy were certainly significant. The faster and more reliable communication between the Solway ports and markets beyond contributed much to the prosperity of the farming economy in the mid-nineteenth-century age of 'high farming'. Even parishes inland felt the stimulus of far-reaching demand for farm produce. In the Nithsdale parish of Closeburn, for example, 'steam navigation was a great stimulus to the fat-stock trade'.[118] The port of Annan revived considerably after the arrival of the steam packets. Despite the difficulties of navigation on the upper Solway, four steamers, *City of Carlisle, Newcastle, Victoria* and *Solway*, totalling 1,338 tons, maintained passenger and goods services to Port Carlisle, Whitehaven and Liverpool. Cattle, sheep, pigs and horses were important elements of trade.[119] Another steamer, *Cumberland*, lay off Dornock and Port Carlisle, while sloops and lighters from either shore ferried goods and passengers for transport to Liverpool.[120] Some attention has already been devoted to the effect of steamers farther west in Galloway proper.

It is perhaps ironic that the steamers succumbed to railways so quickly in the 1870s while the sloops and barks which had carried the Solway trade for centuries survived till the harbours themselves became moribund in the last decades of the nineteenth century. Some indication of the importance of steam shipping in 1846 is afforded by the table below, which shows vessels and tonnages arriving at Galloway ports. Steamboats represented 11·9 per cent of vessels and 27·4 per cent of tonnage. The years immediately prior to 1850 were probably the heyday of Solway coastal shipping. After the arrival of the railway in south-west Scotland a very different picture emerged, with the slow strangulation of shipping and ultimate decay of all but the largest ports.

An important ancillary industry was shipbuilding and repairing, carried on at most of the larger harbours. Sir James Hunter-Blair actively encouraged the industry at Portpatrick and several shipwrights were active there in the 1790s. At Stranraer shipbuilding relied on naval stores and timber imported from the Baltic.[121] At Glencaple, on the lower Nith, twenty-five ship's carpenters and sailors combined shipbuilding and repairing when not at sea c 1793.[122] At Boatgreen and Port McAdam, the ports of Gatehouse, there was a small industry in the 1830s, and at Garlieston vessels of up to 100 tons were regularly launched. Here too, was a ropeworks, manufacturing rope and sail-cloth 'for shipping and rural purposes'.[123]

Vessels & Tonnage Arriving at Galloway Ports 1846

Port	Coastal			Foreign		Vessels Registered
	Vessels	Tonnage		Vessels	Tonnage	Tonnage
Dumfries	697	16,385		9	1,683	8,669
	62	8,005	(S)			
Annan	695	66,640		3	658	
Baldoon	63	1,721				
Barlochan	259	8,375		1	253	
Carsethorn	98	1,647		6	1,205	
	31	4,068	(S)			
Carty	70	2,496				
Creetown	293	20,270				
Garliestown	143	5,141		2	598	
	20	2,900	(S)			
Gatehouse	99	2,619				
Kirkcudbright	307	7,943		3	716	
	64	12,330				
Port William	115	4,413				
Whithorn	88	2,408				
Wigtown	154	4,501		1	193	3,729
	32	6,824	(S)			
Stranraer	258	18,446		4	1,044	1,799
	260	28,860	(S)			
Drummore	65	2,389				
Port Logan	18	457				
Portpatrick	50	1,081				
Totals	3,941	229,919		29	6,350	14,197

(S) indicates steamships

Source: PP. 1847, XXXII, *Report on Tidal Harbours*

Kippford or The Scaur on the lower Urr was for long a shipbuilding port. The industry was begun c 1820 by Henry Cumming, a native of the district who had been apprenticed shipwright in Whitehaven and later emigrated to the United States. Returning to his home he entered into partnership with his brother, John, and started ship-building at The Scaur, concentrating mainly on brigs under 100 tons. After Cumming's death, his nephew carried on the tradition. The last vessel built at Kippford was the *Balcary Lass* of 240 tons, launched in 1884. She was lost during her third voyage after being wrecked on the coast of Newfoundland. Repair of wooden vessels continued until the turn of the present century, when navigation came to an end in the Solway.[124] Farther up the Urr at Dalbeattie there was a modest shipbuilding industry in the mid-nineteenth century.[125]

Annan made a notable contribution to the history of shipbuilding during the first half of the nineteenth century. The firm of John Nicholson & Co built small sloops of under 100 tons at their Welldale yard on the River Annan. Canadian and Baltic timber soon displaced local timber and the tonnage of vessels began to increase, particularly after 1827 when a brig, *Annandale*, of 338 tons was launched. Clippers were built after 1853, the first being *Burns* of 375 tons. The largest clipper built on the Solway was *Elizabeth Nicholson* of 904 tons, launched in 1863. Nicholson & Co built sailing vessels totalling over 8,000 tons which navigated the world during the great age of sail. The yard closed in 1867 and the firm concentrated on contracting. Later, in the 1890s, shipbuilding was revived by the boiler manufacturers, Cochran & Co, who built twenty vessels before the closure of their yard in 1901.[126]

RAILWAYS

The 'Railway Age' reached the confines of Galloway at Dumfries in 1850, when the 'Nithsdale' line of the Glasgow & South-Western Railway between New Cumnock and Gretna was opened. Following the passage of the parliamentary bill establishing the Glasgow, Dum-fries & Carlisle Railway in 1846 (the G & SWR after 1847) there was a rush of schemes proposed for south-west Scotland, the majority so ludicrous that financial reasoning soon dismissed them as totally im-practicable. From these early schemes emerged the five lines which were built: the Castle Douglas & Dumfries; the Portpatrick; the Kirkcudbrightshire; the Wigtownshire; and the Girvan & Portpatrick. The table below shows the mileage of these lines. The first two lines were complementary, carrying the railway through the whole length of Galloway from Dumfries to Portpatrick, while the last named line across the moors of Carrick linked the Galloway system to the G & SWR at Girvan. The Kirkcudbrightshire and the Wigtownshire were simply feeder lines to the main Galloway route and the latter line is the subject of the following case-study.[127]

Railway Mileage wholly within Galloway by Company

Castle Douglas & Dumfries (1859)	19½ miles
Portpatrick (1861)	54
Kirkcudbrightshire (1864)	10¼
Wigtownshire (1877)	19⅛
Girvan & Portpatrick (1877)	30¾
	133⅝ miles

The Wigtownshire Railway was the last line built in Galloway. Its aim was to link the Machars district of the county with the existing Dumfries–Portpatrick line. It presents a particularly interesting example of a branch line constructed and operated almost entirely on local capital and initiative and though lacking major engineering features is not without interest to the industrial archaeologist. It provides an interesting case-study of the effects of railway development in an isolated agricultural district, which traditionally relied upon sea links through the Solway ports to its markets in north-west England.

Many suggestions had been put forward for a branch line to serve the Machars and at least one detailed survey was carried out in 1863.[128] Action was not taken till September 1871, when 'a public meeting of Gentlemen favourable to the extension of Railway Communication from Newton Stewart by Wigtown to Whithorn' was held in the Town Hall at Newton Stewart. Among many local gentry, officials and

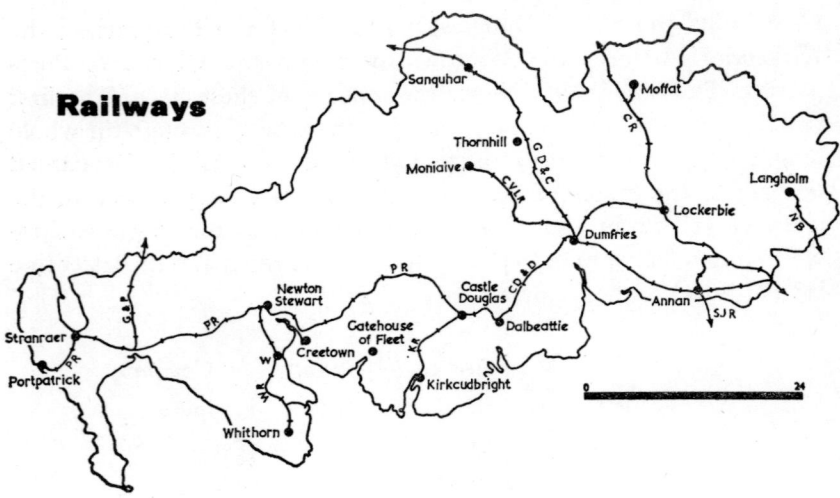

merchants who attended were the Earl of Stair, Lord Garlies, R. H. Johnstone Stewart of Glasserton, R. Vans Agnew of Barnbarroch, Colonel McDowall of Logan and Provost McLean of Wigtown. The meeting was at one in its desire for a railway, which 'was much required for the increasing traffic of the district' and it was agreed that a committee should be appointed to seek subscriptions, to ascertain the extent of support possible from the Portpatrick Railway and to decide on the necessary survey of possible routes.[129]

By October the route had been surveyed and after some disagreement was settled by majority vote. The line was to run 'from Newton Stewart, passing West of Barrhill to the East of Wigtown, thence proceeding to Kirkinner, thence going by Whauphill to a point within $\frac{3}{4}$ mile of the village of Garliestown, thence to Whithorn'. The estimated cost was between £80,000 and £90,000, though by this time a total of £33,570 had already been raised or promised in subscriptions, the majority from gentry, farmers and merchants in parishes ultimately served by the line.[130] 'Few railways', it was recorded, 'started under such promise', for Lord Garlies himself 'had assurances of support from very influential quarters'. The Wigtownshire 'would pass through a rich agricultural district from which a large traffic would be derived' and even the giant Caledonian Railway had expressed interest in working the line.[131]

Julian Tolmé and Robert Johnston were appointed engineers and shortly afterwards reported that the cost of constructing the $19\frac{1}{8}$ mile line would be £96,000, including a tramway from Sorbie to Garlieston harbour. By spring 1872 Lord Garlies was guiding the Wigtownshire Railway Bill through Parliament and on 18 July the Act of Incorporation received the Royal Assent. Garlies was appointed chairman of the Board of Directors, which included most of the local gentry. Opposition from the landed interest was minimal and apart from one isolated incident there were few problems about land acquisition.[132]

The most immediate problem was finance, for despite the favourable start, over £40,000 was still unissued in spring 1873. The directors and engineers hesitated over contracts and there were even suggestions that it would be wiser to build a light railway. Yet undaunted by lack of capital and the unfavourable conditions stated by the 'Cally' for working the line, the directors placed contracts for the permanent way and construction was begun in autumn 1873. The Newton Stewart–Sorbie section (just over 13 miles) was constructed by John Granger of Aberdeen, the railway sleepers being furnished by a local firm, R. & W. Callander of Minnigaff.[133] The work was 'well advanced' in January 1874, when over £10,500 had been spent on earthworks, bridges, rails and sleepers. A call of £2 on every £10 share was immediately made.

During 1874 negotiations proceeded with the 'Cally' about working agreements. The terms were so stringent that the directors resolved in August to work the line on their own. It was all too clear that everything was not well with the company and it soon found itself with a heavy overdraft from the City of Glasgow bank to meet debts to contractors. Another indication of the financial position was the decision to build the branch from Millisle to Garlieston only if the chairman and other interested individuals subscribed the full capital cost.

M

When future prospects looked particularly grim, an offer came from Thomas Wheatley (formerly of the North British Railway) to work the line. For 65 per cent of gross receipts Wheatley offered to manage the line, supply locomotives, carriages and wagons, uphold the permanent way and pay all wages of staff. By the spring the directors had agreed to Wheatley's terms and seemed well pleased to have acquired a manager 'with great experience in Railway matters'. Wheatley himself promised that 'the public will be well accommodated and the traffic of the district thoroughly developed'.[134]

The Newton Stewart–Wigtown section was opened on 7 April 1875 and by that time good progress was being made with the line to Sorbie and with the stations at Kirkinner and Whauphill. To meet building costs the company borrowed £20,000 at 4½ per cent interest. By 2 August the line was open as far as Millisle with intermediate stations at Wigtown, Kirkinner, Whauphill and Sorbie (plate, page 144). Meeting in the autumn, the directors seemed well pleased with traffic figures for the first few months of operation and expressed a high degree of optimism for the future:

April	£199 – 3 – 1
May	230 – 11 – 0
June	252 – 2 – 7
July	278 – 16 – 7
August	527 – 2 – 3½
Sept	475 – 8 – 2
October	507 – 9 – 2[135]

The short branch to Garlieston was operational by April 1876 and at a meeting of directors at that time it was decided to press ahead with the remainder of the line to Whithorn 'as soon as capital [was] subscribed'.[136] The engineers' estimate for the final section of the line was around £21,000. Though another call of £2 on each share was made (which produced enough to cover costs on work done and the interest payments) it became increasingly obvious that the project might well be cut short at Garlieston. But increasing exertions on the part of the chairman, the Earl of Galloway (formerly Lord Garlies), made the construction of the Whithorn section possible by raising £18,500 in subscriptions, mostly on his own account, but including additional subscriptions from other local gentry. The line was opened to passenger traffic on 31 July 1877 and the Wigtownshire ran its first through trains from Newton Stewart to Whithorn.[137] The only difficulty met with regard to land purchase occurred on the Whithorn stretch. Broughton & Cally estates were paid £1,940 in compensation. The Murray-Stewarts were somewhat averse to railways and had earlier caused the Portpatrick Railway some considerable expense for land on the Cally estates.[138]

Improved 'train arrangements' and timetabling with the Portpatrick and Girvan & Portpatrick were of mutual benefit and increased both goods and passenger traffic on the Machars line. But as early as autumn 1879 the directors were voicing alarm about the level of traffic and recording in their minute book that 'the continued depression in trade and agriculture left no room to expect an increase'.[139] Thomas Wheatley estimated working costs at £411 8s per month or just over £4,936 per annum. Of the monthly expenditure, £222 3s accounted for wages and £189 5s for materials and repairs, though these calculations did not include the purchase price of five engines, 22 carriages and 21 wagons which worked the line. Since monthly traffic returns ranged from £500–£700 at this time, it is hardly surprising that Wheatley realised 'only a bare living' from his position as manager of the Wigtownshire Railway.[140]

After Thomas Wheatley's death in March 1883 the Wigtownshire was managed by his son, W. T. Wheatley, but it was just a matter of time before it lost its tenuous independence. A Bill for the transfer of the Portpatrick and Wigtownshire railways to the 'Cally', G & SWR, L & NW, and Midland railways was submitted to the board of directors in December 1884. The Wigtownshire and Portpatrick were amalgamated as a joint committee of these four companies in August 1885, the G & SWR took over operations and though the other three companies retained working agreements, only the 'Cally' ran regular services over the line. Thus the Wigtownshire—a local concern built by local interests—was finally integrated into the greater railway network of the G & SWR.

Although differing in chronology, the history of the Wigtownshire Railway is fairly typical of other lines built in south-west Scotland. The Kirkcudbrightshire, a 10¼ mile line from Castle Douglas to the county town of the Stewartry, was opened in 1864 and passed into the hands of the G & SWR the following year. The Castle Douglas & Dumfries and Portpatrick railways were both heavily subsidised by the G & SWR, the former being merged with the company in 1865. The important Girvan & Portpatrick Railway was not completed until 1877 and working was immediately put in the hands of the G & SWR, which acquired the whole undertaking in 1887.

The history of railways in Galloway reads almost like the history of a branch line. Its feeder line was itself served by branches, which were gradually closed because of the rising competition from road transport. The Stranraer–Dumfries (with its famous 'Paddy' trains) has since closed, and so rapid has been the lifting of track, that little more than deserted stations now remain.

(*See pages 251–4 for notes*)

SECTION TWO

Inventory

MANY of the sites mentioned in Section One are included in the following inventory. Grid references for location are given, together with full structural and other details where possible. Numerous sites and features not mentioned in the text have also been included. The inventory is drawn from a larger card index of industrial and rural features in Galloway compiled during 1965–9. The inventory is arranged under the following categories:

A/1   Mills and Farm Processing
A/2   Breweries and Distillery
A/3   Tanneries
A/4   Timber and Sawmills
A/5   Smithies and Country Forges

B/1   Wool Mills
B/2   Linen Mills
B/3   Cotton Mills
B/4   Paper Mills and Weavers' Dwellings

C/1   Quarries
C/2   Metal Mines
C/3   Lime Quarries and Kilns
C/4   Brick and Tile Works

D/1   Roads and Associated Features
D/2   Canals and Navigations
D/3   Ports and Harbours

A/1   MILLS AND FARM PROCESSING

Derelict meal mills, threshing mills, windmills and corn kilns exist in profusion in Galloway and only those with remains of interest to the industrial archaeologist are detailed here.

Corsewall Mill (NX 020702): large multi-level, three/four-storey mill complex with central building and several additions at various levels, 1 mile NW of Kirkcolm. Buildings of rubble/slate with sandstone quoins and additions in brick. An interesting water-power site on natural stream fall, with former mill-pond upstream. Originally the mill has had a large overshot wheel but converted to turbine about 1900, water being piped from the sluice above. Power was supplemented by a steam engine (c 1870) housed in a lean-to adjacent to original wheel-house. The large brick stack indicates that this has probably been a powerful engine. Interior intact, though most of the actual milling machinery has been removed. Flooring at each of the four levels survives, with stairways, conveyor belts, hoppers and pulleys. The kiln, complete with plates of cast iron, is built into the main mill range and is 20ft square. It was loaded from the level above the drying floor and carried off directly for milling by hoppers and conveyors—unusual arrangements even in a large mill. The mill dates from the late 18th century and has clearly been extended many times since. It has been a very large and important mill locally. The complex is approached by a bridge over the mill race, the parapets of which are composed of old millstones (six altogether) complete with casing. One has an oval plate inscribed 'Peter Reid Millstone Builder Glasgow' (a well-known firm of millwrights) and is probably about 100 years old.

Mills of Craigoch (NX 012669): there are few remains at this site on the Soleburn where until the mid-19th century there were three mills for corn, carding and lint.

Soleburn Mill (NX 032642): this mill is mentioned in tacks as early as 1673 and was probably of much earlier origin. It stands on the Soleburn about a mile E of Leswalt, but little remains of interest for the mill building is incorporated in a farm steading. The lade can still be traced.

Mill of Little Galdenoch (NW 974635): is another very old mill on the Agnew lands on the Galdenoch burn about a mile from the shore.

In 1674 Sir Andrew Agnew had a quarter share of these mills, which were described in 1719 as 'new built in timber and stone'. Few remains.

Lochans Mill (NX 072566): about ¼ mile E of Lochans village a small two-storey range, in rubble and slate, formerly a meal mill dating from the late 18th century. Wheel at the side is of cast iron, three-section, six spoke on cast-iron axle, 12ft in diameter by 4½ft wide. It has cogged drive from the rime. It was high-breastshot to wooden paddles. Stone supports at the side have carried the lade to the wheel. The mill is now used as a byre and there is no internal machinery.

Dinvin Mill (NX 003547): small traditional two/three-storey mill of late 18th century date now converted to hotel. Lade and wheelpit can be traced at the side.

Ardwell Mill (NX 101486): about a mile S of Sandhead, a three-storey mill complex in long range of rubble and slate, whitewashed. It ceased working as a meal mill in 1967 and is now used as a granary. Wheel at side (probably about 15ft diameter by 3ft wide, overshot) was replaced by a turbine in 1945. Turbine in turn replaced by electric motor 1955. Large kiln in main range (about 20ft square) had square cast-iron plates and was last used in 1963. Internal machinery largely modern. The mill had four sets of stones, three being for meal, the other for beans. Formerly powered from mill-pond and lade. The damaged coul lies behind the mill, having being blown from the kiln top in a recent storm. The turbine was shortly to be gutted at the time of visit (April 1968).

Logan Mill (NX 116436): like Ardwell, another estate mill and part of an interesting group of sites, including windmill, sawmill (plate, page 36) and corn kilns. The former meal mill (probably built to replace the windmill sometime in the late 18th century) is a compact two-storey traditional mill range in local rubble and slate. The wheel has been situated on the S gable, though only the axle-hole remains. The kiln has been at the N end. The interior is totally gutted and is now a byre. It was formerly driven off a mill-pond upstream of the nearby sawmill (see below).

Drummore (NX 137367): Old Drummore Mill is a total ruin but Wyllie's Mill, nearer the harbour, survives. It is of mid-19th century date and consists of a long, three-storey range in brick and slate. It is now used as a grain store. At the side is a small breastshot wheel 8ft in diameter by 2ft wide, which powered the mill prior to its conversion to electricity. The wheel is cast iron with zinc buckets.

Bridge Mill of Park (NX 190574): the site of an old mill mentioned in tacks as early as 1695. There are traces of stonework and a lade beside the Water of Luce and a millstone is set up by the roadside near the site of the mill. The mill house survives.

Kirkchrist Mill (NX 215544): in Milton fermetoun, 2 miles SE of Glenluce, a very old but much altered and reconstructed meal mill dating back to at least the early 17th century. It is a three-storey twin-gabled mill range in rubble and slate with kiln adjoining, overall dimensions about 50ft by 40ft. A kiln (18ft by 20ft) adjoining has arched brick interior and fireplace. Internal flooring is complete and some machinery survives, including driving gears, hoppers, pulleys etc. It had a large internal wheel, now removed. This is an interesting mill, reconstructed in the 18th century. Ceased working as a meal mill before 1914.

Elrig Mills (NX 323473): about ¼ mile S of Elrig village a complex series of buildings, formerly bone and meal mills. This widespread site, which covers both sides of the Elrig burn, mostly dates from the late 18th and early 19th centuries, and has probably been the largest mill in the Machars. The whole series of buildings are in a ruinous condition and are part roofless. There is much ruined machinery, both wood and cast iron as well as millstones and gearing. Bone grinding was a most important industry here and bones were imported through nearby Port William.

Port William Mill: large T-shaped range adjoining the harbour is of three storeys in rubble and slate with adjoining warehouses. Former kiln is in main range and has a high ventilator. Interior is much modernised and the mill is still working, though driven by electricity. Formerly it was powered by large internal wheel driven off Killantrae burn. Interesting stone lade. Much altered 18th century mill, built at time of expansion in grain growing (NX 339436) (illustrated on page 17).

Bysbie Mill (NX 476366): on Drummullin burn overlooking Isle of Whithorn harbour, a rectangular, three-storey mill range in rubble and slate, whitewashed. The wheel was at the side nearest the burn and cast-iron axle and centre surrounds survive, indicating that wheel was 15ft diameter by 4½ft wide in stone-lined wheelpit. It was breastshot from a stone lade. Interior largely gutted but the first floor is complete with cast-iron supporting columns to beams of 2nd floor. The former kiln adjoining had a high ventilator on roof. The mill is in poor internal condition. Four millstones on the quayside are from the old mill. These were made and supplied by 'Davies & Sneade Liverpool Est. 1817' and are 4ft 7in in diameter. Bysbie replaced an older mill about two miles south-west.

Garlieston (NX 478465): now demolished, this mill was three-storey in rubble and slate with a wheel at side 18ft in diameter by 5ft wide in cast iron and having cast-iron axle. The mill was water-powered until about 1940 when an electric motor was installed. A kiln was built into the main range. There are a number of interesting old granaries at the nearby harbour.

Creech Mill (NX 436477): about ½ mile N of Sorbie, a T-shaped two-storey and attic mill building in whinstone/sandstone rubble and slate, adjacent to the creamery. It had a breastshot wheel at the side about 15ft in diameter and an axle hole 2ft square remains to give location, though the wheelpit has been partially infilled. Lade is stone-lined. The mill was gutted 'many years ago' and there is little internal machinery. There is a millstone nearby of granite, 5ft in diameter by 9in thick. It is marked 'Mill of Criech' on Ainslie's map of 1782. Probably a reconstruction of a much older mill, probably dating from the 17th century.

Mill of Airies (NX 417481): three-storey rectangular mill building in whinstone rubble with sandstone quoins and windows and slate roof. Ball finials to gables. Built into the stream bank with entrances at upper and lower levels. The wheel was housed in a lean-to on the S side and was probably breastshot. Machinery is long-gutted and the mill is now used as a byre. The location of the millstones can be seen from beneath, where strong beams support the floor which carried the stones. Axle hole blocked up at basement level. There are traces of the infilled lade above the mill. The building is in good structural order. A fairly early mill site and a fine example of the typical Galloway meal mill of the late 18th century.

Milldriggan Mill (NX 422522): a full description of this interesting working mill is given in the main text. It dates from the medieval period and is marked on Roy's map as 'Miltown Kirkinner'.

Newmilns (NX 402552): on River Bladnoch 2 miles W of Wigtown, small, T-shaped mill range of three storeys built into the river bank. The interior is completely gutted and the mill is now used as a store and byre. The wheelpit is at the rear and the remains of a breastshot wheel with wooden axle and cast-iron rims can be seen. It has been about 16ft in diameter by 5ft wide.

Torhouse Mill (NX 396553): about ½ mile upstream of Newmilns, the remains of a similar mill also incorporated in a farm steading. The wheelpit and lade can still be traced.

Barhoise Mill (NX 340618): on Bladnoch 1 mile NE of Kirkcowan village a T-shaped, two-storey and attic mill in granite, whinstone and slate, becoming ruinous. It was driven by a wheel at the side, of which the wooden axle-tree remains. There is a datestone on the door lintel AM 1827', but the mill is certainly a reconstruction of a much earlier one. Extensive weir and long lade off the river drove the wheel.

Minnigaff Mill (NX 411663): on the bank of the River Cree a substantial mill range of four storeys in granite with hipped slate roof. The main building is about 60ft by 40ft with a two-storey addition at the N end. It had a large cast-iron breastshot wheel probably 20ft in diameter by 5ft wide. The wheelpit is intact and the lade is traceable to the weir upstream. There is a datestone on the wall near the wheelpit 'IB 1823' and according to *Pigot's Directory* for 1825–6 John Black was miller at Minnigaff and it was certainly he who reconstructed the mill at that period. It was used as a meal mill till c 1900 and later became a carpet factory. It is now a henhouse. A substantial mill of its period still in good structural order.

Skyreburn Mill (NX 567553): remains of a two-storey and attic mill range in rubble and slate, largely gutted. Wheelpit at side has contained large overshot wheel and the lade is partly visible. Millstones nearby and the millhouse has recently been restored. An interesting mill site, marked on Roy's map 1747–55.

Barley Mill (NX 602573): on Barley burn ½ mile N of Gatehouse a small, two-storey rubble and slate mill range converted to a garage. There is little machinery and only the wheelpit and axle hole can be seen. Former miller's house nearby is a fine period dwelling. The mill is clearly very old, though it is not so ancient as that at nearby Fleuchlarg, which is farther up the Barley burn. Barley was let by Alex Murray of Broughton in 1714 to John Ramsay and again to John Thomson in 1742. Wm Ewart of Potterland obtained a lease in 1794 and the mill was rated at £28 in 1870 when it was worked by John Houston. It is marked on both Roy and Ainslie.

Kirkandrews Mill (NX 601482): on Pulwhirrin burn above Kirkandrews Bay, there are foundation remains of this very old mill, which dates back to at least the early 18th century. The wheelpit and line of the lade can also be traced. A tack of James Murray of Broughton, dated 1759, records the lease of the mill to Hugh Gordon 'miller at Kirkanders parish of Borgue' (SRO GD 10/1225) and again let to his sons John, Anthony, Robert and David Gordon from 1777–94.

Mill of Borgue (NX 638528): this mill on Pulwhirrin burn dates from the period of extensive mill building, although it probably is a much older mill site. It is an L-shaped, two-storey and attic mill range in whinstone rubble and slate with granite quoins. The wheelpit to the rear has axle hole and the remains of timber axle 18in in diameter. Wheel, removed, has been 15ft in diameter by 4ft wide. Some fine internal machinery including the main driving gears survive, mostly of wood and cast iron. Otherwise the interior is gutted and falling into disrepair. The flooring has collapsed with the exception of that supported by the main beams near the driving machinery. An internal square kiln, also much ruined, has an arched fireplace of brick and cast-iron plates and doorway at first-floor level. Ruined datestone (restored on site) in red sandstone is inscribed 'WG 1813'. A very interesting mill site with original machinery in situ (plate, page 17).

Kempleton Mill (NX 683552): about 2 miles NE of Twynholm on the Tarff Water, a long three-storey mill range (70ft by 24ft) in rubble and slate with datestone above main door 'JL DS 1785'. This is a substantial mill, worked until 1958 and has most of its machinery complete, including wheel, gearing and milling machinery. A square kiln and granary are built on to the main range. The wheelhouse (6ft 3in wide) contains an internal cast-iron wheel of light construction with ci cross-spokes and axle. The wheel is 12ft in diameter by 3ft 4in wide with wooden slats 3ft 10in by 1ft, powered from ci trough off the short lade. Most of the internal driving machinery is complete, mostly of cast iron but some wooden. There are three sets of millstones complete with casing and hoppers. The former miller in interview said that he milled a wide range of grains including meal, pease, barley, wheat and animal feeding stuffs. It was a good mill with a fine water supply, never short in summer. Backwater was only a problem three or four times a year, but salmon often got caught in the wheel and caused a lot of damage. Kempleton has been worked by his family for over 50 years and he can remember carts stretching $\frac{1}{2}$ mile along the road waiting to come to the mill. The Murray family also worked Grennan, Holm, Southwick and Torhouse (Wigtownshire) at various times. It is marked on Roy's map.

Kirkcudbright Old Mill (NX 688515): in Millburn St an L-shaped, two-storey and attic range in rubble, brick and slate, whitewashed. There is a kiln with ruined vent to the rear and a brick steam-engine stack. Ruined wheelhouse at side. Little machinery of interest and now used as a pottery.

Laurieston Mill (NX 682650): foundation remains of small meal mill, once the estate mill of Woodhall. It was burnt down about 50 years ago, local tradition having that the fire was caused by grain being left unturned in the kiln overnight. Late 18th century, marked on Ainslie.

Blates Mill (NX 677669): a two-storey L-shaped mill NE of Wood-hall Loch, about 2 miles N of Laurieston. Of rubble and slate it is part roofless and becoming ruinous. One wing has recently been restored as a garage. Marked on Roy and Ainslie.

Barnboard or Glentoo Mill (NX 712620): about 2 miles NW of Bridge of Dee the remains of an L-shaped mill in granite, whinstone and slate, mostly ruinous but with kiln and some walling surviving. Traces of lade and wheelpit. No machinery. This mill dates from the late 18th century and has been out of use for many years. Marked on Ainslie's map of 1797.

Crossmichael Mill (NX 740676): about 1 mile NE of Crossmichael village on Mill burn and located just below Erncrogo loch, remains of a two-storey and attic mill in granite and slate, L-shaped and built into the steep bank of the burn. Part roofless and becoming ruinous it has been out of use 'for thirty years' and little machinery survives. Wheel-pit at side suggests overshot wheel of average size. Marked on Ainslie and rated at £85 in 1870 when operated by James Houston, Bridge of Urr. A typical up-country mill of late 18th century date.

Parton Mill (NX 718691): adjacent to mill house (now a farm), a long, low, multi-level single-storey and attic range in whinstone and slate, becoming ruinous and part roofless. Wheel was at side and lade above is part rock cut. Has been out of use as mill for at least 25 years. Marked on both Roy and Ainslie.

Ironmaconnie Mill (NX 667754): about 3 miles SE of Balmaclellan village on Shirmers burn, a substantial country meal mill situated below a waterfall. It is three-storey L-shaped built into steep bank, with kiln adjoining, of rubble and slate construction part replaced by asbestos roof. Ground front entrance gives on to stones floor and granary. There are three sets of stones with casings and hoppers, though supporting floor becoming unsafe. Above is attic store and granary. Entrance to basement is past kiln fireplace (kiln arched stone-work with small grate) which leads to meal floor with gear cupboard at far end (illustrated on page 17). Survives substantially complete with spur wheel and all associated machinery and gearing to stones mostly in wood and cast iron. On NE gable is large all cast-iron wheel, 13ft diameter by 4ft wide with ci cross-spokes and axle. Wheelpit is built up and very well constructed. This has been a powerful overshot wheel, with spectacular drop from trough to mill race. At the other end of the mill, near the basement entrance, is a small ci wheel 4ft in diameter by 1ft 3in wide, which has had wooden buckets and been overshot, probably used to power bellows for the kiln or to drive a hoist. Kiln had ci plates and coul intact at kiln head. This mill is in remarkable condition, despite having been out of use for some time. It is clearly older than 18th century, but much of the machinery seems to date from this period, while the wheel is mid-19th century. Marked on Ainslie as 'Ernmacanie Mill'.

Grennan Mill (NX 644803): this picturesque mill dates from 1506 and has been extensively reconstructed many times since. It worked till 1949 and has since been beautifully maintained by a sympathetic owner. For full description see main text (illustrated on page 18).

Crogo Mill (NX 758780): traditional, small two-storey mill in rubble and slate, becoming ruinous. Little machinery but wheelpit and lade can be traced. This 18th century mill stands at about 500ft, a mile N of Corsock village, and was certainly milling grain almost on the margin of cultivation.

Old Bridge of Urr Mill (NX 776677): extensive two-storey rubble and slate range, the mill L-shaped with store adjacent on SE and lean-to wheelhouse and former sawmill on NW side. Across the yard is a most unusual self-standing kiln with associated stores and granaries. The interior is becoming ruinous and is mostly gutted of machinery except for millstones and millstone beds, hoist driving gear and a small lathe, powered from the waterwheel. Flooring and stairs sound, though unsafe in parts. It had three sets of stones, all of which lie outside near main ground-floor entrance—maker 'Kay & Hilton, Fleet Street, Liverpool, 1800' (dimensions 5ft diameter by 9in thick). In lean-to is breastshot wood and ci wheel (wheelpit 7ft 3in wide) which has ci rims, axle and gearing with wood spokes and buckets—all tarred. Wheel is 16ft diameter by 3ft 8in wide and has geared drive from axle to former sawmill. The nearby kiln has had a large arched fireplace with access to hearth from doorway at ground level. Cast-iron supports for ci plated floor, replaced with tin. Ornamental coul to roof. Ceased working only a few years ago. Marked on both Roy and Ainslie and reconstructed in late 18th century.

Spottes Mill (NX 806673): about 1 mile N of Haugh of Urr in the wooded Glen of Spottes, a two-storey and attic mill building in granite and slate. It is built into the steep bank above a waterfall on the Spottes burn. A weir upstream diverted the water to a lade which led it to the wheel on the N gable of the mill. The wheelpit is 4ft 6in wide and the breast wheel was about 16ft in diameter. A ci axle remains and part of a ci rim, indicating a segmental wheel with wooden buckets. Marked on Ainslie. Nearby is former miller's cottage, a symmetrical period dwelling. Mill used as implement store.

Lochpatrick Mill (NX 792710): located about ¾ mile N of Kirkpatrick-Durham on burn from Loch Patrick, a two-storey and attic mill building in rubble and slate with kiln adjacent and sawmill in wooden lean-to. Wheelpit on E gable 5ft 8in wide indicates position of large overshot wheel probably about 15ft diameter by 5ft wide— almost certainly of cast iron. Internal machinery gutted, though worked till c 1945—but by electricity. Marked on Ainslie as 'Kirkpatrick Mill'. Probably built at end of 18th century by Rev David Lamont, the local improving landlord.

Glen Mills (NX 924755): on Cargen Water 3 miles W of Dumfries, the ruins of a three-storey sandstone and slate mill, partly roofless, with cast-iron multi-pane windows. It has had an overshot wheel at the side. Formerly housed saw and lint-scutching machinery, probably driven off same wheel. This is a very old mill site but the present mill is of early 19th century date.

Milton of Buittle (NX 814644): remains of two-storey rubble and slate mill with small wheelhouse near single-arch bridge over Buittle burn. In farm garden are some fine early medieval querns found at

N

nearby Mote of Urr. An early mill, marked on Roy's map 1747–55.

Halketleaths Mill (NX 800634): small two-storey and attic T-shaped rubble and slate mill with sandstone quoins and lintels. Granite wheel-pit at side. Had ci wheel with wooden buckets. This and internal machinery only recently removed though long idle as meal mill. Reconstructed in late 18th century.

Kelton Mill (NX 745603): three-storey L-shaped range in rubble, harled and whitewashed, with stores and former granary. Remains of sluice behind but wheel and most internal machinery removed. Mill now houses electric drying kiln. Miller's house nearby. A neat traditional group of buildings.

Gelston Mill (NX 773588): at foot of Gelston village, small L-shaped two-storey mill, last worked about 1950. On extensive ground floor was located a store and gear cupboard, having most of machinery removed. All was of cast iron and gutted at same time as wheel. Upper floor has milling machinery complete including three sets of stones, with casing and hoppers. Hoists complete. Entrance to kiln at this level, about 15ft square. Fired using husks from ground meal. Formerly had ci plates but replaced with tin-sheeting. Wheel was high breastshot about 16ft in diameter by 4ft wide. Had wooden axle and buckets with ci rims and spokes. Interesting natural fall site.

Tongland Mills (NX 698539): the extensive mills which formerly were located here were partly demolished to make way for the Tongland Power Station of the Galloway Electric Power Co in the 1930s.

Fagra or Oroland Mill (NX 748467): two-storey and attic multi-level built into bank of Abbey burn about ¾ mile SW of Dundrennan, is L-shaped in rubble and slate with whitewashed exterior. Had ci overshot wheel at side with wooden buckets—now scrapped. Internal machinery gutted at same time, 'because of good scrap value'. Had two sets of stones, bruiser and grinder. Kiln had ci plates, replaced by punched tin. In interview former miller said during 1939–45 war mill 'worked night and day'. Says turning grain and cleaning kilns was 'a hot and dirty job'. Marked on Ainslie's map.

Dundrennan Mill (NX 799515): at foot of Auchencairn village on

Hass burn L-shaped two-storey rubble and slate range. Wheelpit at side and ci axle. Becoming ruinous.

Barlochan Mill (NX 822570): near Palnackie harbour, shell of three-storey mill now used as garage. Had overshot wheel driven off Glen burn, which was led by conduit under the village street.

Dalbeattie Corn Mill (NX 832612): lowest water-power site on Dalbeattie burn, this former two-storey mill is converted to a garage. The extensive *Barrbridge Mill* (NX 839614) of Jas Carsewell and Son dates from 1837. The original mill building has been extended several times.

Barnhourie Mill (NX 889553): on Fairgirth Lane near Sandyhills Bay, two-storey and attic mill building in rubble and slate with 15ft breastwheel in cast iron and wood. Now the garage of private house and little of interest internally.

Southwick Mill (NX 927579): also known as Mainsmill this stands on Southwick burn. It is a picturesque range of buildings, two-storey, L-shaped and rubble and slate, whitewashed. Had kiln adjacent. Now much altered internally and used as a barn. After it ceased as a meal mill c 1918, the wheel was removed and a small turbine installed c 1925 to provide electricity for Southwick House. This still operates and has a very fine lade system. An old mill, marked on Roy.

Prestonmill (NX 965576): on Prestonmill burn just below a natural fall site, a two-storey traditional rectangular building in rubble and slate. It had a wheel at the E gable, probably overshot, and the wheelpit and axle hole can be seen clearly. The kiln was housed in a square lean-to. Gutted of machinery but flooring apparently complete. Clearly a very old mill, appearing on Roy and a number of Register House Plans, the earliest being 1761.

Monksmill (NX 963662): this complete and well-preserved mill stands in New Abbey village near the bridge over the pow, and was last worked as a meal mill in 1949. It is a traditional rectangular mill range in rubble and slate with square kiln and former miller's house adjoining. At the rear is a ci sectional wheel with wooden axle and buckets, $14\frac{1}{2}$ft in diameter by 5ft wide. The two-mile long lade brings water from Loch Kindar to a pond immediately above the mill. Water is brought to the high breast-wheel through a pipe to a wooden trough supported on a granite pier. The kiln (approx 18ft square) has had ci plates 1ft 6in square and has a ci fireplace by Caldaw & McKinnel, Dumfries. The stones (three sets) are by W. J. & T. Child of Leeds and are dated 1851. The gear cupboard is in very fine order and much of the mill's internal machinery is in working order. A classic example of the Galloway country mill (plate, page 18).

Dumfries Town Mill (NX 970759): there has been a mill on this site since early medieval times and by the late 17th century there were several meal and wauk mills belonging to the burgh of Dumfries. The present mill dates from the 1780s and was built to a design of Andrew Meikle, following the destruction by fire of an earlier structure. The surviving mill is a three-storey, T-shaped structure of sandstone, with a range of outbuildings. The famous caul on the Nith below Devorgilla Bridge is also of early origin—built originally of stakes but reconstructed many times in timber and rubble. Although the lade is infilled the site of the sluice gate at the S end of the caul can still be seen. Flooding was a constant problem at this mill and others in Dumfries and Maxwelltown.

Barmeal (NX 383412): farm threshing mill in rubble and slate with remains of wheelpit at side. Wheel has been breastshot, approx 14ft in diameter. Ruined thresher by Messrs McCartney, New Cumnock, probably of mid-19th century date. Wheel also drove elevator to top floor of threshing barn.

Larroch (NX 372408): similar threshing barn to that above, now used as farm store. Water was channelled through earthenware pipe to the wheel, now removed.

Blairbuie (NX 362420): probably the best-preserved threshing mill in Galloway. Threshing barn is long two-storey range in rubble and slate, with large ci wheel to rear in partly sunken wheelpit, about 16ft in diameter by 5ft wide having geared rim drive to thresher. Water comes from nearby pond by sluice and lade to wooden trough. Overshot wheel in full working order and thresher (since scrapped) last used in autumn 1966. Wheel is reported to be by McCartney of New Cumnock (very active in this district) and of mid-19th century date. A very fine wheel, seen working on visit, 19 April 1968.

Hill (NX 727609): interesting farm group with period farm dwelling house and courtyard with surrounding outbuildings including round, rubble and slate horse mill.

Barnboard (NX 716619): courtyard farm buildings with threshing house in rubble and slate and open horse gin having slated roof supported on cast-iron columns. Internal machinery gutted.

Drumglass (NX 690680): traditional farm group with rectangular threshing barn in rubble and slate and wheelpit at side.

Low Carleton (NX 620470): two-storey stone threshing mill with roof vents and horse gin adjoining.

Upper Senwick (NX 652467): circular horse mill adjacent to interesting farm group.

West Logan (NX 807635): traditional farm buildings set round courtyard with circular horse gin at S end.

Wheatcroft (NX 745637): hexagonal horse mill in rubble and slate adjoining threshing barn. Farmhouse is dated 1791.

Castle Farm (NX 917588): fine rubble and slate circular horse gin, whitewashed adjoining threshing barn.

Southwick Home Farm (NX 937569): threshing barn with fine wood and cast-iron breast-wheel about 15ft in diameter by 4ft 6in wide with rim driving to internal machinery. Driven off extensive pond near the side of the road. Little internal machinery. Used as store. Well-preserved mill of 19th century date.

Logan Windmill (NX 115438): on hill overlooking Logan Mills, remains of substantial vaulted-tower windmill. The tower is about 25ft high, internal diameter 10ft on walls 3ft thick. Doorway at ground level measures 7ft by 3ft. The vaulted chamber on the N side extends 30ft from the base of the tower, is 8ft high and 11ft wide. The whole structure is strongly built of whinstone rubble and boulders from the beach. For a diagrammatic reconstruction see Chapter Two. This is a most interesting Galloway example of this type of early Scottish windmill, which dates from the late 17th century and is mentioned by Symson c 1684.

Stoneykirk Windmill (NX 096524): about 300yd NE of Low Culgroat farm remains of small, round windmill tower 12ft in height and with internal diameter of 8ft on walls 2ft thick. A single door 5ft by 3ft is the only opening. It seems probable that this was the base of a turret post mill, though it could also have been an 'amateur' windmill built by a local farmer. Group of trees in which it stands known as Windmill Plantation.

Barwhanny (NX 410494): unusual farm windmill adjacent to steading is built of rubble and stands 25ft high, ground diameter external 14ft, internal 7ft on walls 3½ft thick. Tapers to about 3ft internal diameter at top. Probably powered threshing mill or possibly water pump. Late 18th or early 19th century.

Cannee (NX 687502): substantial stone windmill tower adjacent to farm steading, which local knowledge takes to have been a windpowered cider press. It stands 24ft high and is 15ft in diameter. It has been converted to a doocot for it has four string courses round the exterior at various levels. There are several very substantial orchards in this district and Scottish Development Department Historic Buildings List does not dispute cider press story.

Whithorn (NX 444398): small windmill stump at top of High St, the sadly reduced remains of a much larger tower. This mill dates from the late 18th century and appears in a print of the town dated 1825. It approaches the Scottish tower mill in its form and in the print is shown with four large sails. Undoubtedly it has been the town mill and was probably fairly important locally in this relatively drier part of the southern Machars.

Dumfries Town Windmill (NX 968758): on Corberry Hill the remains of much altered 18th century tower mill. It was originally about 50ft high with ground diameter of 25ft, being built in 1798. Since 1834 it has formed part of the Dumfries Burgh Museum. The windmill section of the museum was recently modernised and the internal structure of the mill is now seen to advantage. This has been a very large and important windmill.

A/2 BREWERIES AND DISTILLERY

The majority of small town breweries have disappeared or been converted to other uses. Only one distillery survives, Bladnoch, which re-opened after a long period of inactivity in 1957.

Newton Stewart Brewery (NX 410660): long two-storey and attic range with fine period dwelling known as Brewery House adjoining. Brewery building now used as store by Campbell, Hope & King, the Edinburgh brewers. Last used as brewery 'before last War'. Probably dates from the early 19th century, and certainly working in the mid-1820s (plate, page 35).

Whithorn Brewery (NX 446403): near the High Street and adjacent to former tannery, a single-storey and attic range which was probably the brewery. Now used as store.

Gatehouse Brewery (NX 599563): near Fleet Bridge, large three-storey brick and rubble building with slated hipped roof, probably dating from the 1780s, when a 'Brewery Company' was operating in Gatehouse. Part garage and house conversion. This brewery was still operating in 1870, when it was worked by Thomas McKean. Its annual value was £30.

Bladnoch Distillery (NX 420542): this extensive distillery on the River Bladnoch near Wigtown was founded by John and Thomas McClelland in 1817. It was described as 'extensive' in 1825 and by 1845 employed 20 workers, converting 16,000 bushels of barley into spirit per annum. According to Barnard who visited it c 1887, Bladnoch consisted of 'a square pile of buildings round a courtyard'. The distillery was enlarged and modernised in 1878, when it covered over two acres. An overshot waterwheel drove the machinery, including the barley and malt mills. Barnard's description still holds good, for the distillery is little altered. The malting house was a three-storey rubble and slate building, the ground floor being for malting. Adjoining were two similar barns and a pair of kilns (only one survives) with cast-iron plates. The excise house and the distillery offices were ranged round a second courtyard and nearby were four bonded warehouses. The annual output at the time of Barnard's visit was 51,000gal. The present production is over 8,000gal weekly—all malt for blending (plate, page 35).

A/3 TANNERIES

Whithorn (NX 446403): this building stands on the burn which flows through the burgh in the centre of the High Street. It is a two-storey structure, roughly built of rubble with a timber-framed and slatted upper storey, though it has obviously long ceased to operate as a tannery. Probably that which figures in the case described above in Chapter Two.

Newton Stewart (NX 410655): a two-storey building in rubble and slate, now used as a store, served as a tannery till about 1870.

Gatehouse: there were two tanneries in Gatehouse on either bank of the Water of Fleet. The most interesting survival is at NX 599562 and is a single-storey and attic range, dating from the late 18th century. The tanpits were in front of the building and water was supplied by a lade from the sawmill dams at the NE end of the town. Little remains of the other tannery (which also has open tanpits marked on the first OS six-inch map) at NX 597561. Both had gone out of business by the 1860s.

Castle Douglas (NX 764622): a two-storey building in Queen Street was probably a tannery, though it was disused by mid-19th century.

A/4 TIMBER AND SAWMILLS

Sawmills were numerous in Galloway and only the best survivals are described below. Practically all timber sawing is now carried out in modern mills.

Logan (NX 116436): a two-storey and basement range in whinstone rubble and slate in good structural condition but gutted of all internal machinery. Large overshot wheel to rear of cast iron 20ft diameter by 4ft wide with ci axle and spokes. It has geared drive from the rim with zinc buckets. A wooden trough brought water to the wheel from millponds a few hundred yards upstream. An interesting mid-19th century wheel (plate, page 36).

Galloway House (NX 476462): small single-storey range in whin-stone rubble with timber framing and slate roof. Timber shed adjacent. Between the two is breastshot wheel 12ft in diameter by 4ft 6in wide made by 'J. GIBSON MILLWRIGHT 1835'. It is cast iron with wood slats and spokes and powered from a stone-built lade. It has a cogged drive from the middle of the wheel. A fine wheel in superb condition, but somewhat overgrown and becoming ruinous. Early 19th century.

Kirkdale (NX 517533): on Kirkdale burn, small single-storey saw-mill of sandstone and granite with timber and slate roof, 35ft long by 20ft wide. Wheelpit is sunk in ground at E side with fine cast-iron wheel 13ft in diameter by 3ft 9½in wide. Geared drive from internal edge of wheel rim to surviving internal machinery, which includes drive to saw and timber runners. Lade of wood and stone is 3ft wide. Water running to wheel, but long disused.

Twynholm (NX 665543): two-storey range in random rubble, brick and slate. Has ruined cast-iron breast-wheel at side 12ft in diameter by 3ft wide. Formerly powered sawmill which went out of operation c 1900. The building is still used as a joiner's shop.

Drumburn (NX 979621): on Drum burn 2½ miles N of Kirkbean, small single-storey and basement sawmill in whinstone rubble, L-shaped with slate and tile roof. It has an overshot wheel on the N side which is ci sectional with wooden buckets 14ft diameter by 4ft 1in wide. It has a wooden trough with sluice. Still fully operational and driving rotary saw used by local joiner. Probably the last working wheel in Galloway.

New Abbey (NX 958662): the former wool mill was converted about 1900 to a sawmill and is still operated as such. Beside the ruined mill a large cast-iron waterwheel still survives, though long disused. It is sectional with ci spokes and wooden buckets, high breastshot, 17ft in diameter by 5ft 1in wide. Rim drive from the inside of the wheel.

Bridge of Urr (NX 776677): a sawmill adjoins the meal mill and was powered by the same wheel (see description of mill above).

Dalbeattie: had several bobbin and pirn mills until the late 19th century and the industry was carried on at several modern mills until fairly recently. One of the oldest, the High Pirn mill (NX 835614) survives as a garage. The wheelpit can still be seen at the side.

Gatehouse (NX 599564): the old cotton mills were converted into bobbin factories and the Birtwhistle mill is still known locally as the 'Bobbin Mill'. The industry was begun here by William and Thomas Helme, the Dalbeattie bobbin makers and timber merchants c 1850.

A/5 SMITHIES AND COUNTRY FORGES

Numerous country smithies grew up by the wayside to service the farming community of Galloway and the turnpike road traffic. Many survive unaltered and a number are still operating as agricultural engineers, garages, and in the rare instance, as blacksmith's shops.

Malzie Smithy (NX 371541): small single-storey smithy by edge of Water of Malzie. Has small breastshot wheel at side driven off the burn, 8ft in diameter by 1ft 9in wide, constructed of cast iron with zinc buckets 6in deep. A fairly modern wheel (replacing an earlier one), it still drives a lathe, drill and bellows. A remarkable country smithy still in daily use by elderly blacksmith.

Buittle Smithy (NX 805602): traditional single-storey smithy in rubble and slate with central doorway and symmetrical windows. Still working.

Knockmulloch Smithy (NX 621486): small smithy adjoining fine period farmhouse, now used by agricultural engineers.

Maidenholm Forge (NX 842613): on bank of Dalbeattie burn at Maidenholm, below the main weir and sluice to Barrbridge mills, the substantial and well-preserved remains of an early 19th century forge and smithy (plate, page 36). The forge-house is single-storey of granite and slate with cast-iron multi-pane windows. On the SE gable is a well-preserved, high breastshot ci wheel with wooden buckets, ci spokes and axle, fed from a lade above. The wheel is 16ft in diameter by 5ft 10in wide and sits in a wheelpit 6ft 9in wide. It has a small plate engraved 'J. B. A. MCKINNEL, MAKER, DUMFRIES'. The interior is much altered, but the wheel drove a tilt-hammer and some internal gearing can still be seen. John Elliot, a local smith, expanded his business to Maidenholm c 1835, producing ploughs, spades, axles and other castings, as well as undertaking millwrighting. It later became a granite-polishing mill and about 1916 was taken over by the Dalbeattie Electric Light Co, who installed a turbine on the NW gable. This is still used by the Barrbridge Mills for power.

B/1 WOOL MILLS

As indicated in the figure on page 75, there were over 30 small country woollen mills operating in the south-west c 1850. The majority of them have since been converted to other uses, but the remains of several are of considerable interest to the industrial archaeologist.

Dyemill (NX 106476): long single-storey range on coast near Ardwell formerly a small carding mill. Converted to cottages.

Ardwell (NX 103488): rubble wall remains on Ardwell shore below the meal mill of rectangular building. Marked on Roy's map c 1750 as 'Waukmill' and on first OS six-inch (1847) as 'Lint Mill'. Traces of wheelpit and lade, but clearly long disused.

Bar Mill (NX 319462): at West Barr on Elrig shore, the roofless ruin of wool-carding and spinning mill. The structure of whinstone and granite rubble is 45ft long by 18ft wide on walls 2ft thick. The two-storey mill has been powered by a small breastshot wheel about 13ft in diameter by $4\frac{1}{2}$ft wide (see figure on page 69). It has been powered by a short lade off the burn. This is a very early mill, marked on Pont's map (1654), Roy (c 1750) and Ainslie (1782). Probably disused since late 19th century.

Waulk Mill (NX 434475): a two-gabled, two-storey and attic range adjacent to farmhouse, with lean-to and other additions, all in whinstone rubble and slate. This is probably the reconstructed shell of a wool mill (the earliest on the site is marked on Roy's map) and was quite likely a linen mill by the early 19th century, associated with the local Sorbie and Kirkinner damask industry. Little machinery, but traces of lade and wheelpit.

Milldriggan (NX 420520): opposite the meal mill is the site of a wauk mill marked on Roy's map, which like Waulk Mill (above) was probably converted to a lint mill in the late 18th century.

Tarf Mills (NX 331603): complex of mid and late 19th century factory buildings with central two-storey mill range and weaving sheds. The original mill dates from the early 19th century but has been greatly extended since. Tarf Mills manufactured woollen blankets and continued in operation until the early 1950s when it was forced to close. The machinery was removed shortly after and the mill is becoming ruinous. Little of the early mill survives. Many of the houses in Kirkcowan village were built by the two wool mills to house workers.

Wauk Mill, Kirkcowan (NX 333603): for the history of Wauk Mill see main text. The original mill, founded by Robert Milroy in the late 18th century, was enlarged and rebuilt in 1821 and again extended in 1835. This building is a long three-storey range in granite and slate with cast-iron multi-pane windows. There are dormers to the attics. The original power was from a waterwheel on the S gable. Wauk Mill was further enlarged in the 1880s when a series of weaving sheds were added on the N side, power being supplied by a steam engine. The large brick stack survives. Wauk Mill was still being worked by descendants of the Milroys as late as 1945 and the plant was used for weaving and spinning by the Cree Mills Co of Newton Stewart in 1966 (plate, page 54).

Cumloden Waulkmill (NX 414669): this interesting mill survives in almost original condition and dates from the late 18th or early 19th centuries. Its history is given in the main text, a scale drawing is shown in the figure on page 73, and it is illustrated on page 53.

Creetown Waukmill (NX 477586): originally built as a cotton mill, probably on the site of an earlier wauk mill, this wool mill stands on the Balloch burn about a ¼ mile upstream of Creetown. It consists of a large roofless ruin of rubble, three storeys high, 60ft long by 40ft wide, built into the steep banking. The wheelpit is in the basement and measures 25ft by 12ft, with a large axle hole. There are windows at each level, some blocked up. The structure is much ruined and badly overgrown.

Old Bridge of Urr Carding Mill (NX 776677): opposite the meal mill at old Bridge of Urr, a small two-storey whitewashed building in rubble and slate built into the river bank. No machinery or wheel, but traces of lade and partly infilled wheelpit. Marked on Ainslie's map (1797).

Newbank Mill (NX 805694): on Spottes burn at S end of Springholm village, L-shaped two-storey mill range in sandstone and slate, former wool-carding and weaving mill. The mill dates from c 1804 and was operating until 'the last War'. Formerly powered by 16ft breastshot wheel and 'smaller one', which was overshot. The lade and weir are complete and the present owner has installed a turbine for domestic electricity supply. Internal machinery gutted.

Rosedale and Troqueer Mills (NX 9775): this large factory complex on the Maxwelltown side of the Nith at Dumfries dates from the third quarter of the 19th century and formed one of the largest tweed mills in Scotland by 1900. It continued to operate under the founding company until closure in the 1920s. Nithsdale Mills (NX 975754) on the Dumfries side is a similar Italianate structure in brick, dating from the late 1860s.

Kindar Mills (NX 958663): remains of two-storey mill with outbuildings adjoining, now part of a sawmill. Described above.

Kingholm Mills (NX 976736): this extensive tweed mill complex built by Robert Scott after 1830 consists of three ranges of three- and four-storey mills with cast-iron multi-pane windows at all levels. Much altered and now used as granaries and stores.

B/2   LINEN MILLS

There were at least twenty mills in Galloway, but the locations of many are unknown. Most lint mills appear to have been worked in conjunction with wool-carding or meal-milling machinery, or were later converted to other uses; hence little survives to interest the industrial archaeologist.

Craigoch (NX 012669): little remains except surface traces of foundations of this former lint, carding and meal mill, marked on Ainslie's map of 1782.

Ardwell (NX 103488): marked on Roy's map as 'Waukmill', but later converted to a lint mill. Few remains.

Glenluce (NX 207576): on Lady burn at top of Glenluce village, there are traces of this mill, marked on Ainslie and OS six-inch map 1847.

Shirmers Burn (NX 663742): about a $\frac{1}{2}$ mile NE of A 713 and one mile downstream of Ironmaconnie Mill, the foundation remains and walling of an old lint mill with traces of wheelpit and lade off the burn.

Skyreburn Lint Mill (NX 572548): there are foundation remains and traces of both lade and wheelpit here. This mill stood near Skyreburn bridge and is marked 'Lint Mill' on Ainslie's 1797 map.

Kelton (NX 745603): opposite the meal mill, there are traces of this lint mill, marked on Ainslie and OS six-inch map 1850–1.

Crofthead (NX 825688): a similar site with few surface traces apart from foundations and lade, marked on OS six-inch map 1850–1.

New Abbey (NX 964659): one of two lint mills in New Abbey village. Few traces, except for lade and some low walling.

B/3   COTTON MILLS

Of the three major cotton mills in Galloway, only Gatehouse shows substantial remains. The smaller ones have virtually been lost without trace, save for that at Creetown, which survived for a time as a wool mill.

Creetown (NX 477586): for description see section B/1 above. Many blocked out windows at various levels indicate that this has almost certainly been a cotton mill. Its short history as a cotton mill began c 1790, though it probably did not survive the Napoleonic Wars.

Gatehouse: there were four cotton mills here, all fairly substantial, the history being given in the main text (plate, page 71). The Birtwhistle complex (NX 599564) is much ruined and overgrown, though one of the original mills (four storeys high) still has its walls standing. On the S gable is the axle hole of its former breastshot waterwheel. The upper mills survive as mere foundations, though the large wheelpit and lade indicate the size of wheel which drove them (about 25ft in diameter by 8ft wide). The remains of the lade system to the Birtwhistle mills are, however, extensive, running from former milldams above the town and powering various plants before reaching the cotton mills. The former Scott's Cotton Mill (NX 603564) survives structurally intact. After being abandoned as a cotton mill it became a sawmill, powered from the same dam as the Birtwhistle complex. Gatehouse has some fine period dwellings and some interesting workers' housing, many of which seem to have been cotton weavers' dwellings (plate, page 71).

Newton Stewart: the site of this cotton mill is that of the Cree Wool Mills and the lade upstream is probably that built to power the cotton mill.

Castle Douglas: there is no known record of the site of this second cotton mill built by Sir William Douglas in the 1790s. Its name survives in 'Cotton Street', where there are a number of former weavers' dwellings.

B/4 PAPER MILLS AND WEAVERS' DWELLINGS

Tongland Mill (NX 699539): this paper mill (see figure on page 106), of which little now remains, dates from the late 1780s, and was demolished during the construction of the Tongland Power Station. All that remains are foundations and traces of the wheelpit. For history see text.

Mount Pleasant, Dalbeattie (NX 836614): this partly roofless three-storey building of sandstone and granite rubble stands on the lade in Dalbeattie. Adjacent are outbuildings and small, brick chimney-stack, indicating the use of a steam engine to supplement the wheel. The wheelpit can still be traced. The building is becoming ruinous, though a fine period dwelling adjoins. The mill was last used as a paper mill c 1925. For history see text (plate, page 54).

New Galloway: there are some fine weavers' cottages off the High Street, mostly of late 18th and early 19th century date.

Sorbie: this interesting street village consists almost entirely of former domestic weavers' and damask workers' housing, mostly of early 19th century date. Most of the dwellings are low but have a large window and often attic dormers to the former work rooms.

Gatehouse: as indicated above many of the houses in Catherine Street and Birtwhistle Street are former domestic workers' dwellings, typical of many in the villages of Galloway.

Kirkpatrick-Durham: is a similar village with many weavers' houses of late 18th century origin.

C/1 QUARRIES

There were a large number of quarries throughout Galloway and the following inventory provides details of only the most important.

Lochryan: there are five former slate quarries in the neighbourhood of Cairnryan village. Polymodie (NX 059705) is located on the shore about 1½ miles north of Cairnryan, while in the valley of the Glen Burn, there are two smaller quarries at NX 069698 and 071695. Above Lochryan House at NX 069689 are two old slate quarries, which were opened in the late 18th century and were still operating c 1850.

Portpatrick (NX 000538): a stretch of the cliff face has been extensively quarried for harbour works and building during the late 18th and early 19th centuries.

Glasserton: at Laggan (NX 397376) there is an old millstone quarry, and at Fell of Carleton (NX 401381) about $\frac{1}{2}$ mile to the north-east, a former slate quarry. Both were disused before the mid-19th century.

Kirkmabreck: the history of these famous quarries is given in the main text. The earliest granite workings were in the Glebe and Kirkmabreck quarries (NX 485567), opened by the Liverpool Dock Trustees in 1830. A tramroad carried the granite to a large quay about $\frac{3}{4}$ mile to the east on the banks of the River Cree (NX 4756) and traces of this can still be seen. Later, in the 1860s, new quarries were opened farther up the hillside, known as Fell, Fell Hill and Silver Grey (NX 4956). In 1904 the Kirkmabreck quarries employed 268 workmen. The quarries are still operating, but on a much reduced scale.

Bagbie (NX 490551): a large quarry opened c 1870 to exploit a granite outlier is located $\frac{1}{2}$ mile north-east of Carsluith. Bagbie employed 43 labourers in 1904.

Dalbeattie: there are many old granite quarries in the neighbourhood. The largest, Craignair (NX 8160) covers many acres and was first worked in the 1820s by the Liverpool Dock Trustees and later by Andrew Newall, founder of the Dalbeattie granite industry. Little remains of the 19th century working, save sections of old tramway and a granite pier near the road, which supported the Craignair terminus of the rope-way to the granite-crushing plant at Dalbeattie railway station. Near the latter is Cowpark (NX 827816), a smaller granite quarry opened in the mid-19th century. Steadstone (NX 8358), farther down the valley of the Urr, has an old quay used for shipment of granite.

Caledonian Quarry, Kippford (NX 841553): dates from the latter half of the 19th century and in 1904 employed 41 workers. It was linked to a small quay at Kippford on the Urr estuary by tramroad. It is still in use for the provision of roadstone.

Glenstocking (NX 864527): a famous millstone quarry dating from

o

the late 18th century; continued in use until the turn of the present century.

C/2   METAL MINES

There were many metal mines in Galloway, the majority worked at various times during the last two centuries. There are a number of small mines and trials in the Newton Stewart, Creetown and Gatehouse districts and only the most important are described here. The *Special Reports on the Mineral Resources of Great Britain: Vol XVII The Lead, Zinc, Copper and Nickel Ores of Scotland* (1921) contains much valuable information on activities in south-west Scotland.

Knockibae (NX 190665): this old lead mine is located about 2 miles NE of New Luce village and is reached by a very rough track over the moors from the farm of Barnshangan a mile to the S of the workings. Knockibae was first exploited about the middle of the 18th century when several cwt of rich ores were obtained. Another attempt was made c 1790 and the mines appear on Ainslie's map of 1789. A company was formed to work the mines in 1866 and reports on the ores obtained in trials were provided by Captain John Kitto of Laxey Mines, Isle of Man. An adit has been driven in along the vein for some distance and there are also several old shafts and slag heaps. These are marked on the OS six-inch map 1847. Little else survives.

Woodhead (NX 5293, 5393): the remains of this large lead-working and mining complex are considerable, although little of the plant survives entire. Woodhead is located about 3 miles W of Carsphairn and is approached by a farm track from Garryhorn. At least 12 shafts were sunk at various periods during the working life of the mines to tap two main veins (Woodhead and Garryhorn) and three drainage adits at depths of 9, 18 and 31 fathoms, known respectively as Top, Middle and Deep to carry off water to the Garryhorn valley. All these levels would appear to be blocked and many of the shafts are sealed off. The ruined remains of the large smelting plant are situated 200yd N of the present shepherd's cottage. It was demolished 'before the first world war' and is so badly damaged as to evade all possible reconstruction. The outline of a lade and infilled wheelpit can be traced, possibly the location of the large wheel mentioned in the *New Statistical Account*. On the hill overlooking the smelter is a fine rubble-built chimney and the hillside is a maze of flues (rough-hewn stone and brick), constructed to carry off fumes from the furnaces. Refuse dumps and slag heaps cover both sides of the Garryhorn valley. About ½ mile uphill from the plant are the remains of Woodhead village, consisting of three workers' cottages and a large building which has probably been the school or church (plate, page 72). The history of Woodhead is detailed in the text.

Coldstream Burn (NX 386696): this is probably the oldest of three lead and zinc mines in the valley of the Cree N of Newton Stewart. The earliest workings date from the 19th century although ore was mined here as late as the turn of this century. Three shafts were sunk to tap the same vein which occurs at the Wood of Cree mine and these were connected by three levels. Little surface evidence survives save an old powder magazine and the stone foundations of what was probably a water-pressure beam engine, similar to that at Wanlockhead. The slag heaps cover a wide area.

Wood of Cree (NX 386694): is located about 250yd S of Coldstream Burn and was first worked about 1870. Ore Supply Ltd, a syndicate which worked a number of mines in the area including the Blackcraigs, before and during World War I, were fairly active here. Although a shaft and two levels were sunk the ores were mainly worked open-cast. In 1918 the mine produced 105 tons of zinc ore. There are few remains, apart from foundations of buildings, slag heaps and the old level mouths (plate, page 72).

Silver Ridge (NX 3772): the third mine is situated about 2½ miles upstream of Wood of Cree and was first worked in the mid-19th century. There are few remains now although in 1920 'the ruins of workmen's houses and a water wheel' could be seen.

Cairnsmore (NX 463633): this old mine is situated on Cairnsmore estate about ¼ mile S of Strathmadie. It was worked on a small scale before 1845 when the Kirkcudbrightshire Mining Co, which held a lease from the Broughton & Cally estates to work minerals in the Gatehouse area, developed the mine. In eight years of frenzied activity the company raised 3,280 tons of ore valued at £36,000 (an average of £11 per ton), which was shipped south for smelting through the harbour of Palnure. The company was dissolved and although another mining concern headed by Thomas Field tried to work the mine the tonnage raised was so low that work was finally abandoned c 1859. The main vein was worked by three principal shafts (Stewart's, Keith's and Gilpin's) and there were at least ten levels. Rails were laid in all the levels and ore raised to the surface by Stewart's shaft in hutches. Surface remains consist only of ruined buildings and dumps.

Englishman's Burn, Creetown (NX 488588): this old mine is located about ¾ mile from Creetown in the steep-sided valley of Balloch Burn. It has only been worked on a small scale and between 1862 and 1864 yielded 11½ tons of lead ore. Marked on later editions of OS six-inch maps.

Pibble Gulch (NX 523615): this long abandoned trial is located on a tributary of the Moneypool Burn about ¼ mile upstream of the old military road. A level has been driven in along the vein and farther up the burn a few shafts have been sunk to reach it. There is a large grass-grown tip.

Pibble (NX 525608): is situated about ½ mile NE of Pibble farm and is reached by a rough track across the moors. Working here probably dates from the 1840s and several levels and shafts have been driven in to reach the vein. These and later workings have resulted in several large dumps. Near the level mouth the remains of washing and dressing plant can be made out.

Dromore (NX 538622): was both a lead and copper mine, probably opened in the 1840s. A small shaft was sunk, though the various mineral veins were mostly worked open-cast. For a short period before and during World War I Dromore was worked for copper and zinc. According to the *List of Mines* (1915) the Dromore Mining Co employed four workers here, two below and two above ground.

Enrick (NX 618552): the remains of this interesting copper mine are located 2 miles SE of Gatehouse-of-Fleet and are partially overgrown by a plantation of trees. The vein was accidentally discovered in the 1820s and a company with its headquarters in Cornwall was formed to mine and extract the ore. At first mining was confined to short shafts and levels and the ore raised shipped via Gatehouse to Wales. Gradually the shallow levels were worked out and sinking operations resumed. By 1837 the mine had reached a depth of 270ft, where new levels were driven off. Rich copper ores were discovered and exported south to Swansea for smelting. There were three main shafts (Engine, Nicholson and Horse) and one of the levels was 1,240ft long. Inclined shafts linked one level with the other. Lease of Enrick was latterly held by the Cally Mining Co which carried on operations until 1857, when the mine was abandoned. This company renounced its lease the following year. In 1908, the Cally Mines Development Syndicate (capital £12,000) attempted to re-open the mine, installing winding-gear and pumping equipment. Nearly 40 workmen were employed to clear the old levels but after a time work was again abandoned.

Drumruck (NX 581628): was opened before 1914 and is located on the E bank of the Little Water of Fleet opposite Scrogs of Drumruck, 5 miles N of Gatehouse. Col Murray Baillie of Cally 'spent a considerable sum on the adventure' of working this mine, possibly a reference to the activities of the Cally Mines Development Syndicate mentioned in connection with Enrick. Three levels were driven into the hillside and these can still be clearly traced.

Lauchentyre (NX 559572) and *Kings Laggan* (NX 562578) are two old copper mines on either side of the old military road near farms of the same names, about 2 miles NW of Anwoth. Both consisted of single shafts and levels, and were apparently worked on a small scale. They were probably opened by lessees of the Cally estates in the 1840s and 1850s, for at least one lease was granted to work ores in the parish of Anwoth.

Hestan Island (NX 8350): these old copper mines are located near the N end of the rocky island of Hestan, situated at the mouth of

Auchencairn Bay. They were probably first worked in the late 18th century and re-opened by an English company before 1845. Ore was shipped to Swansea. On the W of the island two levels 15yd apart have been driven inwards from just above sea-level, and 30ft higher up there is another level. Farther up, the sites of two old shafts can be traced and on the other side of the island there is further evidence of mining activity.

Rascarrel (NX 816484): is located ¼ mile SW of Airds farm about 100yd from the coast. A shaft was sunk to the vein and a cross-cut driven from the bottom of the shaft to the cliff-foot.

Colvend (NX 872532): is located at the head of a rocky inlet about a mile SE of Colvend kirk. This area is well known for the diversity of its minerals, though few are available in workable quantities. This is a very old copper mine, which according to the *Statistical Account* (1796) was first worked c 1770, when a considerable quantity of ore was raised. Evidence of mining activity is slight, though an old shaft can be traced at the cliff-top.

Tonderghie (NX 440347): known as Mary Mine is located 2½ miles SW of Isle of Whithorn on the coast near Burrow Head. Hugh Stewart of Tonderghie granted a lease to an English company to work the minerals some time prior to 1795. Both copper and lead were mined though the exploit was short-lived. A Welsh company tried c 1845 but it too abandoned the work after trials. An old shaft and adit-level can still be traced.

Blackcraig (NX 4464): the history of these mines is given in the main text. The West mine was the more extensive of the two, and numerous levels worked out the galena to 25 fathoms depth. Some work was carried beyond this after 1917, when the mine was revived for a few years. The East mine was shallower, though one shaft—Engine—was sunk to 133 fathoms. Surface remains include ruined smelters and chimneys.

Wanlockhead (NS 8613): the remains in this extensive lead-working district are numerous, but much ruined by continuous working. The majority of plant still in situ dates from the 1860s (plates, page 89).

C/3 LIME QUARRIES AND KILNS

Portpatrick (NW 999540): built into former raised-beach at the harbour near the landward end of the South pier, is 20ft high and 15ft wide roughly built of local rubble and having double-arched fireplace. Clearly has been gravity-loaded from above and is now infilled. This kiln dates from the early 19th century, having been built for use at the time of the extensive harbour works. Marked on OS six-inch map 1846–7.

Mossdale (NX 662707): just to the north of New Galloway railway station there is evidence of quarrying activity in a localised limestone pocket. The OS six-inch map 1850–1 has a limekiln marked and this may have been built to supply lime during the period of land improvements in this area during the early 19th century.

Torrorrie (NX 963572): about a half-mile south-west of Prestonmill, the remains of a small limestone quarry and kiln bank with traces of stonework, probably the outline of a single small kiln. Ainslie's map 1797 indicates a 'Marle Pit' and two kilns, although the OS six-inch map 1850–1 has only one kiln marked. Torrorrie limeworks were probably developed in the late 18th century to supply lime to neighbouring farmers.

Arbigland (NX 979571): about one mile west of Arbigland House, the rubble remains of another limekiln marked on Ainslie's map. This kiln, like that above, was associated with the activities of the famous agricultural improver, William Craik of Arbigland, who was a great advocate of liming.

Southerness (NX 972543): about a half-mile west of Southerness lighthouse on the raised-beach, the surface remains of an old lime quarry. Nearby is an artificial mound into which is built a now ruined stone limekiln. This also made use of the Kirkbean limestone series although it has been abandoned for over 100 years. Ainslie does not have it marked and it is described as 'old quarry' on the OS six-inch map 1850–1. This kiln must have been active for about thirty years as the *NSA* says that 'a lime-kiln has lately been erected at Southerness'.

Closeburn (NX 907913): the history of these limestone quarries is detailed in the text. Remains are extensive, particularly at Croalchapel (NX 912915) where there are old limestone and sandstone quarries. The fine limekilns at Park date from the late 18th century (plate, page 90). They are built into the natural banking above the flooded quarry, constructed of red sandstone, and are 30ft high and 60ft long. There are three arched, single-draw kilns, the centre one being 90ft broad at the entrance, 8ft high and 11ft deep to the fireplace wall in the interior. The latter is constructed of brick, measuring 4ft by 5ft, with cast-iron door. The kilns are brick-lined and the tops measure 9ft in diameter (plate, page 90). The limestone for burning has been loaded from the top, having been raised from the quarry by an inclined wagon-way, traces of which can still be seen. The OS six-inch map 1856 indicates an 'old limekiln' to the north of the quarry with the existing kilns on the south-west, but there is no trace of the former. These works remained in operation until c 1888, although they probably produced lime intermittently until about 1895. Park village nearby has some interesting traditional single-storey dwellings, probably erected in the late 18th or early 19th centuries by the Menteiths to house quarrymen and limestone burners.

Barjarg (NX 883902): about 300yd west of the River Nith, a bank of single-draw kilns, three in number, similar to those described above. On the opposite side of the road the surface remains of the former limestone quarry can be clearly seen. This works dates from 1788 and its history is given in the main text. It was operating in 1888 but had closed by 1904. Nearby is a row of former workers' cottages.

Porterstown (NX 874912): the third limeworks in mid-Nithsdale is located one mile north-west of Barjarg. Its remains consist of derelict twin single-draw kilns of sandstone construction, extensive quarries on both sides of the road, and a row of cottages and smithy. The works dates from the late 18th century and continued to operate until c 1880.

The lime produced was of 'a scorching quality' used for building and land.

C/4 BRICK AND TILE WORKS

Many of the small works have disappeared, having been little more than single kilns and a clay pit. Even the larger brick and tile works have left little to interest the industrial archaeologist.

Terally (NX 121408): abandoned works 4 miles N of Drummore opened c 1840. Remains consist of small bank of twin kilns, brick-built, 40ft by 30ft, arched and floored internally in brick (plate, page 107). Operational till 1953. Flooded claypit and former workers' houses nearby. Kilns in good order. Interesting small country tile works, of type once common in Galloway.

Monreith (NX 359415): about a ½ mile N of village, foundation remains of similar tile works, operated by Monreith estates.

Carty (NX 431625): working tile works with 12 kilns in single range and drying sheds nearby. Uses local clays and produces a wide range of tiles for agricultural purposes.

Gatehouse (NX 595562): the remains of the small early 19th century works can be seen in a field, known locally as 'Brick Field'.

Sanquhar: there were two works here but only the Buccleuch Brick Works has any remains, but these are substantial. It consists of a large rectangular brick shed, 7 conical kilns (ground diameter 18ft by 30ft high) illustrated on page 107, 1 oven and a large steam boiler and associated pipes. For the history see the main text. The works closed in November 1958.

D/1 ROADS AND ASSOCIATED FEATURES

Remains of pack routes, drove, military and turnpike roads are widespread in Galloway. There are some specially fine bridges and tolls of the turnpike era.

Roads: there are many sections of disused drove road, though much of the original military road is obscured by later development. The Old

Military Road is best seen between Glenluce (NX 2057) and Shennanton Bridge (NX 3463), Creetown (NX 4758) and Anwoth (NX 5856), where there are some interesting old bridges, Gatehouse (NX 6156) and Bridge of Tarff (NX 6856), and lastly between Castle Douglas (NX 7763) and Drungans (NX 9474), where the road nears Dumfries. The last section is particularly interesting because of its long, straight stretches. Turnpike roads abound and virtually all 'A' class roads follow the original turnpike routes. An interesting early example is the Old Edinburgh Road—running from Newton Stewart to New Galloway across moorland districts of the Kells, which dates from the early 18th century.

BRIDGES:

Bridge of Park (NX 192573): whinstone-built, two-arched bridge dating from late 18th century over the Water of Luce.

Shennanton Bridge (NX 344633): traditional two-arched stone bridge dating from late 18th century which carried Dumfries–Portpatrick turnpike over River Bladnoch. Now by-passed.

Bridge of Cree (NX 412656): this fine, five-arched granite bridge with toll was built to the design of John Rennie in 1813 (plate, page 108).

Skyreburn Bridge (NX 573546): single-arched stone bridge over notorious Skyreburn is 19th century reconstruction of an earlier bridge.

Fleet Bridge (NX 598562): similar single-arched bridge in whinstone and sandstone; dates from early 18th century. Recently replaced by modern cement and aluminium bridge.

Ken Bridge (NX 640783): the original bridge, designed by Rennie and built in 1811, was destroyed by floods soon after completion and the present structure (also by Rennie) was not built until 1821–2. It consists of a fine five-arched granite structure 340ft long with an 18ft 3in carriageway, with former coaching inn adjoining W end.

Glenlochar Bridge (NX 732645): a very similar five-arched bridge over the River Dee; dates from the early 19th century.

Threave Bridge (NX 737604): three-arched granite bridge over the River Dee built c 1825 (probably to a design of Telford) on the Dumfries–Portpatrick turnpike, to replace the much older Bridge of Dee nearby.

Old Bridge of Dee (NX 734599): four-arched stone bridge of whinstone and granite dating from early 18th century crosses the River Dee near Bridge of Dee village. Until 1825 this carried the main route through Galloway, but was replaced because of its narrowness and difficulty of access.

Tongland Bridge (NX 692533): built 1804–8 to a design of Telford, this replaced the older bridge upstream. Smiles describes it as 'bold and picturesque', with its wide arch of 112ft span and six pointed arches (three on either side). Tongland is undoubtedly one of Telford's best Scottish bridges, built as it is at a very difficult site posing quite considerable engineering problems.

Low Bridge (NX 684778) and *High Bridge of Barlay* (697786) are fine traditional single-span bridges over the Barlay Burn.

Old Bridge of Urr (NX 775677): interesting two-arched bridge with centre buttress over River Urr near the old meal mill. Dates from late 18th century.

TOLLS:

Barlae (NX 276603) and *Low Knockbrex* (395642) are fine tollhouses on the Glenluce–Newton Stewart section of the Portpatrick turnpike, while that at *Gatehouse* (602566) with its bow fronts is probably among the most picturesque in Galloway. *Kelton Toll* (NX 750612) is very simple by comparison, the only ornate feature being the Gothic pointed-arch windows (plate, page 108). Numerous other toll-houses of standard design can be seen by the wayside in Galloway.

MILESTONES:

These exist in such numbers that it would be a major task to list them. All of the main types are seen in Galloway, but the most common are the simple granite stones with cast-iron mileage plate, either on the face or the head of the stone (plate, page 125). Many of the later turnpikes (such as those in Wigtownshire) have solid cast-iron milestones. The distance stone (giving mileage from the nearest major centre) is also common, especially on the moorland roads.

Coaching Inns: survive in great numbers in the towns and villages of Galloway. Castle Douglas has several, including the Douglas Arms (which has an interesting mileage plate on its wall), the King's Arms and the Imperial. Gatehouse has its famous Murray Arms, a coaching inn dating from mid-18th century, while Glenluce has the Crown Inn and Old King's Arms. Change-houses also abound along the main turnpikes, particularly the Dumfries–Portpatrick road.

Smithies: are equally numerous and usually consist of a traditional, single-storey cottage with smithy adjoining, invariably having the forge and chimney on one gable and wide central door. See section A/5.

D/2 CANALS AND NAVIGATION

The history of canals and navigations in Galloway is given in the text. This inventory provides details of surviving features.

Fleet Canal: constructed in 1824 to improve navigation on the Water of Fleet to the port of Gatehouse at Boatgreen and later Port McAdam. The canal cut runs from the saltings 1,000yd north-west of Calley Mains farm (NX 586546) to Port McAdam (NX 595558) and is approximately one mile in length. It varies in width from 50 to 75yd, the actual channel being about 25yd wide, depending on the state of the tide. From Cardoness Castle south-west to Fleet Bay the channel is unembanked, but between the castle and Port McAdam, a distance of 750yd, earthen and in some places stone embankments line the edge of the canal. Opposite the castle (and about half-way along the length of the canal) are the remains of a swing bridge (marked 'draw bridge' on OS six-inch map 1850–1), consisting of the granite supporting piers extending into the canal and a derelict keeper's cottage on the Cally bank (plate, page 126). The canal continued in use until the late 19th century and is still navigable to small boats. (See figure on page 166.)

Carlingwark Canal: now known as Carlingwark Lane, this former canal runs from Buchan Bridge (NX 762614) by the edge of Carlingwark Loch to a point opposite Threave Island (NX 744625), where it enters the River Dee. At the Buchan Bridge end the canal is about 15ft wide and 3ft deep. There are traces of stonework beneath the bridge, but this does not seem to last for any distance. The canal has long been abandoned and is badly silted up throughout the whole of its $1\frac{1}{2}$ mile length. Built c 1765, it is marked on Ainslie's 1797 map. (See figure on page 163.)

Glenkens Canal: a short section of this canal was built on the River Dee below Glenlochar Bridge at Culvennan. The channel was about $\frac{1}{2}$ mile in length, leaving the Dee from a point $\frac{1}{4}$ mile west of the Fortalice of old Greenlaw (at NX 735635) and entering again opposite Boatcroft (at NX 734643). Near the north end of the canal was a single lock (marked on the OS six-inch map 1850–1) but no trace survives of this feature. The canal itself is little more than a ditch. (See figure on page 164.)

Nith Navigation: much of the original embankment along the river bank survives, as does the breastwork at Dockfoot, Kingholm, Lagall, Kelton and Glencaple quays. For history and descriptions see text and inventory D/3.

D/3 PORTS AND HARBOURS

Cairnryan (NX 062687): long a popular port for the cattle trade, little was done to improve this harbour until the early 19th century, when a small quay was built. When Stranraer was developed as the packet station for Ireland after the 1860s Cairn Point lighthouse became important because it lit the entrance to Loch Ryan. Little remains of the original pier, following the extensive alterations made at Cairnryan during World War II.

Stranraer (NX 0561): in 1791 there was no artificial harbour and vessels larger than 100 tons were forced to anchor offshore. The first pier, built at a cost of £4,500 in 1820, extended 200yd in a NNE

direction and was maintained by the burgh authorities. It provided
11ft depth, but only at high water. The East pier was erected in 1863
prior to the opening of a ½ mile branch line from the Portpatrick
Railway, and was later extended when Stranraer became the permanent packet station on the short sea route to Ireland.

Portpatrick (NW 9954): for the history of this harbour see Section
One. Only a short section of the South pier survives, though much of
the inner harbour is maintained in good order. The harbour is now
used by fishing boats, yachts and a lifeboat (plate, page 126).

Port Logan (NX 095405): the first pier built in this bay (the only
safe anchorage on the whole Rhins coastline) dates from c 1680, the
work of Robert McDowall of Logan. By the 1790s this was in ruins
and Drummore was considered the safest harbour in Kirkmaiden
parish. Port Logan occupied a central place in the argument over the
best harbour for the Galloway end of the Irish packet service. Its role
in this connection is discussed in the main text. Improvements suggested in *Telford's Report* (1809) were implemented in 1818 under the
active encouragement of Colonel Andrew McDowall, who contributed
£3,000 towards the cost of a pier, lighthouse, sea-wall, inn and road
approaches. It was used mainly for the import of Irish cattle, on which
McDowall exacted proprietor's tolls. After the decline of this trade
Port Logan was little used, except as an outlet for local produce. The
remains are derelict but impressive. The pier is 180yd long, the
landward end consisting of massive rubble remains. The seaward end
is fairly complete with a splendid granite and sandstone light-tower
25ft high and 10ft in diameter (plate, page 125). It has an ornamental
light chamber and doors at ground and first-floor levels. Access to the
light was by ladder. There are several fine granite bollards. Thomas
Telford is believed to have designed Port Logan. Nearby is the former
lifeboat-house, a model of its kind built in 1907. Port Logan village
has some interesting early 19th century dwellings.

Drummore (NX 138369): this harbour, the most southerly in Scotland, was built in the early 19th century, and although described in
the 1840s as 'very limited in extent' provided a valuable outlet for

local farm produce. The pier runs north-west across the bay and gives good shelter from most south and north winds. A plan of 1864 in the Stair Papers shows the quay to be about 270ft long with a dredged sandbank on the landward side 120yd wide. The harbour is now badly silted up, though a small stream keeps the part near the pier fairly clear. The pier is built of rubble with an additional section added during World War II. Stair Estates carry out some repairs, but only the odd fishing boat now uses the harbour.

Stair Haven (NX 208537): was formerly known as the Crow's Nest. The Bay of Kirkchrist in which Stair Haven is located was one of three landing stages serving Old Luce parish in 1795. The pier at Stairhaven dates from the early 19th century and was extended in by the Earl of Stair. A plan in Stair Papers indicates the size of the pier, 'a gigantic structure for so modest a port', according to C. H. Dick. Until the coming of the railways, sloops imported lime and coal for the surrounding neighbourhood and exported farm produce. Only the landward end of the pier remains.

Port William (NX 338437): Sir William Maxwell of Monreith founded and gave his name to this small port village c 1776. In 1796 it was described, as 'a small neat village, consisting of low houses, well built, facing the sea'. A small pier was probably erected at this time, though the existing one dates from around 1800. It was built by subscriptions and 'dues levied by mutual consent', soon becoming 'highly useful to the trade of this part of the country'. A substantial jetty 120yd long runs along the south side of the harbour, leaving an entrance between it and the north wall about 100ft in width at the landward end. The harbour dries out at low water, and the shifting beach has been a problem since its construction. Port William was an important harbour for the export/import trade of the southern Machars and even after the opening of the Wigtownshire Railway retained its trade. As late as 1916 C. H. Dick was able to photograph a two-masted sloop tied up at the harbour. There are several interesting warehouses adjoining the harbour, all of early 19th century date.

Isle of Whithorn (NX 477363): the earliest harbour built here was

under authority of James IV of Scotland. Bishop Pococke describes
Whithorn in 1760 as 'a little harbour formed by a pier' into which
ships of 300 tons could enter. Its trade at that period consisted in the
export of barley and imports (according to Pococke) of plank and iron
from Sweden. The pier was extended with the aid of the Convention
of Royal Burghs in 1790 and was improved from time to time during
the 19th century. The L-shaped pier is about 100yd long and provides
good shelter from SW and N winds, but is difficult of access due to
tidal races and rocks. The pier dries out at low water. On the landward
side of the harbour are a range of former grain stores and warehouses,
the Steam Packet Inn (with a painting above the door of the steamer
Countess of Galloway) and a fine period Customs House. The harbour
is used by fishing boats and pleasure craft.

  Garlieston (NX 4846): is a planned port village, laid out before 1790
by Lord Garlies, son of the Earl of Galloway. A pier existed by this
period and Garlieston was one of the most important ports in the
Machars district, having its own vessels trading to London, Liverpool,
Dublin and Glasgow. The present pier was erected by subscription
in 1838 at a cost of £2,600. It is over 100yd long and is partly sheltered
by a breakwater 140yd long. A tramway connected the harbour to the
branch extension from the Wigtownshire Railway and a short length
of this can still be traced. There are several interesting warehouses and
granaries in the harbour area, mostly now used for storage of grain.
Garlieston was a port of call on the Galloway–Liverpool steamer
service. The harbour was 'almost deserted' when Dick visited it in
1916, though an excursion steamer still sailed to the Isle of Man in
the summer months. Today the desertion is complete (plate, page
143).

  Baldoon Quay (NX 428538): located on the S bank of the River
Bladnoch about ¾ mile from Bladnoch village, this quay is about a mile
upstream of Wigtown harbour. The pier and road to it were constructed in the early 19th century by the Earl of Galloway to service
the N end of Kirkinner parish. Like many other small quays, Baldoon
provided an outlet to markets in the north of England and for the

import of lime, coals and other products. In 1846, 63 vessels of 1,721 tons arrived at the quay. Now derelict and grass-grown.

Wigtown Harbour (NX 438546): for the history see main text. The present quay on the Bladnoch is about ¾ mile SE of the town and is becoming derelict. It was built in 1818 because a change in the course of the river made the older pier inaccessible. The cost of construction was paid by the burgh and the harbour was described as 'well adapted to the coasters that ship the agricultural produce of the neighbourhood'. In 1832, 160 vessels used the port, while in 1846 154 vessels (excluding steamers) of 4,501 tons used the port. Wigtown was one of the ports of call of the Liverpool steamer *Countess of Galloway*, but this service did not survive long after the opening of the Wigtownshire Railway and the collapse of coastal trade. Dick found 'one small rowing boat' at the old quay in 1916.

Kelly Port (NX 448613): derelict remains of small 19th century quay on River Cree 1½ miles SE of Carty Port.

Carty Port (NX 432626): remains of earth, stone and wooden quay near St Ninian's Creek on upper Cree estuary, 2 miles SE of Newton Stewart. Known as New Quay, this harbour was constructed by the Earl of Galloway in the early 19th century to replace an older jetty about ½ mile upstream. Carty could be reached by vessels of up to 40 tons, importing lime and coal—and exporting local farming produce. The brickworks adjoining the quay are still operating.

Creetown (NX 473586): located on Cree estuary near the mouth of Moneypool burn and adjacent to centre of the town is a small granite stone jetty with associated breastwork, erected in late 18th century when Creetown was established as a planned industrial village, along the lines of its neighbour, Gatehouse. Creetown has a long tradition of shipping, dating back to the period when it served as a ferry point for passage over the Cree.

Palnure (NX 455631): this creek was used by sloops of up to 50 tons as late as 1850. It was an important outlet for ships transporting lead ore from Blackcraig lead mines during late 18th century.

Kirkmabreck (NX 4756): large jetty, still occasionally used, built

P

c 1830 by Liverpool Dock Trustees for export of granite. Linked to quarries by tramway.

Gatehouse: the old harbour was just below Fleet bridge at Boatgreen (NX 598561), which dates from late 18th century. The Fleet canal, opened 1825, permitted vessels of 160 tons to reach harbour. Port McAdam was built by David McAdam, a local merchant and ship-owner 1836–7 (NX 595557) and continued in use until early 20th century. (RHP 8812; OS six-inch map 1850–1.)

Kirkcudbright (NX 683511): the port of Kirkcudbright has a long history. The river bank was quayed in late 18th century and a small basin constructed. The latter was filled in at the turn of the century and the harbour extensively altered. Kirkcudbright is still a very active harbour used by a coastal tanker, fishing boats and yachts (plate, page 144).

Brighouse Bay (NX 636453): small rubble-built jetty and former fish house, probably of late 18th century date, used for landing lime and coal for local farmers in this isolated district.

Carsethorn (NX 994598): the remains of the wooden jetty which stretched from the shore to the main channel of the Nith can still be seen at low water. The 'Steam Packet Inn' is a reminder of the fact that this port once had regular steamer services to Liverpool.

Glencaple Quay (NX 994687): for the history of this Nith port see main text. The remains are substantial—consisting of a large quay of massive rubble blocks with associated breastwork and stores. Glencaple village has a number of fine period houses and an inn.

Kingholm Quay (NX 975736): quay and dock on the Nith, about 1 mile S of Dumfries, with stores, inn and former Custom House, all of late 18th century date. Some fine period frontages on the former seamen's dwellings and interesting two and three-storey granaries and stores. Nearby are the former Kingholm tweed mills.

Dumfries Dockfoot (NX 977748): uppermost of the Nith quays, this extensive length of wharfage was built in the early 19th century below the Whitesands. It could only be used by small vessels, except at high spring tides.

Notes and References

THE following abbreviations are used in the chapter notes and bibliography:
BTA—British Transport Archives (Edinburgh)
COS—Court of Session
Dumf—Dumfries
GV—General View of the Agriculture of . . .
IA—Industrial Archaeology
Kirk—Kirkcudbright
Mun—Muniment
MB—Minute Book
MGSS—Memoirs of the Geological Survey of Scotland
NSA—(New) Statistical Account
OSA—(Old) Statistical Account
PP—Parliamentary Papers
PSAS—Proceedings of the Society of Antiquaries of Scotland
RHP—Register House Plan
SJPE—Scottish Journal of Political Economy
SL—Signet Library, Edinburgh
SRO—Scottish Record Office
TDGNHAS—Trans of Dumfries & Galloway Natural History & Antiquarian
          Society
TNS—Trans of the Newcomen Society
TSA—Third Statistical Account
UP—Unextracted Process (Court of Session)
VR—Valuation Roll
Wig—Wigtown
Numbers in italics indicate volume in a series, eg OSA, *1*, 599

CHAPTER ONE: THE REGIONAL ECONOMY OF GALLOWAY 1700–1900

1   Mantoux, 247, 312; Dodd, Forbes and Wilson have useful general references;
    Somervell, McCutcheon, Green and Butt (1967) provide useful parallels from
    regions similar to Galloway.
2   Rostow, 307–18; Mathias (1969), 121–78; Deane & Cole give valuable indi-
    cators on the development of the national economy.
3   Butt (1967), 17–18
4   Handley, 25, 40, 49; Symon, 111
5   Morton, 231–62; Prevost (1967), 196–204
6   Haldane has many references to the cattle trade from Ireland and to droving in
    Galloway.
7   PP 1895, XVII, *Royal Comm on Agriculture in Scotland*, 523–4

8 McDowall, 788
9 *Pigot's Commercial Directory of Scotland 1825–6* lists local brewers.
10 Barnard, 342–3
11 Hamilton (1963), 131–4, 407–9
12 Smout, T. C. *Lead Mining in Scotland 1650–1850* (in P. L. Payne (ed), *Studies in Scottish Business History*, 1967), 103
13 *List of Quarries 1904* provides details of working quarries.
14 Simpson and others, 31
15 TSA Dumfries, 61; *List of Quarries 1904*
16 Anderson provides a valuable account of the history of road development in the Stewartry.
17 Mackenzie, 2, 490–2; PP 1847, XXXII, *Report of Comm on Tidal Harbours*, App to 2nd Report gives much detailed information on ports.
18 Highet, C. *The Glasgow & South-Western Railway* (Oakwood 1965) and Smith, D. *The Little Railways of South-West Scotland* (Newton Abbot 1969) provide outlines of railway development in south-west Scotland.
19 For a short account of tourist developments see Donnachie, I. L. *The Economy of Galloway in Historical Perspective* (in the *Galloway Project* 1968)

CHAPTER TWO: AGRICULTURAL PROCESSING AND RURAL CRAFTS

1 TSA Kirkcudbright & Wigtown, 353–6
2 Donnachie & Stewart, 276–99
3 McKerlie, *1*, 457; *2*, 473
4 SRO, *Hay of Park Papers* GD 72/453 Tack to the millers of Kirkchrist 1636; /464 Tack to John McCulloch 1676.
5 Ibid, GD 72/537 Tack of Milnton of Larg 1730; /536 Poinding by Sir Charles Hay 1725.
6 SRO, *Agnew of Lochnaw Mun* GD 154/435 Tacks of the mill and mill lands of Soleburn; /452 Tacks of the mill of Lochnaw; /460 Survey of Milns in the Parish of Leswalt 1718–41.
7 Ibid, GD 10/1219 Bond of thirlage by Alex Gordon yr 1729
8 Symon, 163–72; Mathias (1959), 393 emphasises the importance of barley as a rent crop on poor soils of the upland districts of Scotland.
9 Information from Mr Arthur Harrison of Grennan.
10 Information from Mr John McDowall of Milldriggan; *Pigot's Directory of Scotland 1825–6*
11 Information from Mr J. Allan Nicol of Monksmill, Mr Charles Stewart and Mr George Alexander.
12 SRO, RHP 4740 Plan of Ravenstone c 1850 with Specifications for the Building of a Meal Mill; ibid, RHP 4948 Plan of Sandmill Grain Mill 1861 and RHP 4951 Machinery in Sandmill 1861
13 PP 1895, XVII, *Report of the R C on Agriculture (Scotland)*, 538
14 Frew, 120–1; *Maxwell's Guidebook to the Stewartry of Kirkcudbright* (Castle Douglas 1908), 42
15 Donnachie & Stewart, 276–83
16 Symson, 89
17 Donnachie & Stewart, 287; McLaren, 6–14
18 Somerville (1805), 75–7

19   Smith, 370–5
20   Singer, 135–6; Atkinson, 31–55
21   Nicholson, 147–53
22   Symson, 120–1
23   OSA *1*, 362; ibid *5*, 125
24   SRO, *Broughton & Cally Mun* GD 10/1273 Copy of feu disposition to James
     Davitts 19 July 1797
25   Heron II, 159, 191, 256
26   SRO RH 15/397 Sequestration of Hugh Gibson & Co 1804
27   OSA *16*, 294
28   SL, *Session Papers* 415/54 Anthony Sloan v John Milroy 1800, Answers for
     Milroy, 4
29   Ibid 209/19 Petition of Anthony Sloan, 10–11
30   Bremner, 355–9
31   Singer, 424; *Pigot's Directory 1825–6*, 316–23
32   NSA *4*, Kirk, 340
33   McDowall, 788
34   Butt (1967), 44–5
35   Bremner, 437; Mathias (1959), 399
36   Hamilton (1963), 105
37   Singer, 422–3; 35 Geo III c 113 1794–5, *Sale of Beer Act*; OSA *1*, 195;
     ibid *11*, 313
38   SRO RH 15/158 Sequestration of John McGeorge, Merchant in Dumfries
     1816; *Pigot's Directory 1825–6*, 316–23; Singer, 423
39   SRO GD 10/1265 Tack of two fields occupied by the Brewery Co 1784; ibid,
     VR 106/14 Stewartry of Kirk, 1870–1, Parish of Girthon
40   Mathias (1959), 393 and many refs in OSA and NSA
41   Hamilton (1963), 107–8; Bremner, 449; Barnard, 346
42   OSA *16*, 294 and 7, 188; ibid *15*, 80; ibid *1*, 197
43   SL, *Session Papers* 415/49 Wm Hyslop v A. McGuffogg & Co 1800, Answers
     for A. McGuffogg; 429/28 Petition for Creditors of A. McGuffogg & Co 1801;
     452/22 Answers for David Dickson, Trustee on Sequestered Estate of A.
     McGuffogg 1803
44   SRO, COS, UP McNeil A 14/12 Sequestration of Arnott & Co 1826; Barnard
     348
45   NSA *4* Dumfries, 66, 345; Barnard, 344
46   Barnard, 342–3; information from Bladnoch Distillery Co
47   OSA *1*, 360; *15*, 128; *19*, 449; *9*, 524
48   OSA 7, 514; *4*, 55; *4*, 529; *4*, 261
49   Anderson (1967), *2*, 86–7; Webster, 10; NSA *4* Kirk, 138–9
50   Anderson (1967), *1*, 450–1; *2*, 109
51   NSA *4* Kirk, 252, 288; OS 6 In maps 1847–51
52   OSA *13*, 262; ibid *19*, 449
53   Frew, 135; SRO, VR 106/14 St of Kirk 1870–1
54   Gray, 124, 155
55   NSA *4* Kirk, 236
56   NSA *4* Wigtown, 214; OSA *17*, 562; ibid *11*, 32
57   OSA *2*, 53; ibid *17*, 562
58   Adams, 153–62

59 Dick, 351; SRO, *Agnew of Lochnaw Mun* GD 154/451 Declaration by Patrick & Rbt McDowall re their Salt Pan 1688; Symson, 89–90; GD 154/460 Survey of Milns (Leswalt) 1791
60 OSA *2*, 53; NSA *4* Wigtown, 124
61 Heron II, 279; Singer, 530; Haldane, 225–6; OSA *1*, 248

CHAPTER THREE: TEXTILES

1   Symson, 94–5
2   Ibid, 94–6
3   Lindesay, P. *The Interest of Scotland Considered* (Edinburgh 1733)
4   Wilson, P. N. (1964), 28
5   SRO, *Hay of Park Papers* GD 72/530 Tack to Wm Ker 1711
6   Ibid, GD 72/489 Precept of Poinding against John Baillye 1681
7   OSA *14*, 485; ibid *2*, 255 and Heron II, 107; OSA *15*, 80
8   OSA *4*, 55; ibid *17*, 588; ibid *1*, 362
9   NSA *4* Kirk, 198
10 Milroy Family Papers, examined April 1968
11 NSA *4* Kirk, 138–9
12 PP, 1839, XLII, *Reports from Assistant Handloom Weavers' Commissioners*, 298–9; 310–11
13 NSA *4* Wigtown, 198
14 Singer, 425
15 PP 1839, XLII, *Reports from Assistant Handloom Weavers' Comm*, 310–11
16 McDowall, 702
17 Singer, 595; NSA *4* Dumfries, 536
18 Butt (1967), 75–81
19 Heron II, 256
20 OSA *6*, 457
21 Singer, 425–7
22 Brown, J. (1891), 362
23 McConnel, 18–19
24 PP 1839, XLII, *Asst Handloom Weavers' Comm*, 517–18
25 Brown, J. (1891), 363–5
26 NSA *4* Kirk, 341–2
27 PP 1839 XLII, *Asst Handloom Weavers' Comm*, 298–9; 310–11
28 SRO, VR 106/14 St of Kirk 1870–1, Kirkmabreck Parish
29 OSA *5*, 125; McDowall, 786
30 Bremner, 200
31 McDiarmid, 9–10
32 Bremner, 201; NSA *4* Dumfries, 18
33 Butt (1967), 77; McDowall, 787
34 McDowall, 787–8
35 Campbell, 115
36 Beattie, 24
37 NSA *4* Dumfries, 424
38 McDowall, 790
39 Ibid, 791; Bremner, 202
40 McDowall, 792

41 PP 1839, XLII, *Asst Handloom Weavers' Comm*, 517–18
42 Bremner, 203
43 Beattie, 17–24
44 OSA, *9*, 428
45 Hamilton (1963), 131–4
46 Brown, J. (1891), 334; Corrie (1910), 133
47 Singer, 262
48 NSA *4* Dumfries has references in parish accounts
49 Hamilton (1963), 407
50 Butt, 58–9; Hamilton, 135–6; Campbell (1964), 27
51 SRO, *Records of the Board of Trustees*, NG1/19/1 Reports from the Stamp-masters Anent Lint Mills 1772, 23
52 OSA *9*, 421
53 OSA *7*, 243; *7*, 312; *3*, 143; *10*, 159
54 Heron II, 74; ibid, 277
55 OSA *1*, 157; *1*, 362; *3*, 135
56 Chalmers, G. *Caledonia* (3 vols London 1810–24), *3*, 403
57 OSA *1*, 363; *2*, 53
58 Heron II, 279
59 Hamilton (1963), 406–9
60 NSA *4* Kirk, 43, 288, 353; Ainslie's map 1797
61 OSA *7*, 235
62 Ibid *1*, 166; Singer, 421; *Pigot's Directory 1825–6*, 327
63 OSA *9*, 421
64 Campbell (1965), 99
65 Butt (1967), 72
66 Trotter, 135
67 SRO, *Abercromby of Forglen Mun* GD 185/40 Submission & History of the House of Douglas & Shaw 1823
68 Ibid
69 SRO, *Melville Castle Mun* GD 51/1/32/1 James Shaw to Henry Dundas 17 June 1796
70 Ibid GD 51/1/32/5 Shaw to Dundas 29 March 1796
71 Heron II, 254–5
72 GD 51/1/32/1; NSA *4* Wigtown, 186; Valuations of the Sun Fire and County Offices; SRO, COS, UP 1 Sh/ Misc Bundle 10/3, Spinning and Reeling Book of Douglas, Dale & McCall
73 SRO, *Abercromby of Forglen Mun* GD 185/40
74 Trotter, 135–6; Pryde, 81
75 Heron II, 128
76 SRO, GD 51/1/32/1
77 NSA *4*, 186
78 SRO, GD 51/1/32/4 Shaw to Dundas 10 Sept 1795
79 Heron II, 190
80 OSA *11*, 56
81 Ibid *14*, 486
82 OSA *15*, 80; *15*, 553; NSA *4* Kirk, 341–2
83 Trotter, 436
84 Beattie has photo

85 OSA *13*, 607
86 Singer, 422
87 PP 1840, X, *Report from Sel Comm on the Act for Regulation of Mills & Factories* (4th Report), Appendix, 120
88 OSA *19*, 451
89 Singer, 422
90 PP 1843, LVI, *Return of Factories in the United Kingdom* (1839), 340–1
91 NSA *4* Dumfries, 528
92 Butt (1966), 127–37
93 Heron II, 217–18
94 Ibid, 219; SRO, *Broughton & Cally Mun* GD 10/1266 Feu to Birtwhistles 1785
95 OSA *11*, 314
96 Ibid, 310; GD 10/1267 Contract between James Murray and John Thomson for making a drift and channel from Loch Whiney 1785; /1268 Estimate by Miners for making the Cut 1787
97 PP 1840, X, *Report on Regulation of Mills & Factories*, App, 121
98 SRO, VR 106/14 St of Kirk 1870–1, Girthon Parish; Harper, 140
99 OSA *14*, 485; *1*, 174; *11*, 518
100 Sinclair, Sir John. *Analysis of the Statistical Account of Scotland* (Edinburgh 1826), *1*, 183
101 SRO, RH 15/40 and 41, Account Books of David Laird 1814–16; COS, UP Currie Dal C 12/21 James Cooper v David Laird 1817; SL, *Session Papers* 561/16 Sequestration of James McGowan 1816
102 NSA *4* Dumfries, 269
103 PP, 1834, X, *Report from Sel Comm on Handloom Weavers' Petitions*, 118; ibid, 1839, XLII, *Asst Handloom Weavers' Comm*, 519; NSA *4* Dumfries, 61
104 SRO, *Buccleuch Mun* GD 224/511 Letters re the State of Manufactures at Canonbie & Sanquhar 1842, State of the Woollen & Cotton Manufactures at Hawick, Langholm & Sanquhar, State of Outlay for Sanquhar Weavers 1841–2
105 Ibid, Return re Cotton Weavers of Sanquhar Dec 1842
106 *Asst Handloom Weavers' Comm*, 521, 552; *Handloom Weaver's Pet*, 49–50, 109
107 NSA *4* Wigtown, 32–3
108 Butt (1967), 81; Coleman, 148–50
109 OSA *11*, 75; *Pigot's Directory 1825–6*, 445; PP 1852, L, *Return of Number of Paper Mills* (1851), 556; information from Mr William Heron, Carlisle, and Dr A. Thompson, Royal Scottish Museum
110 SRO, *Broughton & Cally Mun* GD 10/1230 Lease to Wm McWhinnie 1788; ibid /1431 Corresp re Farina Mill feu 1846; RHP 8813
111 Singer, 420

CHAPTER FOUR: MINING AND QUARRYING

1 OSA *1*, 157; *15*, 553; *13*, 268; *19*, 449; *6*, 22
2 Heron II, 298; OSA *16*, 284; *1*, 186; NSA *4* Wigtown, 284; OSA *2*, 290; Heron II, 180
3 OSA *17*, 108; Bremner, 409; Harper, 254
4 Heron II, 113
5 Bremner, 410
6 NSA *4* Kirk, 210

7   Ibid, 339
8   Ibid, 340; Bremner, 411
9   *Maxwell's Guide Book* (1908), 38–40; Harper, 254–5
10 Harper, 167
11 Bremner, 410; Callan, 111–20
12 NSA *4* Dumfries, 16, 86–7, 284
13 *Mines & Quarries Report* 1900
14 Howe, 156
15 Lewis, 203–10
16 PP 1893–4, LXXII, *Report on the Condition of Labour in Open Quarries* (1893), 12; *List of Quarries* 1904; *Mines & Quarries Reports* 1900–20
17 Smout (1967), 103
18 Ibid, 104–7
19 Smout (1960–1), 144–58; Brown, R. (1925–6), 58–78
20 NSA *4* Kirk, 280–1; PP 1843, XV, *R Comm on Children's Employment*, App to 1st Report, Part II, 861
21 Smout (1960–1), 152
22 SRO, *Buccleuch Mun* GD 224/666 Misc Letters re Wanlockhead Lead Mines 1813–22
23 Ibid /722 Wanlockhead Lead Accounts 1811–22
24 Smout (1960–1), 153–4; Butt, Donnachie & Hume (1968), 58
25 Wilson & Flett (1921), 26; Brown (1925–6), 69–71
26 OSA 7, 54
27 SRO, *Clerk of Penicuik Mun* GD 18/1164 Letters from Cuthbert Readshaw re prospecting 1755
28 Ibid /1167 Mining Lease by P. Heron Jan 1764
29 Ibid /1169 Articles of Copartnership
30 Ibid /1172 Rough Plan of Blackcraig 1768
31 Ibid /1173 Memorial for George Clerk 1770
32 OSA *4*, 54–5
33 SRO, GD 18/1174 Letters re Craigtown Mining Co 1778–87
34 Ibid, Mure to Clerk 23 Feb 1782; RHP 3850, 3849
35 Ibid, Mure to Clerk 19 Jan 1782
36 Ibid /1182 Abstract of the Produce of the Craigtown lead Mines & of the Shot Miln 1782–6
37 Ibid /1177 Note of the number of men employed 1780
38 Ibid /1183 Sederunt of the Craigtown Mining Co; OSA *15*, 553
39 GD 18/1182
40 Ibid /1174 Carruthers to Clerk 4 Jan 1783
41 GD 18/1182 Produce of the Shot Miln
42 GD 18/1183 Sederunt of the Craigtown Mining Co 1783
43 OSA *4*, 54–5; SRO, *Seaforth Mun* GD 46/17/5 Robert Scott to Keith Stewart 21 July 1792
44 Ibid GD 46/17/3 Charles Dunbar to Stewart 11 March 1790; /17/5 Copy of the Bargains Set 1792; ibid, Report by Robert Scott 1792
45 Ibid, Scott to Stewart 17 Aug 1792
46 Ibid, Report by John Taylor of the state of Admiral Stewart's mines at Blackcraig in Galloway 4 Oct 1792
47 Ibid, Scott to Stewart 21 Aug 1792

48 OSA *13*, 584
49 Ibid, *16*, 284
50 Ibid, *4*, 263
51 Smout (1967), 106
52 Harper, 158
53 NSA *4*, Kirk, 280–1
54 PP 1843, XV, *R Comm on Children's Employment*, App to 1st Report, Part II, 861
55 NSA *4*, Kirk, 280–1
56 Ibid
57 Harper, 158; Wilson & Flett (also cited as *Lead Ores*), 50
58 NSA *4*, Kirk, 120, 138; *Lead Ores*, 52
59 SRO, *Broughton & Cally Mun* GD 10/1246 Mem re a lease to the Kirkcudbrightshire Mining Co 1845
60 *Lead Ores*, 48–51
61 NSA *4* Wigtown, 53–4
62 SRO, GD 10/1247 Memorial to John Nicholson 1849; /1249 Memorial to Geo Fowke 1852; *Lead Ores*, 123
63 Stewart, J. (1912), 124–7
64 OSA 7, 514
65 NSA *4* Kirk, 361
66 McConachie & Sulley, 31–3
67 McCracken, 140–8
68 OSA *11*, 525–8; Singer, 23–4
69 McCracken, 146–8
70 MGSS, *Arsenic & Antimony Ores* (1920), 54; *Lead Ores*, 63–4
71 Dron, 18–28; Simpson, J. B. and others (1936), 31; Lumsden, G. I. and others (1967), 160–1
72 Brown, J. (1891), 343
73 McConnel, 16
74 Brown, 175–7
75 OSA *6*, 454
76 SRO, *Buccleuch Mun* GD 224/473 McNab Leases 1805
77 Ibid, 1821
78 Brown, 177
79 McConnel, 19; Brown, 342
80 McConnel, 21–2
81 Ibid, 27; Brown, 345
82 McConnel, 30
83 Ibid, 35
84 *List of Mines* 1915, 49
85 SL, *Session Papers*, 8/81 Francis Hetherington v John Henry Book et al 29 June 1724; Information for JHB and Thomas Dod 3 July 1724
86 SRO, *Buccleuch Mun* GD 224/240 Journal of the Canonbie Coal 1768–70
87 Ibid, 2
88 Ibid, 11, 31
89 Ibid, 54, 60–1
90 Ibid, 105–6; OSA *14*, 415
91 NSA *4* Dumfries, 486

92 Singer, 26, 675–7
93 OSA *14*, 424, 428
94 SRO, GD 224/511 Letters re State of Manufactures and of the Colliers at Canonbie & Sanquhar 1842
95 GD 224/526 Canonbie Colliery Account 1856–61, Output & Accts 1860–1; Credit Accts 1856–7
96 Lumsden (1967), 214; *List of Mines* 1905
97 Butt (1967), 99; Skinner, B. C. *The Lime Industry of the Lothians* (Edinburgh 1969) provides an excellent survey of the lime quarrying and burning industry in eastern Scotland.
98 Symson, 63–4
99 OSA *1*, 251; *4*, 139; *14*, 475
100 Brown, 340
101 SRO, GD 224/240 Journal of the Canonbie Coal 1768–70, 54, 60–1, 64
102 OSA *13*, 240
103 SRO, *Closeburn Writs* GD 19/405 Contract between Alex Farquharson, trustee for Sir James Kirkpatrick & John Kelleck Jr 1781
104 Ibid /406 Agreement between Alex Williamson & Kirkpatrick trustee 1783
105 Ibid /407 Valuation of Tools at Closeburn, March 1783
106 NSA *4* Dumfries, 79
107 OSA *13*, 233, 240–1
108 Singer, 540–8
109 Singer, 40
110 Ibid, 541
111 Ibid, 41
112 NSA *4* Dumfries, 86–7
113 SRO, *Hunter of Barjarg Mun* GD 78/233 Accts re Rev Dr Hunter's lime quarry at Barjarg 1793–1811, Acct for 1793
114 Ibid, Arrears on 10 March 1794; OSA *12*, 80
115 NSA *4* Dumfries, 464
116 OSA *9*, 427; ibid *7*, 306
117 Singer, 594–5; NSA *4* Dumfries, 284
118 NSA *4* Kirk, 236

CHAPTER FIVE: TRANSPORT AND TRADE

1 Hamilton (1963), 228–9
2 Arnott, 120–34; Haldane has many references.
3 Anderson, 44, 209
4 SRO, *Broughton & Cally Mun* GD 10/547 Report on Survey of Proposed Road c 1757
5 Ibid
6 Arnott, 121
7 Ibid, 131
8 Anderson, 210
9 SRO, *Seaforth Mun* GD 46/13/9 Act for Repairing Highways & Bridges in the County of Wigtown 1778
10 37 Geo III c 153, 1797; SL, *Session Papers* 300/4 Alex McMillan v David McCulloch 1813

11   SRO, GD 46/13/9 Draught Bill 1793
12   SRO, *Agnew of Lochnaw Mun* GD 154/733 Act for Repairing Roads in Wigtownshire 1802, 5
13   Ibid, 16
14   PP 1809, III, *Report from the Sel Comm on Telford's Report & Survey relative to Communication between England & Ireland*, 612, 672
15   Ibid, 612
16   Ibid, 615
17   PP 1810–11, III, *Report from the Sel Comm on Roads between Carlisle & Portpatrick*, 791–3
18   Public Works, Roads & Transport Congress, *British Bridges: An Illustrated Technical & Historic Record* (London 1933), 463
19   Anderson, 214
20   PP 1823, V, *Report from the Sel Comm on the Glasgow & Portpatrick Roads*, 155
21   Ibid, 166, 168
22   Ibid, 198
23   Vale, E. *The Mail-Coach Men of the late Eighteenth Century* (Newton Abbot 1967), 28
24   PP 1860, XXXVIII, *Report of the Royal Comm on the Public Roads of Scotland*, 114
25   Ibid, 68–9
26   Ibid, 776
27   Lindsay, 178–94
28   OSA *14*, 102–3
29   Lindsay, 178
30   NSA *4* Dumfries, 397
31   Singer, 413–14
32   NSA *4* Dumfries, 37–8
33   Singer, 413–14
34   PP 1847, XXXII, *Report of the Royal Comm on Tidal Harbours*, 598–9
35   OSA *1*, 169–70; NSA *4* Kirk, 146–7
36   SL, *Session Papers* 262/9 Shawes v Douglas and others 1811, Petition of Richard & Robert Shawes, 5
37   OSA *4*, 261
38   Pet of Richard & Rbt Shawes, 5
39   Ibid, 27
40   OSA *1*, 170
41   Answers for Sir Wm Douglas, 15
42   Pet of Richard & Rbt Shawes, 17–18
43   Priestly, 309–10
44   Pet of Shawes App X (quoting Sir Alex Gordon's letter from John Spalding 21 Dec 1801
45   Ibid, 6–7
46   42 Geo III c 114 Glenkens Canal Bill; Answers for Sir Wm Douglas, 31–2
47   Pet of Shawes, 1
48   Ibid, 5–6
49   NSA *4* Kirk, 146–7; ibid, 192
50   NSA *4* Kirk, 292, 375
51   SRO, *Broughton & Cally Mun* GD 10/1288 Statement re Port McAdam 1849

52 Brown, P. H. (1891), 180
53 Ibid, 180–1
54 Symson, 114–15
55 Ibid, 115
56 Defoe, D. *A Tour through Great Britain* (London 1727)
57 OSA *16*, 293
58 Ibid *4*, 53–4
59 *Report on Telford's Survey* and *Report on Carlisle & Portpatrick Roads*
60 Brown, P. H. (1891), 180–1; Symson, 54
61 OSA *14*, 475–7
62 *Report on Tidal Harbours* app to 2nd Report, 773; NSA *4* Wigtown, 6
63 Fraser, 233–4
64 Smout (1958–9); Truckell (1954–6); Murray (1965)
65 McDowall, 597
66 Ibid, 597–8
67 Ibid, 598
68 OSA *5*, 125–6
69 Singer, 430–2
70 *Tidal Harbours*, 774
71 McDowall, 691–2
72 51 Geo III c 147 Nith Navigation Bill, 17; *Tidal Harbours*, 598
73 Priestly, 510
74 Nith Navigation Bill, 3
75 COS, UP Adams Mack g 9/115, Gordon v Knox 1814–16 contains a copy of
     Hollinsworth's plan
76 *Tidal Harbours*, 598
77 Ibid
78 Gordon v Knox 1814–16, Specification for a New Channel 1811
79 McDowall, 693; *Tidal Harbours*, 774
80 *Tidal Harbours*, 774
81 Ibid, 609
82 NSA *4* Dumfries, 19–20
83 Ibid, 20–1
84 McDowall, 777–8
85 Ibid, 778
86 *Tidal Harbours*, 774; OSA *11*, 63
87 Frew, 142
88 Frew, 119
89 Ibid, 62–3
90 Ibid, 141–2
91 Green, 76
92 *Report on Telford's Survey*, 637
93 Ibid, 672
94 Ibid, 672–3
95 Ibid, 625
96 Ibid, 618
97 Ibid, 625–6
98 Green, 76; NSA *4* Wigtown, 155
99 Dick, 340–1

100   Harper, 374
101   *Tidal Harbours*, 772
102   Green, 76; PP 1831–2, XVII, *Report from the Sel Comm on Post Communication with Ireland*, 6
103   Carter, 286
104   Harper, 375
105   OSA *1*, 250; *17*, 566, 584–8
106   Ibid, *11*, 7–20; *9*, 322–3
107   Ibid, *15*, 122; *2*, 127
108   SRO, COS, RH 15/397 Wm McLellan & Co, Timber Merchants Sequestration 1816–17, 2–3
109   Ibid, 21
110   Ibid, 38
111   Ibid, 26–7
112   Ibid, 76, 78
113   Ibid, 79
114   SRO, COS, UP McNeill M 42/2 Samuel McKnight Jr Sequestration 1819
115   OSA *19*, 449
116   Fraser, 234
117   NSA *4* Dumfries, 241
118   Ibid, 85
119   Ibid, 529
120   Ibid, 259
121   OSA *1*, 42, 360
122   Ibid, *6*, 26
123   NSA *4* Wigtown, 33
124   Fraser, J. *Colvend During Fifty Years*, TDGNHAS 1894–5, 38–55
125   Frew, 119
126   TSA Dumfries, 266–7
127   Carter, 141, 278, 286, 377, 410; Dunbar, 20–44; David Smith, *Little Railways of South-West Scotland* (Newton Abbot 1969)
128   BTA (Edinburgh) Wigtownshire Railway Company, Minutes & Reports, MB *1*, 6 (8 Sept 1871)
129   Ibid, 2
130   Ibid, 8 (2 Oct 1871)
131   Ibid, 15 (quoting Lord Garlies to Portpatrick Railway Co 1 Sept 1871); 17 (quoting Garlies to Caledonian Railway Co 23 Sept 1871)
132   Ibid, 25, 49–54
133   Ibid, 100–9
134   Ibid, 219 (quoting T. Wheatley to WR Co 31 March 1875)
135   Data from MB *1*
136   MB *2*, 17 (25 April 1879)
137   Ibid, 62–70
138   SRO, *Broughton & Cally Mun* GD 10/552 Papers re Compensation paid by WR Co 1878–80; GD 10/550–551 and 1413–16 Papers re Compensation paid by Portpatrick Railway Co 1856–63; MB *2*, 55
139   MB *2*, 135 (27 August 1879)
140   Ibid, 153–9

Bibliography

MANUSCRIPT SOURCES

Signet Library: Session Papers
Scottish Record Office:
Records of the Board of Trustees for Fisheries, Manufactures & Improvements in Scotland, NG 1
Abercromby of Forglen Muniments GD 185
Agnew of Lochnaw Muniments GD 154
Broughton & Cally Muniments GD 10
Buccleuch Muniments GD 224
Clerk of Penicuik Muniments GD 18
Closeburn Writs GD 19
Fergusson of Craigdarroch MSS GD 77
Hay of Park Papers GD 72
Hunter of Barjarg Muniments GD 78
Melville Castle Muniments GD 51
Seaforth Muniments GD 46
Stair Papers GD 135
British Transport Archives (*Edinburgh*) (now at SRO):
Wigtownshire Railway Minute Books

PARLIAMENTARY PAPERS

Report relative to the distilleries in Scotland (1798), 1803, XI
Report from the Sel Comm on Telford's Report & Survey relative to communication between England and Ireland, 1809, III
Report from the Sel Comm on roads between Carlisle and Portpatrick, 1810–11, III

Report from the Sel Comm on the Glasgow and Carlisle road, 1814–15, III

Report from the Sel Comm on the Glasgow and Portpatrick roads, 1823, V

Eleventh Report of customs and excise (1825), 1824–5, XIII

Accounts relating to malt and spirits, 1826–7, XVII

Report from the Sel Comm on the state of the northern roads between London and Edinburgh and London and Portpatrick, 1830, X

Report from the Sel Comm on Children in mills and factories of the United Kingdom, 1831–2, XV

Report of the Sel Comm on Handloom weavers, 1834, X

Account of Soap Made, Exported & Imported, 1837–8, XLV

Return relative to the Duty on bricks 1837–8, 1838, XLV

Reports of the Assistant Handloom Weavers' commissioners, 1839, XLII

Report from the Sel Comm on the act for the regulation of mills and factories, 1840, X

Report of the Children's employment commission, 1843, XV

Return of factories in the United Kingdom, 1843, LVI

Return relative to real property, 1845, V

Report of the Commissioners on tidal harbours, 1847, XXXII

Return of the number of paper mills at present working in England, Scotland, Wales and Ireland 1851, 1852, L

Agricultural statistics for Scotland 1854, 1854–5, XLVII

Report of the Royal Comm on the public roads of Scotland, 1860, XXXVIII

Report of the Royal Comm on depressed conditions of the agricultural interests, 1881, XVI

Report on the condition of labour in open quarries, 1893–4, LXXIII

Report of the Royal Comm on agriculture (Scotland), 1895, XVII

Royal Comm on metalliferous mines and quarries, 1914, 2nd report

Reports of the Inspectors of mines 1874–1900

List of mines worked in the year 1888 onwards
List of quarries 1904

BOOKS

Anderson, M. L. *A History of Scottish forestry*, 2 vols (Edinburgh 1967)

Bald, R. *Report of a survey of minerals around Dumfries* (Dumfries 1837)

Barnard, A. *The whisky distilleries of the United Kingdom* (London 1887)

Beattie, D. J. *Lang Syne in Eskdale* (Carlisle 1950)

Boyd, J. S. *The royal & ancient burgh of Stranraer 1617–1967* (Stranraer 1967)

Bremner, D. *The industries of Scotland: their rise, progress and present condition* (Edinburgh 1869) (new edn Newton Abbot 1969)

Brown, J. *The history of Sanquhar* (Dumfries 1891)

Brown, P. Hume (ed). *Early travellers in Scotland* (Edinburgh 1891)

Butt, J. *The industrial archaeology of Scotland* (Newton Abbot 1967)

Butt, J., Donnachie, I. L. and Hume, J. R. *Industrial history in pictures: Scotland* (Newton Abbot 1968)

Campbell, R. H. (ed). *States of the annual progress of the linen manufacture 1727–54* (Edinburgh 1964)

—— *Scotland since 1707: the rise of an industrial society* (Oxford 1965)

Carter, E. *An historical geography of the railways of the British Isles* (London 1959)

Coleman, D. C. *The British paper industry 1495–1860: a study in industrial growth* (Oxford 1958)

Corrie, J. M. *The droving days in the south-western district of Scotland* (Dumfries 1915)

—— *Glencairn (Dumfriesshire): the annals of an inland parish* (Dumfries 1910)

Deane, P. and Cole, W. A. *British Economic Growth 1688–1959* (Cambridge 1967)

Q

Defoe, D. *A tour thro' Great Britain* (London 1727)

Dick, C. H. *Highways & byways in Galloway and Carrick* (London 1916)

Dodd, A. H. *The industrial revolution in north Wales* (2nd edn Cardiff 1951)

Dron, R. W. *The coalfields of Scotland* (London 1902)

Fraser, G. *Wigtown and Whithorn: historical and descriptive sketches* (Wigtown 1877)

Frew, D. *The parish of Urr, civil and ecclesiastical: a history* (Dalbeattie 1909)

Gray, M. *The highland economy* (Edinburgh 1957)

Green, E. R. R. *The industrial archaeology of County Down* (Belfast 1963)

Haldane, A. R. B. *The drove roads of Scotland* (Edinburgh 1952)

Hamilton, H. *The industrial revolution in Scotland* (Oxford 1932)

—— *An economic history of Scotland in the eighteenth century* (Oxford 1963)

Handley, J. E. *Scottish farming in the eighteenth century* (London 1953)

Harper, M. M. *Rambles in Galloway* (Dalbeattie 1896)

Heron, R. *Observations made in a journey thr' the western counties of Scotland in the autumn of 1792* (Perth 1799)

Highet, C. *The Glasgow & South-Western Railway* (Oakwood 1965)

Howe, J. A. *The geology of building stones* (London 1910)

Hudson, K. *Industrial archaeology: an introduction* (London 1963)

Johnston, B. *General View of the agriculture of Dumfries* (London 1794)

Kyd, J. G. *Scottish population statistics* (Edinburgh 1952)

Learmonth, W. *Kirkcudbrightshire and Wigtownshire* (Cambridge 1920)

Lewis, J. Parry. *Building Cycles and Britain's growth* (London 1965)

Lindsay, J. *The canals of Scotland* (Newton Abbot 1968)

Lumsden, G. I. and others. *The geology of the neighbourhood of Langholm* (Edinburgh 1967), *Memoir of the Geological Survey of Scotland*

McConnel, J. C. I. *The upper Nithsdale coalworks from Pictish times to 1925* (Dumfries 1962)

McDiarmid, J. *Picture of Dumfries and its environs* (Edinburgh 1832)

McDowall, W. *History of the burgh of Dumfries* (Edinburgh 1867), 2nd edn 1887; 3rd edn 1906

McIlwraith, W. *The visitor's guide to Wigtownshire* (Stranraer 1875)

Mackenzie, W. *The history of Galloway from the earliest times*, 2 vols (Kirkcudbright 1841)

M'Kerlie, P. H. *History of the lands and their owners in Galloway* (Paisley 1877)

Mantoux, P. *The industrial revolution of the 18th century* (London 1961)

Marwick, W. H. *Scotland in modern times* (London 1964)

Mathias, P. *The brewing industry in England 1700–1830* (Cambridge 1959)

—— *The first industrial nation* (London 1969)

Maxwell's Guide book to the Stewartry of Kirkcudbright (Castle Douglas, 8th edn 1908)

Maxwell, H. *A history of Dumfries and Galloway* (Edinburgh 1896)

Nicholson, J. *Minute book of the Stewartry covenanting war committee* (Kirkcudbright)

Pannell, J. P. M. *Techniques of industrial archaeology* (Newton Abbot 1966)

Payne, P. L. (ed). *Studies in Scottish business history* (London 1967)

Peacock, J. *An east Galloway parish: Troqueer* (Dumfries 1896)

Porteous, J. M. *God's treasure-house in Scotland: a history of mines and lands in the southern Highlands* (London 1867)

Priestly, J. *Historical account of the navigable rivers, canals, and railways throughout Great Britain* (London 1831)

Pryde, G. S. *The burghs of Scotland: a critical list* (Oxford 1965)

Public Works, Roads & Transport Congress, British bridges: an illustrated technical and historic record (London 1933)

Robertson, J. F. *The story of Galloway* (Castle Douglas 1963)

Rostow, W. W. *The process of economic growth* (Oxford 1960)

Simpson, J. B. and others. *The geology of the Sanquhar coalfield* (Edinburgh 1936) *Memoirs of the Geological Survey of Scotland*

Singer, W. *General view of the Agriculture of the county of Dumfries* (Edinburgh 1812)

Smith, D. *The Little Railways of South-West Scotland* (Newton Abbot 1969)

Smith, S. *General View of the Agriculture of Galloway* (London 1810)

Smout, T. C. *Scottish trade on eve of Union* (Edinburgh 1963)

Somerville, R. *General view of the Agriculture of East Lothian* (London 1805)

Stark, W. A. *The book of Kirkpatrick Durham* (Castle Douglas 1903)

Symon, J. A. *Scottish farming past and present* (Edinburgh 1959)

Symson, A. *A large description of Galloway (1684)* (Kirkcudbright 1841)

Trotter, A. *East Galloway sketches* (Castle Douglas 1901)

Warden, A. J. *The linen trade* (London 1864)

Webster, J. *General view of the Agriculture of Galloway* (Edinburgh 1794)

Wilson, G. V. and Flett, J. S. *The lead, zinc, copper and nickel ores of Scotland* (Edinburgh 1921) (cited as *Lead Ores*)

ARTICLES

Adams, I. H. 'The salt industry of the Forth Basin', *Scot Geog Mag* 81 (1965), 153–62

Anderson, A. D. 'The development of the road system in the Stewartry of Kirkcudbright', *TDGNHAS* 44 (1967), 205–22

Arnott, M. C. 'The military road to Portpatrick 1763', *TDGNHAS* 28, 120

Atkinson, F. 'The horse as a source of rotary power', *TNS* 33 (1960–1), 31

Barbour, J. 'The Glenkens in olden times', *TDGNHAS* 12 (1895–6), 135–47

Brown, R. 'The mines and minerals of Wanlockhead', *TDGNHAS* 13 (1925–6), 58–79

Bryson, A. 'Gatehouse of Fleet: its history & antiquities', *The Gallovidian*, 13 (1911)

Butt, J. 'The industrial archaeology of Gatehouse of Fleet', *IA* 1966, 127–37

Callan, I. A. 'Dalbeattie granite industry', *The Gallovidian* 1902, 111–20

Crosbie, S. M. 'The water of Urr: its sailors and shipping', *The Gallovidian Annual* 1931, 64–8

Donnachie, I. L. and Stewart, N. K. 'Scottish windmills: an outline and inventory', *PSAS* XCVIII (1964–6), 276–99

Donnachie, I. L. 'The economy of Galloway in historical perspective' (in *Galloway Project: a study of the economy of south-west Scotland*, Glasgow 1968)

Donnachie, I. L. 'The classification of industrial monuments', *IA* 6 (1969)

Dunbar, A. G. 'Notes on proposed railway companies 1845', *Scottish Railways*, 2 (1968), 20–44

Forbes, R. J. 'Power to 1850' (in Vol IV of *Hist of Technology*, Oxford 1958)

Fraser, J. 'Colvend during fifty years', *TDGNHAS* 11 (1894–5), 38–55

Leftwich, B. R. 'Selections from the customs records of Dumfries', *TDGNHAS*, 17 (1930–1), 101–31

McConachie, G. and Sulley, P. 'Notes on Rerrick', *TDGNHAS* 13 (1896–7), 31–3

McCracken, A. 'The Glendinning Antimony mine', *TDGNHAS* 42 (1965), 140–8

McCutcheon, W. A. 'The application of water power to industrial purposes in the north of Ireland', *IA* (1965), 69–81

McIntire, W. 'The fords of the Solway', *Trans Cumberland & Westmorland Soc* 39 (1939), 152–70

McLaren, T. 'Old windmills in Scotland', *PSAS* LXXIX (1944–5), 6–14

Milne, R. W. 'Some notes on estate management in the 18th century', *TDGNHAS* 24 (1911–12), 146–55

Morton, A. S. 'The Levellers of Galloway', *TDGNHAS* 19 (1933–5), 231–62

Murray, A. 'The customs accounts of Dumfries and Kirkcudbright 1560–1660', *TDGNHAS* 42 (1965), 114–32

Prevost, W. A. J. 'The drove road into Annandale', *TDGNHAS* 31 (1952–3), 121

——— 'Sir John Clerk's journey into Galloway in 1735', *TDGNHAS* 42 (1965), 133–9

——— 'Letters reporting the rising of the Levellers in 1724', *TDGNHAS* 44 (1967), 196–204

Scott-Elliot, J. 'A grain drying kiln in Dumfriesshire', *TDGNHAS* 39 (1960–1), 80–2

Smout, T. C. 'The foreign trade of Dumfries and Kirkcudbright', *TDGNHAS* 37 (1958–9), 36

——— 'The lead mines at Wanlockhead', *TDGNHAS* 39 (1960–1), 144–58

——— 'Scottish landowners and economic growth 1650–1850', *SJPE* (1964), II, 3

Somervell, J. 'Water power and industries in Westmorland', *TNS* 18 (1937–8), 235–44

Stewart, J. 'Copper mining in the parish of Girthon', *The Gallovidian* 1912, 124–7

Stone, J. C. 'The early printed maps of Dumfriesshire and Galloway', *TDGNHAS* 44 (1967), 182–95

Truckell, A. E. 'Early shipping references in the Dumfries burgh records', *TDGNHAS* 33 (1954–5), 132 and 34 (1955–6), 29

Williams, B. J. 'Past and present industries in the Stewartry', *The Gallovidian*, 16 (1914), 113–22

Wilson, P. N. 'The influence of water power upon the industrial revolution', *Water Power* 1954, 309–16

——— 'Water driven prime movers' (in *Engineering Heritage*, London 1964)

MAPS AND PLANS

Register House Plans consulted are fully detailed in the chapter *Notes* above. There are several medium-scale maps of the eighteenth and nineteenth century which give details of interest to the local historian and industrial archaeologist, including:

Ainslie, John. *The County of Wigtown*, 1782 and 1789
—— *The Stewartry of Kirkcudbright*, 1797
Crawford, Wm. *Map of Dumfriesshire*, 1804
OS Six Inch Maps:
>   *Wigtown*, 1846–7
>   *Kirkcudbright*, 1850–1
>   *Dumfries*, 1856

Modern OS Maps (Seventh Series) sheets 67, 68, 69, 70, 73, 74, 75, 76, 79, 80, 81

Acknowledgements

ONE of the great pleasures in writing a book is the opportunity it affords of thanking many friends without whose help it would have proved a daunting task. My first debt is to Dr John Butt of the Department of Economic History, University of Strathclyde, who many years ago introduced me to industrial archaeology. When I later undertook formal research in the subject (of which this book now forms part) his enthusiasm was only matched by his willingness to provide advice whenever occasion demanded. Another former Strathclyde colleague, John Hume, put his wide knowledge at my disposal and kindly provided information and photographs of several sites in Galloway. My period as a Research Assistant in the department working on the Galloway Regional Study gave me an opportunity to examine the economy of the region both past and present in some depth. I acknowledge with gratitude the help and encourage-ment of Professor S. G. E. Lythe and Mr (now Professor) Glyn Davies during this time.

Much of the documentary research was undertaken between 1966–9 and I thank the staffs of the following libraries and institutions for their constant help: Andersonian Library, University of Strath-clyde; Glasgow University Library; the Mitchell Library; the Scot-tish Record Office; National Library of Scotland; the Signet Library; National Museum of Antiquities of Scotland and Alexander Fenton; Royal Commission on the Ancient & Historical Monuments of Scot-land and Miss Catherine Cruft; the Ewart Library, Dumfries; Dum-fries Burgh Museum and A. E. Truckell; the Stewartry County Library; Broughton House Library, Kirkcudbright; Wigtown County Library; Ministry of Public Building & Works; and the Scottish Development Department and David Walker.

The fieldwork would have been an impossible task without the help of countless Galloway people. It is my pleasure to accord thanks to farmers and businessmen who gave up so much of their valuable time to answer my questions and provide me with facilities to inspect and photograph their premises. Their patience was boundless and their interest and hospitality a great encouragement.

My publisher, David St John Thomas, was as always, sympathetic to the problems of a hard-pressed author and editor.

Lastly, I accord thanks to my wife, Norma, who helped in so many ways that I could not start to list them.

Edinburgh 1970 I. D.

Index

The index does not include references to specific sites. These are listed by industry in the Inventory. References to illustrations are in italics.

266